BY GERALDINE DERUITER

If You Can't Take the Heat

*All Over the Place: Adventures in Travel,
True Love, and Petty Theft*

IF YOU CAN'T TAKE THE HEAT

CROWN
NEW YORK

IF YOU CAN'T TAKE THE HEAT

TALES OF FOOD, FEMINISM, *and* FURY

GERALDINE DeRUITER

Published in the United States by Crown, an imprint of the Crown
Publishing Group, a division of Penguin Random House LLC, New York.

Crown and the Crown colophon are registered trademarks of
Penguin Random House LLC.

Library of Congress Cataloging-in-Publication Data
Names: DeRuiter, Geraldine, author.
Title: If you can't take the heat / Geraldine DeRuiter.
Description: First edition. | New York: Crown, [2024] |
Includes bibliographical references.
Identifiers: LCCN 2023034136 (print) | LCCN 2023034137 (ebook) |
ISBN 9780593444481 (hardcover) | ISBN 9780593444498 (ebook)
Subjects: LCSH: DeRuiter, Geraldine—Travel. | Adventure and
adventurers—United States—Biography. | Bloggers—United
States—Biography.
Classification: LCC G226.D47 A3 2024 (print) | LCC G226.D47 (ebook) |
DDC 070.4/496415092 [B]—dc23/eng/20231016
LC record available at https://lccn.loc.gov/2023034136
LC ebook record available at https://lccn.loc.gov/2023034137

Printed in the United States of America on acid-free paper

crownpublishing.com

2 4 6 8 9 7 5 3 1

First Edition

Editor: Aubrey Martinson
Text designer: Susan Turner
Production manager: Angela McNally
Managing editors: Allison Fox and Sally Franklin
Proofreaders: Julie Ehlers, Alissa Fitzgerald, Ruth Anne Phillips
Publicist: Bree Martinez
Marketer: Melissa Esner

For the Palazzo Pals

CONTENTS

IF YOU CAN'T TAKE THE HEAT

1

THE FIRST TASTE OF DEFIANCE

When people find out I'm a food writer, they immediately want to know what my first food memory is. It's like the pissing contest of the culinary world—whose first gastronomical imprint is the best. I've read enough culinary memoirs to know that's where the seeds of someone's entire relationship with food supposedly begin. There is nary a cooking competition where the chefs are not required to create an entire menu around that memory.

These recollections are always so lyrical—the sizzle of sofrito, the brine of an oyster, the scent of cookies fresh from the oven. Memory, distilled into flavor and scent. The taste and feeling become locked into the electrical wiring of our brains, more so than first kisses. First kisses can be absolute disasters, too clammy or taste of Cheez-Its, affronts to the senses, but the first food memories, my *God*. Ask anyone in the food world—the answer is always poetry.

I've concluded that someone *must* be lying.

The first thing you remember eating is soufflé? Not your own coagulated snot, not a dusty jelly bean you found on the floor, not your older brother's farts? Was every chef and food writer in the world born a fully formed adult with a standing reservation at Balthazar? As a kid, I distinctly remember drinking water from a vase that had recently been relieved of flowers. I remember desperately licking Fun Dip off a plastic tablecloth, the granules spilled from the packet, mixed with grains of salt and pepper that were scattered on the table from an earlier meal. I did not care. I know that I ate the paper wrappers that clung to the outside of peanut butter cups, with some sort of hazy understanding that it was dark chocolate around milk (the logic behind this confounds me, because it requires the absence and presence of intellect all at once).

If you want poetry, I can lie to you. I can tell you about my mother diligently stuffing cannelloni and making béchamel from scratch, back when that was the sort of thing she did. I can tell you about all the rustic southern Italian dishes my grandmother tried to get me to eat, meals that I often rejected handily.

If you want to know my actual first food memory, it's this:

The setting is the early 1980s, a time that looks more like the 1970s, really; there are bell-bottoms and big hair, though it could be that my family is just stuck behind the fashion. The carpet is a burnished red, the upholstery of the couch quilted and iridescent gold in the rare Seattle sunlight. It feels like velvet, and when I run my chubby hand along it one way, it is smooth and shiny; the other way, it bristles up like a cowlick. Picture me, a toddler. I have a baby mullet, the hair you see on professional European soccer players, a receding hairline, and a sort of wispy tail hanging off the back of my enormous head. (It is easy to envision me, working through the last few seasons on a premier team, nursing a knee injury, wondering if my supermodel ex-wife still loves me.)

I am dressed, without fail, either like a rodeo clown or in the long underwear of a cartoon prospector, snap buttons that go up the inside of one leg and down the other. They are cold and I will squirm as my mother attempts to button me into them, and once she does, I am free to roam the house like a cat, which is more or less how I am regarded. *Make sure she doesn't get outside. Don't let her climb on the furniture. Did someone feed her?*

My family has just arrived in America. My mother is the last to immigrate. She leaves my father and Europe all at once, claiming that she is coming to America only because she doesn't want to have another baby on the U.S. Army base outside Munich, where my brother was born. He is three when he arrives in America, wide-eyed and confused. He leaves behind my father, the only home he has ever known, and a beloved red biplane that my father built him, with his name—EDWARD—in black block letters painted across the top.

After I am born, my mother tells my father that she is not going back to Germany, where my father is stationed and will live for the rest of his life. My brother does not get the red biplane back. He is softly haunted by the loss of a home and a life he remembers before this one, but for me there is nothing else. There is only the chaos, the noise, the people all around buzzing like a hive of bees. This is all there has ever been. I get lost in it.

The sink in the downstairs bathroom is not high. It is so short that even my petite mother has to bend down to use it. And this is how I score my triumph. In a blissful, unsupervised moment, I grabbed the tube on the counter.

It was not the first time I had reached for it; I remember that desire, unfulfilled, just a feeling, really, unattached to words. I often managed to get my fists—shaped like tiny round dinner rolls, dimpled at the knuckles—around the tube. My mother would whisk it away, after I'd completed the complicated task of grasping it. I was too young to articulate my want. I don't even remember crying; I just remember the ease of her lifting it from my hands, the long curtain of her honey blond waves brushing against me.

But she is not there to thwart my plans this time. After all, what trouble could a toddler possibly get into, unattended, in a bathroom in 1982? (It's a miracle my generation survived at all.) I have concluded the cap must have already been off, because I don't think I had the motor skills at that age to remove it myself. I squeeze the container, and creamy mint deliciousness oozes forth. I press my finger to the edge and deliver it to my mouth, or maybe I just squeeze the tube directly into my open, waiting maw. But there it is: my first food memory. Mint toothpaste, served straight from the tube.

This substance will never be a secret ingredient on *Iron Chef*. Decades from now, the culinary experts on *Top Chef* will not be asked to create a menu around a tube of Aquafresh.

This is because toothpaste is not food. It is a health and beauty product. It is *designed* to be spit out.

In the coming years, manufacturers will realize the untapped market that children present, the willingness of parents to spend endless resources to preserve their progeny's teeth. Toothpaste will be available in banana, in bubble gum, in electric-blue raspberry. A veritable thirty-one flavors of dentifrice in saturated Lisa Frank hues. But these options do not exist in my world. There is only the chalky paste of the standard mint-flavored Crest, bracingly cool and astringent. What kind of desperation leads a toddler to eat toothpaste? How has my brief life gone so astray? I am starved for anything that has even the suggestion of sweetness, because it is entirely absent from my young existence. No one in my family bakes. No one makes cakes or cookies or serves dessert. There is the occasional dusty breath mint found at the bottom of my aunt's purse, which I will pop into my mouth, bits of foil still clinging to it. But toothpaste is the closest I can get to dessert, akin to minty frosting. And eating it is forbidden, which means I want it all the more.

Also, I like mint.

Years later, standard toothpaste instructions state that children under the age of six should be given only a pea-sized amount and supervised to minimize swallowing. Does the tube say this in 1982? It seems improbable, and it also wouldn't have mattered: At this point in my personal history, I am *extremely* illiterate. I doubt it would have made a difference, anyway. These are the early years of Reagan's first term, and supposedly the Russians may destroy us at any moment; I live my toddler life to the fullest. I walk, bravely, unsteadily, ingesting toothpaste as I go. The downstairs is where we live, and my aunt Pia—my mother's oldest sister—lives upstairs. That is where everyone congregates to scream at one another. I stumble up the steps; I have less balance than usual. My hands are now preoccupied with delivering toothpaste into my face and cannot steady me, and my head is breathtakingly large. There is wood paneling on the walls, and I walk through the simulated forest that is late 1970s American home decor.

I manage to make it all the way up the stairs, toothpaste still in hand, neck unbroken, toward sounds of my family having dinner. The scraping of cutlery against dishware, the eternal litigation of age-old family quarrels, the barking laughter, set against my uncle's records. A delicate blend of hostility and affection screamed in two languages, intermingled with the music of Dr. Hook and the Medicine Show, it calls to me like the sea does a sailor. This is all I want—to eat the food of my questionable toddler choosing surrounded by my people. This is all I will ever want. The door at the top of the stairs is closed, which is an insurmountable problem for me. I cannot reach the handle, and besides, my hands are covered in toothpaste.

But miraculously, the door opens. My mother is there. I don't remember how she looks, really, or even grasp the concept of what a mother is. I just know that she is mine. I fill in the gaps in my memory with photos from this time—my Italian mother, large green eyes and masses of blond hair, full lips. A small space between her two front teeth. She will be small and beautiful for always. By the time I am thirteen, I will be taller than her. But that is years away. Now she looms over me, bends down, plucks the tube from my hands.

It's too late, of course. I've already savored it. The sweet taste of *defiance*.

Everything in the world would subsequently fall into two categories:

1. The things my mother wanted me to eat

2. Random shit I would shove into my mouth with frenzied abandon

The Venn diagram of these two items would rarely, if ever, overlap.

But I'd already realized, at a very young age, that there were few things in life I could control. Bedtimes and baths were inevitable. There were few battlefields of independence and self-determination left. Clothes were a great place to wage a war, and occasionally, when I was left unattended with a pair of scissors, my own hair presented an excellent canvas for personal expression. But perhaps the greatest of all of these was food. This was where I fought with the fervor of a tiny Valkyrie with freshly butchered bangs.

No one, I'd decided, would tell me what I would eat. Not even those stiff-collared jerks at Poison Control.

My eating habits were unpredictable and chaotic. Most of the time I simply refused food. My mother would beg and cajole me and go through a list of menu items, and I would decline all of them. I was a nightmarish combination of an iron will and a complete disinterest in my own survival. When I was three or four years old, I got a feverish stomach infection that resulted in my body immediately rejecting whatever liquids you tried to put into me. The doctor told my mother she needed to get me to drink or I'd end up hospitalized for dehydration. Sorry? You want me to drink *liquid*? The same substance you keep demanding I also bathe in? The stuff that inexplicably flows into the toilet after it flushes? I had to put a stop to things before they got further out of hand.

My mother tried to bribe me with full-strength apple juice, not the vaguely apple-tasting diluted variety I was normally fed.

I turned up my nose.

I am fairly certain that in a moment of desperation she offered me Coca-Cola. Here, my determination almost wavered. But I knew she had other motives, and so I held strong, with the sort of impenetrable resolve of someone who literally did not know the meaning of the word "compromise."

She threatened me with hospitalization.

Again, I refused.

The next day, I was hospitalized.

I spent two days in the pediatric wing being treated for extreme dehydration. I had an IV and a nurse who fed me juice (which I drank only because she had pink streaks in her hair and multiple piercings, and this assigned her a legitimacy other adults, with their stupid human-colored hair, lacked). But my point had been made.

I wanted autonomy, even if it killed me. And my mother was constantly telling me it would. She was convinced I was going to be stolen the second I set foot outside, that there was a bustling black market for demonic four-year-olds in early 1980s Seattle. So I was allowed to exist in the confines of our home, and occasionally the yard (though even in these controlled spaces my mother would sometimes burst through a door, wide-eyed and out of breath, screaming my name. Because if I played alone too quietly for too long, I was obviously dead). This was not a treatment my brother or my cousins received. I am the first girl in my mother's family to be born since her. There are seven male grandchildren who come before me. There will not be another girl until my cousin Valeria is born, but that is six long years and an entire continent away. For now, there is only me, and my mother made it very clear that kidnappers were not interested in the boys. They wanted me, for some unfathomable reason.

So I conquered the one domain that was left to me: food. I stole raw potatoes as my mother was cutting them up to roast, popping them into my mouth and demanding more, this time with salt. The wedges would crunch between my teeth, some savory, starchy cousin to the apple. (My mother stared at me, mouth agape, the first time I did this. I was barely two years old. Apparently, my father, whom I scarcely knew, had a penchant for doing the same thing.) I ate pasta, but only with butter and salt, and not the Neapolitan ragu my grandmother spent all of Sunday cooking in a massive pot.

But offer me a plate of tripe dripping in a bright red tomato sauce? I would down an entire plate of it, the honeycomb lining of a cow's stomach catching the sugo. I wouldn't touch hot dogs, but I consumed pig's feet and boiled cow's tongue with all the restraint of an underfed hyena, delighting in my cousins' and brother's horror. There was no logic to it save for this: If it caused someone to raise their eyebrows in a measure of alarm or admiration or exasperation, I would eat it.

On more than one occasion I shoved random berries, torn off a plant, into my mouth (perhaps my mother's fears were not entirely unfounded). I remember the interrogation that followed, the attempts to get me to open my mouth and spit out whatever poison was inside. I remember a vague mention of going to the hospital, and me shouting an emphatic "NO" loud enough to shake the windows. I don't remember if they succeeded in making me throw up, but in any case it's irrelevant: I, stubbornly, survived.

"I think you were just trying to experience the world by tasting it," my mother told me once. Which is a rather beautiful retelling of history.

The truth was this: I was trying to defy everyone by eating what was not to be eaten. They, in turn, were simply trying to keep me alive.

"Eat, eat, eat," is the mantra of any Italian family. And eventually, I did. As a teenager I got more independence (my mother was just exhausted by having spent the previous fifteen years in a state of chronic panic over me) and less combative in my eating habits. The food, by then, was less abundant, and I was hungrier than I'd ever been. My mother worked, my grandmother was older, my aunt lived elsewhere. There was no one to cook for me, and so I made things for myself—frozen pizzas or Hot Pockets or meals that consisted entirely of microwave popcorn and ice cream. There was even fast food when it was financially possible.

Slowly, the message from my younger years had started

to morph. "Eat, eat, eat" still echoed from my childhood, but now there was an addendum, something specific that applied to me now that I was a woman: "But don't get fat."

I hadn't anticipated that part of it. It felt like a cruel betrayal, some weird monkey's paw kind of curse. I was finally eager to do what everyone had been asking of me for years (I would have killed for that slow-cooked, rich red sauce of my grandmother's), but now I was being told doing precisely that was undesirable. I had always been thin through childhood and alarmingly so through my adolescence, but toward the end of high school I filled out. I was round-faced, with a posterior notable enough that a girl who hated me went around with my prom photo ridiculing the size of it. (We didn't even go to the same school.)

As I grew older, my mother's dietary views became clear and they reflected a sort of schism with reality afforded by being naturally thin. She had never been on a diet; she ate whatever she wanted and was always, consistently, a size 4. She was convinced that the only reason people got fat was that they ate dessert, and she conveniently has never had a sweet tooth. "You need to stop eating sweets," she told me, like a soothsayer portending some sort of horrible fate. She refused to accept that perhaps we had different body types, that the Punnett square had left me with a distinct selection of genes different from her own. And more important, she refused to accept that fatness was something people could not control. She was of a generation raised to believe that it was a moral failing, something that could and should be overcome. The one time I asked her to let out a dress, she adamantly refused.

"We don't let dresses *out*," she told me. "That dress is big enough."

It had not yet occurred to me that the awful things said to us by our parents were awful things that were once said to them. They had been subject to this same thinking, been forced to adhere to these same rules. This had been going on for years and years, stretching back generations, starting with some single judgmental asshole who decided that bodies should only look one particular way. (Should I ever find out who he was, I will dig up his corpse and desecrate it.)

In the coming years I'd be inundated with an impossible-to-reconcile duality, a dynamic that would replay itself over and over. There would be books and columns with names like "Hungry Bitch" and "Skinny Shrew" telling me how to replace things I wanted to eat with things I did not in order to be dissatisfied and thin. Fashion magazines would advise me to skip orange juice with breakfast and instead opt for a mimosa, to cut down on sugar. Because who cares if you are drunk at 9:00 a.m. if you've saved ninety calories?

I didn't want to eat when food was around, and now that it wasn't, I wanted to eat, but I shouldn't anyway, because food could make me—*gasp*—fat. In my twenties, a series of diets emerged, all of them remarkably confusing in nature, and I knew about them only through societal osmosis. Carbs were bad but bacon was somehow fine, and now we were told to drink clear alcohols with no mixers in them, because mimosas were too sugary, so let's just have vodka with breakfast. The same magazines that said diet desserts were an overly processed sham that didn't actually help you lose weight were literally advertising those exact desserts.

I'd be lying if I said I was able to ignore all of it, that the words never reached my ears, that I spent all my decades on earth loving the body I was in, unequivocally. That I didn't break down in tears when my uncle came up behind me at the dinner table and asked me, teasingly, if I was "stuffing my face again." There were days when my blood would boil with pure rage at all of it. The doubts and castigations roared in the background while I was simply trying to go about my life, eating lunch, having sex, buying jeans. But I adamantly refused to direct any of that rage at myself, because that was precisely where everyone—television, magazines, occasionally my family—told me it belonged. Defiance kicked in again, and when every source was telling me to count calories and worry about getting fat, I blithely ignored all of it and ate. I always ate. I tried to be healthy, and I tried to eat vegetables, because they're good for you and they aid in pooping, but I never counted a carb or denied myself dessert. The best rebellion I could ever come up with was endeavoring to love myself and hurling every piece of dietary advice out the window with the zeal of someone tossing out a cheating lover's belongings.

And I think, honestly, the toothpaste was to blame. The lesson it taught me was too formative, hit me too early, before the world could teach me to hate food, or myself. I could barely walk, but there I was, eating something I shouldn't have been (something that wasn't even technically food) and enjoying the hell out of it. I was taking full possession of my tiny, sticky, mint-fragranced body. I was reaching out and tasting the world and still demanding to be loved.

2

FOR THE SEAFOOD LOVER IN ME

I have developed a somewhat unfortunate habit. If my husband, Rand, is driving and we happen upon a Red Lobster, I will scream, with the urgency of someone who has been stabbed with something very sharp, for him to stop.

"Absolutely not," he will reply cheerfully.

We have been together for more than twenty years. After such a stretch of time, you learn to read your partner's expressions and the secrets hidden in their sighs. You also learn to ignore any casual fine-dining-related screaming. The latter is an important component in the success of any marriage.

There is no Red Lobster close to us. We live in Seattle, and the nearest one to our home is either thirteen miles north or twenty-seven miles south of us. To encounter one is a rare thing, like finding a truffle in dirt. Red Lobster, it should be noted, offers a truffle lobster mac and cheese on its seasonal Lobsterfest menu. A dinner-sized portion contains 1,460 calories and proudly exceeds the recommended daily intake of sodium and cholesterol. With every bite you are laughing at mortality itself. To eat it is to believe, for a moment, that you will live forever. This is simply part of the excellent value proposition Red Lobster offers. My husband does not realize this. And so, as the restaurant and the strip mall it resides in grow smaller in our rearview mirror, I explain it to him again.

"I need endless shrimp for $19.99."

"No you do not. No one needs endless shrimp."

"Orcas do," I say. This is obviously a winning argument.

"You are not an orca," he replies, and keeps on driving.

I accuse him of not loving me. This is a laughable charge, and we both know it. He adores me so completely that at least three of my in-laws have accused me of sexual witchcraft. But these are desperate times. He sighs, the air flowing out of him slowly, along with some of his resolve.

"Do you really want to go? I will turn around."

"No," I say. "It's fine." The concept of endless shrimp feels environmentally reckless. Perhaps living creatures should not be harvested from the sea in infinite quantities so that we may ingest them with all the restraint of a hungry, hungry Bacchus. We keep driving, this irreconcilable difference washing over us: He knows with all the fiber of his being that Red Lobster is a terrible restaurant. And I know with every fiber of my being that he is wrong.

This knowledge has been instilled in me since childhood, perhaps the only thing I have retained from that time. I am no longer a Catholic, and I have abandoned virtually everything the Florida public school system taught me, which is for the best, since they insisted on teaching both perspectives of the Civil War (or the War of Northern Aggression, as more than one of my teachers insisted on calling it). The state song is a minstrel song, which we were taught to sing in a sort of racist patois. In health class, for reasons that made sense only to her, a teacher showed us the symbol for female—a circle with a cross underneath it—and told us that it was synonymous with abortion. In recent years, they've started pulling books from the shelves for containing words. By now, I assume they've replaced chemistry classes with mixology.

My tan from those years, and even some of the scars on my knees and my heart, have faded. But I still love Red Lobster. It had people who were kind to me, and cheesy biscuits that were served warm, in a little basket. It taught me that life had more to offer. That's a lesson that childhood doesn't always impart. Especially if your childhood takes place in Florida.

When I was halfway through second grade, my mother moved us to the central east coast of the state, in what is called the Space Coast. Presumably the name comes from the nearby Kennedy Space Center. Also, because the more apt "Little Congealed Balls of Petroleum Tar That Wash Up on the Beaches Thanks to Off-Shore Drilling Coast" was too wordy for the Florida board of tourism. Mom appeared to be selecting where we would live based on when it had been most recently featured on *America's Most Wanted.* We ended up in Casselberry and later Indialantic, Florida, places that are notable only because of how many times they are mentioned on murderers' Wikipedia pages.

Florida is a terrible place to live. It's not even a good place to visit. I spent seven years there, in a home without air-conditioning, hoping the thermostat would dip below ninety degrees and offer us a reprieve from the endless summer. My mother, still convinced that someone would make me the eventual namesake of a child-protective crime bill, insisted that I keep my window shut at night. It turned my tiny room into a sauna. I didn't sleep for roughly half a decade, while my brain cooked inside my skull. This is probably why I now frequently spend a lengthy span of time looking for an object, only to find that it's in my hand.

This insomnia was exacerbated by the fact that my mother's boyfriend had followed us to Florida from Seattle, and he had the unfortunate distinction of being the most abusive human being I've ever met. Fortunately for me, the Florida "educational system" spends a great deal of time on how to survive natural disasters (it permanently replaced biology sometime in the 1980s), and much of it was applicable to living with a man who was the human equivalent of a tornado. I learned the important lesson that my surroundings, even when they seemed peaceful, might hurl something large (a piece of furniture, a live cow) at me. I could identify coming storms, kept one eye on the sky in case it darkened, took cover when necessary. It became a kind of normal, the way most fucked-up things do when you're a kid.

At school, I had the sad realization that any child who starts out eating toothpaste, and heads immediately to offal the second her molars come in, is not destined for popularity. My mother's assessment of the situation was incorrect: I was not teased because other children were jealous. I was teased because children are pack animals who know to weed out and destroy the weak and the slow and any creature that is too solitary or strange. They are not above cannibalism. Third graders are basically wolves with opposable thumbs.

My classmates swirled around me like a homogeneous mass. They wore the same brand-name clothing and ate the same brand-name fruit snacks. Teachers would snip open their half-frozen Capri Suns at lunchtime. The girls would flip around on the monkey bars, the soles of their perfectly white Keds never touching the ground, long ponytails twirling around them.

One of the ways of getting through a childhood that wasn't perfect and was maybe, I don't know, sort of shitty (sorry, Mom, but also, *Jesus Christ*) is by telling yourself there are small, tangible things that will put you on equal footing with your peers. My classmates had air-conditioning, and pools, and fathers who were disinclined to hurl things across rooms. I wanted these things, but I needed to be more pragmatic in my demands. Instead, I begged for granola bars with chocolate chips and Ecto Cooler juice boxes and Fruit Roll-Ups that I would peel slowly from the plastic. I thought these things would allow me to blend in seamlessly with my classmates. My childhood was as good as theirs because I had Lunchables just like they did. It was an elaborate lie, one that my mother began when she told me the unlikely story that she'd somehow walked into a closed door. One that I continued when we pretended I believed her.

• • •

Running away is a common motif in childhood. Packing bindle sticks, absconding to live with your best friend or possibly a circus, in order to escape your station and the powerlessness imposed on you by youth. For me, I dreamed of absconding to someplace isolated and cold, with lighthouses and icy waters and ramekins filled with melted butter. This fantasy was due, almost entirely, to the Red Lobster chain of restaurants.

Stepping into a Red Lobster is to partake of dinner theater, an elaborate illusion that unfolds while you attempt to eat several species of crustaceans into near extinction. The interior is a pastiche of New England, with its deep blue walls, wooden wainscoting, and nautical-themed decor, designed by someone who quite possibly has never been on a boat. There are black-and-white photos of crew teams now long dead, signal flags hanging from the walls, brass shades on overhead lamps to evoke a galley kitchen. The exterior of nearly every restaurant has horizontal siding, evocative of a northeast coastal home. It's all a fiction. The first Red Lobster was opened in Lakeland, Florida, in 1968 by William Darden, a restaurateur from Georgia. He had noticed that fish sold well at his other restaurants and decided to dedicate an entire establishment to the cuisine. There are now more than seven hundred locations worldwide. (In the continental United States, the only place where Red Lobster cannot be found is northern New England.)

We did not go to restaurants often when I was young. This is still true among certain members of my family. I have an aunt and uncle who adamantly refuse to go out to eat. I cannot remember the last time my mother voluntarily set foot in a restaurant, though she will steer her car down a drive-thru from time to time. Usually the only time anyone can be tempted is if there is a promise of an all-you-can-eat buffet. They will spend money if they feel as if they were pulling something over on someone, a dynamic that requires unfettered access to crab legs. But when I was young, if there was reason to celebrate, or my mother's boyfriend needed to smooth over some particularly notable rampage, we would go out to eat. Servers would stare at us when we arrived and smile. We looked like a little family. Here is the mother, here is the son, here is the daughter. Here is a vaguely father-shaped human being. No one needed to know that he called me a little bitch or that he referred to my brother with homophobic slurs. When you're a kid, you want the adults in your life to love you and one another. When that seems impossible, you settle for the next-best thing: Cheddar Bay Biscuits.

Sometimes during the summer, my mother's brother would come from Italy to visit with his family. My uncle and his family would stay with my grandparents, all of them crammed into the guest bedroom. I dragged a suitcase over from our house within the first week of their arrival and would sleep on a twin bed crammed into my grandparents' room. My uncle occasionally yelled, but it was Italian yelling, which usually had to do with soccer or politics that I didn't understand, and people yelled back. It wasn't angry; it was just loud, punctuated by laughter. Sometimes when we went out, people mistook me for their daughter. I never corrected them.

We went to the beach almost every day. It was a fifteen-minute walk from my grandparents' house under a scorching sun. We rarely wore sunblock. My cousin Marco and I dug up tiny clams from the beach, collecting them in a pile. My aunt had me carry them back in the bra of my bathing suit, which scandalized me. Later she would make us spaghetti alle vongole, garlicky, dotted with tiny rubbery bivalves that she swore were the same ones we'd dug up. Cooking any sort of seafood was rare in my family. My grandparents were from mountain villages outside Naples. The only fish they regularly ate were anchovies, which I hated with the enthusiasm you would expect from a child. But my aunt's pasta was something altogether different. It tasted elegant. It was of the sea, but somehow Italian, and until that moment these seemed irreconcilable to me. I interrogated her about the clams, refusing to believe they were the ones we'd gathered. She would not admit her deception for another twenty years: They were from a can.

There are currently five pasta entrées available at Red Lobster, four of which contain shellfish, and all of which conveniently exceed the recommended daily sodium intake for adult humans. They are entirely American inventions. My family did not eat grilled Cajun chicken linguini Alfredo in the old country.

Spaghetti alle vongole does not appear on Red Lobster's menu.

Most of the time during these summer visits, we ate at my grandparents' home. My aunt, my mother, my grandmother, and occasionally even my uncle would cook pastas and lasagnas and stewed meats over a hot stove on a stifling ninety-degree day. But at the end of each trip, we would go to Red Lobster as a finale. I don't know how this tradition started. But once every summer, and sometimes twice if our whining was well placed enough, we would pile into our cars and eat (if the menu was to be believed) like admirals. It made their departure bittersweet—an odd thing to look forward to each year, something to take the sting out of having to return to my own home, of school starting again, of being too young to do anything about my unhappiness.

But for at least a moment, Florida's casual dining helped create an illusion of something I thought was inaccessible to me. There was air-conditioning. There were tablecloths. There was the sound of clinking silverware in the distance and a tank of lobsters by the door. I didn't mind when there was a wait, because there was nothing greater than the anticipation—knowing the feast that was ahead of me. That for at least ninety minutes, nothing could go wrong. That no plates would be thrown, no yelling would occur.

I would sit on a bench near the door and stare at the tank of lobsters. Some had rubber bands around their claws, which my mother argued was a cruelty. If you were going to be boiled to death, she reasoned, you should be able to fight back. For some reason, her advocacy on behalf of doomed crustaceans made me irrationally angry. I had no understanding of allegory.

Every meal at Red Lobster comes with a house salad, and we all opted to upgrade ours to a Caesar. The lettuce is covered in garlicky dressing so thick it threatens to wilt, a sprinkle of cheese like fine snow, crowned with a few golden-brown croutons. Sometimes it came with black olives. Caesar salad was first invented in Tijuana, Mexico, by an Italian immigrant named Caesar Cardini. At the age of eleven, I did not know this. I knew only that it cost seventy-five cents extra, but it was allowed, because it was deemed a good value.

I almost always ordered the same thing: shrimp scampi and a fully loaded baked potato. The shrimp swam in a tiny ramekin of butter and garlic that was too hot to touch. Scampi is an Italian word, singular being scampo. It refers to a type of small lobster that is found throughout Europe. I ordered my baked potato loaded because it cost the same as a baked potato with merely butter.

The visiting Italians marveled at the potato, now elevated to affordable lower-middle-class luxury with a dollop of melting sour cream, waxy slivers of yellow cheese, and a sprinkling of tiny green onions, thrown over the top like confetti. They had never seen anything like it. I wanted to impress them with this show of toppings. I wanted them to fall in love with America and with me. I wanted them to move to Florida so I would feel less alone. Also, perhaps they would adopt me. I hadn't asked, but we all got along, and it seemed only reasonable that we move in that direction.

"I've always wanted to go to Italy," one server said to us after overhearing my family speak.

"Yes, yes, it's wonderful," we all said, nodding, though I scarcely had any idea what I was talking about.

The Cheddar Bay Biscuits—arguably the most famous item in the Reb Lobster oeuvre—came out hot in unlimited quantities. They arrived, safely nestled in a basket, like baby Moses upon the banks of the Nile, but with more garlic butter. My mother invariably tucked some in a napkin and smuggled them out of the restaurant in her purse. Later, removed from their natural environment and reheated in the oven, the biscuits' magic would somehow be lost. But they existed as a reminder, a souvenir of our time there. For a moment, I could pretend I was in a restaurant, and that restaurant was pretending to be in New England.

We never ordered dessert. Or soda. Or appetizers. These things, we were reminded, were "how they get you." Restaurant chains were akin to grifters in my family. You needed to constantly have the upper hand. There were infinite add-ons, markups, and traps—ready to prey upon those who were less savvy about their money. This would not be me. I was going to be clever. Money meant I could afford trips to Italy, and Disney World, and shoes with little blue rubber labels on the back. When I begged my mother to leave her boyfriend, money was one of the reasons she said she couldn't. I was going to have it in massive quantities.

I did not mind that we were relegated to merely water and entrées and endless biscuits. I did not feel deprived. There was an abundance before me. Behold the bounty of the sea, dredged up from the depths of the oceans, battered and deep-fried or lounging in butter. My cousin ordered both tartar and cocktail sauce—foreign concoctions that he had never tried before—because there was no need to choose just one. We could have everything. For ninety minutes, we could even have air-conditioning.

They never moved here, and in hindsight I do not blame them. They lived in Italy, and I expected them to leave that behind in favor of a state where toddlers were legally allowed to own firearms. Based merely on anecdotal observation, I am fairly certain the official state bird of Florida is a vulture that drowned in the neighbor's pool. The state's board of health recently declared Funyuns a vegetable. The punch lines come easily—a tight five about the state's many shortcomings, masking the fact that all I ever wanted from it was to fit in, to belong, to have it love me back.

After seven years in the Sunshine State, my family moved back to Seattle. My mother still had the same boy-friend, on and off and on again. When I was in college, he locked me out of her house because I'd cut my hair too short for his liking. I didn't go home often, but instead stayed in the dorms, and later my own apartment. In the tiny kitchen of my studio, I learned to make Red Lobster's Cheddar Bay Biscuits. They are easy to pull together—a basic buttermilk biscuit, with some added garlic powder and cheddar cheese. Making them in my home felt like a power I shouldn't have had, a sort of magic too potent for mere mortals to wield. To have Red Lobster biscuits anytime you wanted—this was why the gods punished Prometheus. You can make them from scratch, but I've found that using a Bisquick mix works just as well. Add milk to the mix, per the instructions, then fold in cheddar cheese and garlic powder. The final step is to brush the freshly baked biscuits with melted butter and more garlic powder, as well as a sprinkling of salt. Parsley or chives can be added if you are inclined, but those are not strictly necessary. They take roughly twenty minutes to make, including baking time. (There is also a premade, fro-zen variant. I have not tried them. I am adamant there need to be more steps to decadence than just a properly preheated oven.)

At this time in my life, it does not yet occur to me that

the things I have always longed for are things I can make myself. That if I want cheesy garlic biscuits, I can bake them. That if I wish to have a loving family, I can create one. I still believe that these things are preordained and inaccessible to me, destined to happen only to the girls with shiny hair and perfect blue tags at the backs of their shoes. I still somehow think that if someone treats you badly, even if you are a child, it is because you deserve it. This is, apparently, easier to wrap my head around than the alternative.

I am in my junior year of college. My dating life, until this point, has been the final scene from *Fight Club* where all the buildings collapse, minus the romantic hand holding. It usually ends with me wailing, "But I love you," and them replying, "But I don't love you," and me more or less sobbing incoherently for what I am certain will be the rest of my life. I assume that this is just the nature of relationships, or at least the nature of relationships for me. When a boy I meet on a bus asks me to dinner, I am anxious, but agree to go. Because I am lonely. Just as, if not more important, I am hungry.

This date takes me to an Italian restaurant. I order the spaghetti alle vongole, and when the waiter comes by, I speak with him in Italian. My date stares, mouth hanging half-open, in a sort of reverence. I cannot see myself clearly, the way none of us can when we are twenty-one and sad and think that maybe no one should love us at all. It is like looking at a painting too close up. And so when he wants to see me again, and again, and again, I am baffled at first. I am baffled for years.

He turns out to be kind, and not inclined to yelling, and

he does not run away in horror when he sees me tear connective tissue from bone like a raptor while eating. I assume he is just going to be a seasonal special, available for a limited time only. But his overwhelming popularity earns him a place on the permanent menu.

What I am saying is this: Eater, I married him.

He learns to make me spaghetti alle vongole, soaking the fresh clams in frigid water so they spit out all the sand. He takes me to Italy, and we eat fried anchovies in waterfront towns. To Portugal, where we eat giant platters of fish while staring at the sea. We sit in chilly restaurants in Boston and bite into lobster rolls in restaurants with tile-lined walls. We eat sushi from a 7-Eleven in Tokyo and marvel at how good it is.

I often ask him why he loves me.

"Because you are great," he says.

"WHY?? WHAT IS BROKEN ABOUT YOU THAT MAKES YOU THINK THAT?" I often scream back.

He usually just shrugs and kisses me, and tells me I am his favorite person. It is still deeply confusing, but twenty years later I no longer think that it is a mistake or that he has me mixed up with someone else.

One year, for my birthday, he surprises me with a dinner at Red Lobster. The gleam of the restaurant has faded, the way things do with time and perspective. After all, what use is an escape when you no longer have anything to escape from? But the air-conditioning is cool, and the salads are still included as part of the meal. I don't remember the lettuce being iceberg, or this wilted. Or the croutons being slightly stale and ... dusty? The biscuits are still excellent because they are filled with cheese and butter and salt (or, as they are known in Tampa, "nutrients"). But the meal, on the whole, is stunningly mediocre. And I do not care. I haven't come to Red Lobster for the salad. I haven't even come to Red Lobster for the lobster. I have come back because this is where I once dreamed of the life I wanted to have, one meal at a time. And now, when I compare it with the life that I do have, the luster of this restaurant is gone. It's a bittersweet thing, to look back at your childhood dreams and know that you've exceeded them, that you were so desperately longing for not that much. I just wanted to feel safe and loved and to maybe eat an environmentally irresponsible quantity of fried crustaceans.

There are no illusions left to maintain, and when people look at us, I hope they see the truth. Here is a woman, happy with who she is. Here is a man who is patient and kind and loves her so much that he will call her bluff and take her to casual fine dining seafood restaurants. Here is the woman's purse. Inside are two Cheddar Bay Biscuits wrapped in a napkin. She has no idea how they got there.

3

I'LL HAVE WHAT I'M HAVING

A statistic that was thrown out repeatedly in my child-hood was that the average American household watched nearly seven hours of television a day. Every time it was mentioned, cultured and well-bred people were absolutely scandalized.

"There is no way that is possible," they would gasp, clutching their pearls and their monocles and their tiny dogs, and whatever fancy things people who don't watch a lot of television clutch. Our teachers read this statistic to us, often, in a sort of preemptive shaming of potential behaviors that would almost certainly lead to unemployment, prison, and an early death. (This pretty much defined much of my early scholastic career: Go to bed early and say the Pledge of Allegiance and don't ever smoke pot or you won't amount to anything. Well, look who is extremely high and laughing now, Mrs. Schmidt.) My classmates were baffled as to how the average was so high, since they were not allowed to watch *that* much television. And there were some kids—extremely maladjusted kids, I might add, who probably grew up to tuck in their shirts with shorts and vote libertarian—who were not allowed to watch any television at all.

I, of course, knew the answer. I was making up for all of them, single-handedly. I sat on the ground, mouth agape, watching hours and hours of sitcoms and talk shows and game shows and unintentionally hilarious edited-for-network-television feature films. Television has always been there for me, so I don't like to bad-mouth it. It was a perfectly adequate parent, reliable and generally trustworthy, week after week, except when my broadcast was interrupted with a very important news bulletin. It was more emotionally intelligent than a lot of people I've met, with music that would help you read the room and live studio audience reactions to help delineate what was a joke and what was not.

Where did it get me, you ask? I am certain that if I am ever on *Jeopardy!* and the categories are "Romantic Comedies of the Early 1990s," "John Stamos," and "Other Episodes of *Jeopardy!*," I would clean *up*. It also gave me a wildly fucked-up impression of the relationships adult women had—not only with romantic partners, but with food, which became allegorical to their messy dating lives. At some point, I started to wonder if the writers of these movies and TV shows based their entire knowledge of women on *other* movies and TV shows and not on actual women. They moved further and further away from the source material so that the result was a derivation of a derivation, a weird caricature with boobs that would fall, clumsily but charmingly, off the screen and hopefully into viewers' hearts as an assortment of Hershey's Miniatures spilled out of her purse.

Women on television, I'd found, were portrayed in only a few ways when it came to food:

1. She doesn't eat. It's not that she's starving herself, at least not canonically. It was just that she's never seen consuming food, ever. It's as though she were the human equivalent of an air plant, sucking nutrients straight from the atmosphere, even as her male counterparts are allowed to go to restaurants and order food and consume calories. I've watched nearly every single episode of *Friends* at least once (it was the 1990s, I was young, mistakes were made, including a haircut that involved "chunky layers." Let's just move on). And without fail, all of the men *eat*. (There's an entire episode where Ross gets justifiably angry when someone eats his Thanksgiving leftover sandwich.) But the women don't. Hell, Monica is a chef, and while she's allowed to talk about food, the only time it's ever close to her mouth is when she puts a turkey on her head (she is shown eating, but it's when she's "Fat Monica"—Courteney Cox in a fat suit that appears in flashbacks and alternate realities. A specific brand of bullshit that I will address in #4.)

2. She eats garbage. She's basically a raccoon with breasts. She doesn't cook for herself, because—I don't know, she doesn't have time, she never learned, her parents died in a nutritionally well-balanced accident

and now she can eat only Hot Pockets. All of that is backstory, and we don't care about that. What we care about is a grown woman who eats candy for dinner, which is a signal that she's just a hilarious mess. This is the domain of Lorelai Gilmore, whose diet can be found on the shelves of a gas station, and Liz Lemon, angrily tucking into her plate of night cheese. Even Leslie Knope and Olivia Pope, who are stunningly competent in their careers and know exactly what they want, eat waffles or popcorn for dinner (Leslie refuses to eat salad because she "doesn't hate" herself). The Sexy Garbage Eater's tendency to eat Runts candy instead of fruit is a window into her disorganized soul, a signifier that despite her intelligence and her accomplishments, she's approachable, she doesn't have it all together, that she just might need someone (read: a rakishly handsome guy with floppy hair) to feed her. But, hey, all of these characters are thin, so it's okay to eat trash.

3. She's extremely picky about food and will therefore die alone. I've seen this scene in countless romantic comedies—a male character on an endless string of dates, wherein his female companion proves herself to be high maintenance based on the specificity of her ordering. In Netflix's abysmal *Love, Guaranteed* (note: Never watch this movie), Damon Wayans Jr.'s character goes on a thousand dates—literally!—all at the same restaurant, looking for love. What follows is

a montage of women who are all wrong for him, as is illustrated by their specificity of ordering meals. One wants dressing on the side! In the romantic comedy universe, she might as well have ordered a flayed kitten. When he ends up having dinner with his lawyer, Susan (played by Rachael Leigh Cook), she orders, simply, a burger and fries.

The server looks stunned, waiting for some sort of augmentation. "That's it?" she asks.

"Extra mayo," Susan replies.

"I like this one," the server says approvingly.

In *How to Lose a Guy in 10 Days,* Andie (played by Kate Hudson) is trying to drive away Matthew McConaughey's character, so she sends him off to get her Diet Coke instead of regular (and openly weeps at the table while yelling that he thinks she's fat). Later, when he cooks her a rack of lamb, she tells him she's a vegetarian and insists he take it out of her sight before she gags. The message is clear: Dieters and vegetarians are unstable drama queens (fear not: Andie is, of course, lying. She eats anything—a sign of her desirability—and is hot and skinny).

In *Sex and the City,* the impetus for one of the biggest fights between Carrie and Big is when she lies about having an allergy to parsley because her aversion to the herb is so strong. It comes to symbolize not only Carrie's fussiness and particularities but also her dishonesty (spoiler: She will later cheat on her fiancé, Aidan, with Big).

Everyone remembers the "I'll have what she's having" scene in *When Harry Met Sally*... when Meg Ryan fakes an orgasm over a sandwich at Katz's to prove a point. But the one that really stuck with me was always when she's ordering at a diner with Harry.

WAITRESS: What can I get you?
HARRY: I'll have the Number Three.
SALLY: I'd like the chef salad, please, with the oil and vinegar on the side. And the apple pie à la mode.... But I'd like the pie heated, and I don't want the ice cream on top. I want it on the side. And I'd like strawberry instead of vanilla if you have it. If not, then no ice cream, just whipped cream, but only if it's real. If it's out of a can, then nothing.
WAITRESS: Not even the pie?
SALLY: No, just the pie. But then not heated.
WAITRESS: Uh-huh.

The scene was apparently inspired by the late, great Nora Ephron's way of ordering food, which was incredibly elaborate. And while Ephron writes her female lead with a lot of charm and depth, this scene becomes a metaphor for why Sally can't find love: She's too particular, she demands too much, and she terrifies Harry. It's not the first time a woman has been portrayed as too picky and too demanding about her food, and therefore too picky and demanding

about life in general. The message isn't subtle: If you
want to be loved, you must have zero special requests.

4. She's fat. She eats. For some reason, this is *hilarious.*
This is the low-hanging fruit on the comedy tree.
Look! A woman who is fat and eating food! Let us
ridicule her for having a round body that consumes
calories. I don't know when this narrative shift
happened—it was way before I was born, and I think
that the makers of aspartame are somehow to blame
in all of this—but fat became something to be
ashamed of, rather than just something that *was,* a
part of our bodies that everyone had. And women
who are hungry for food are often portrayed as
hungry for love as well. Half of the time, these
women aren't even fat. (NOTE: THIS DOES NOT
MEAN IT IS OKAY TO TREAT PEOPLE WHO
ARE FAT LIKE THIS. It just highlights how unrealistic body images are for women that skinny women
are called fat and fat women are told to jump in the
sea.) In *Love Actually,* Martine McCutcheon's character, who is a U.S. size 6, maybe a size 8 (*gasp,* the
horror!), is disparagingly called "the chubby girl" and
described as having "a pretty sizable arse" (in her
workplace! Because we all know that having a big
butt means you can't do your job properly). In *Bridget
Jones's Diary,* the titular character's weight is a constant focal point (and Renée Zellweger's weight gain
for the film was the subject of countless magazine

articles). At the time of filming, she was five feet four inches and 140 pounds—five pounds heavier and an inch taller than my own five-foot-three frame. (It's impossible not to draw parallels. People weren't just talking about Zellweger's body. They were talking about *mine*.)

The Mindy Project attempts to turn this same trope on its head. "I'm not overweight," the titular character says. "I fluctuate between chubby and curvy." Like McCutcheon's and Zellweger's, Mindy Kaling's body resembles that of so many women I know (including my own), and while that feels like a triumph in Hollywood, her character falls prey to the same clichés, the same jokes about weight, the idea that her eating is somehow a laughable offense. Mindy insists that her weight isn't an issue, but it comes up again and again. Her excessive confidence seems to exist in spite of it and becomes a punch line in and of itself.

Other times, the manifestation of this tired joke is just a skinny actor in a fat suit—everyone from Gwyneth Paltrow to Julia Roberts has played the chubby girl who hopes that someone can *somehow* see their inner beauty. Savala Nolan, author and director of the Henderson Center for Social Justice at UC Berkeley School of Law, writes that the fat suit "perpetuates the categorically false and harmful myth that fat people are thin people for whom something went wrong, and that there is a thin person in every fat person who wants ('deserves') to get out." And this framing starts *early*. I remember watching an episode of *Scooby-Doo* when I was a kid that inexplicably featured Cass Elliot—the lead singer of the Mamas & the Papas—as the guest star. Elliot had notoriously struggled with her weight, and the episode itself was peppered with fat jokes (there's a scene where she gets stuck in an air vent and promises to go on a grapefruit diet, and by the end of the episode she's shown eating an entire tray of grapefruits, topped with hot fudge and whipped cream. Everyone has a laugh about it). I probably watched it in the mid-1980s, and remember it clearly forty years later, but it originally aired in 1973. Less than a year after it first aired, Elliot would die from heart failure likely due to drug use and crash dieting. (And yet the rumor persists, to this day, that she choked on a ham sandwich.)

5. She's the "She Doesn't Eat Like Other Girls" Girl. She eats like Joey Chestnut about to win his championship competitive eating title—entire hot dogs swallowed whole in a matter of seconds. She does it to illustrate that she's low maintenance, and "one of the guys," and has no gag reflex. She won't bother her spouse with the particularities of her appetites (be they carnal or emotional or epicurean), won't get upset when he fails to show up at her grandmother's funeral because he was too hungover from hanging out with his fraternity brothers. She is, to put it bluntly, not that particular about what she puts inside her body, and she is free from being food- or

slut-shamed for this because she's hot and thin. And all of this without ever showing any sign of working those calories off, of any of the work involved in being that hot, of the sheer impossibility involved in consuming that much food and being that thin without the aid of a tapeworm, because no one wants to see the effort that goes into being effortless. No one wants to see how the sausage is made (but they will watch a video of her swallowing one whole).

Though easily confused with our trash-eating raccoon with breasts, this archetype eats trash not because of a deep-seated chaos within her soul but because she needs to be appealing to the opposite sex. She is a construct made to reflect the male gaze and has no actual personality. She does not have wants or feelings or needs of her own. Because if you start to express too much emotion or demand too much of a partner or of life in general, you could get labeled as "high maintenance" or "difficult" or— worst of all—"crazy." Once you are branded with it, it will follow you everywhere. It's like an ancient Greek curse where the harder you fight against it, the more it seems true.

Gillian Flynn touched on this concept in *Gone Girl,* in one of the novel's most famous passages. Amy, one of the book's narrators, describes what it means to be a man's ideal: the cool girl.

"Men always say that as the defining compliment, don't they? She's a cool girl. Being the Cool Girl means I am a hot, brilliant, funny woman who adores football, poker, dirty jokes, and burping, who plays video games, drinks cheap beer, loves three-somes and anal sex, and jams hot dogs and hamburgers into her mouth like she's hosting the world's biggest culinary gang bang while somehow maintaining a size 2, because Cool Girls are above all hot. Hot and understanding. Cool Girls never get angry; they only smile in a chagrined, loving manner and let their men do whatever they want. Go ahead, shit on me, I don't mind, I'm the Cool Girl."

There were life lessons that I started to glean from all of this, and there was no one around to tell me not to believe them. You can't be the high-maintenance crazy girl who wants dressing on the side because she goes home alone and unloved. You need to be the sort of girl who can devour a burger while simultaneously looking as if you've never eaten a burger. So I happily drank Mountain Dew and ordered Hardee's or Subway because that's where the guys were going, even though no one likes Hardee's or Subway and Mountain Dew tastes as if the entire product development team were going through a rough divorce. I've never been on a diet, but to say that I haven't denied myself what I've wanted would be disingenuous. I have starved myself in other ways.

By the time I was fifteen, some of these ideas had already started to take hold. That was the year I had my first kiss and began dating my first boyfriend. For the purposes of this essay, I will call him Shane, because my editor rejected the other pseudonym I gave him of "Assmouth."

I was fifteen, and he was a year older—a delta of time

that seemed infinite when I'd spent so little time on the planet. It's why children measure their ages in fractions—because those little increments of time feel bigger when you are young. Or perhaps it was because it always felt as if he were looking down on me. After we'd broken up, I'd point out this tendency of his, and he would usually tell me something like "No one can make you feel inferior without your consent," which is a quotation that's often attributed to Eleanor Roosevelt and repeated by shitty people who want you to feel responsible when they hurt your feelings.

The first time we hung out, he took me to the marina, which was where kids went to make out, but I took him at his word when he said he just wanted to talk. Which we did. We also held hands, and it was rather sweet, and he waited for me to kiss him, closing his eyes expectantly again and again. I worked up the nerve to finally do it. He responded by shoving his tongue into my mouth. He declared I was his girlfriend the next day, stealing one of my Reese's Peanut Butter Cups under the guise of communal property.

On our first official date, he took me to a restaurant where he'd worked the summer before and told me what I should order: fettuccine Alfredo. I rarely had the chance to go to restaurants. If I did go out, I was not going to order pasta, which was something I had in abundance at home. More important, I do not like fettuccine Alfredo.

I ordered the fettuccine Alfredo.

In the early weeks of our relationship, I would be on the defense—trying to fend off his hands as he attempted to grab my chest. He laughed as I swatted them away, as if we were just playing a game of keep-away. I laughed nervously, too, because he was laughing, and maybe this was just a game? Maybe if I stopped trying to fight him off, he'd stop trying, too. But I didn't want to test the theory.

It was the mid-1990s. We were told that "no means no," but no one told us what happened after that. No one told me that "no" would just be perceived as a starting point in a negotiation.

I wanted to be the person that he wanted. So my interests fell into line with his—depressing music, geopolitics, corduroy pants. We made out when he felt like it, when he had time, and if I ever initiated anything, he'd ridicule me mercilessly. As if I'd ceded ground I hadn't meant to. I had a poster for the movie *Speed* in my room, a larger-than-life Keanu Reeves staring at me from the ceiling above my bed. Shane teased me for it. I eventually took it down, not because I wanted to, but because I didn't want the criticism.

He was an asshole, but also: I never walked away. Because that was never part of the narrative. The narrative was how to be appealing to guys. Not how to leave them. So I tried to be what he wanted, which required being less of myself. We dated, officially, for two and a half months. He would finally break up with me, laying out during our lunch break a laundry list of negative attributes I possessed and branding me as overdramatic when I sat there, unable to muster a reply and teary-eyed. When he started dating a friend of mine, I was heartbroken. And when he showed up on my doorstep in the middle of the night a few short months later, telling me he still loved me, but couldn't break up with her for complex reasons, this somehow made perfect sense to me. It was confirmation of my own worth. *Of course we should have a clandestine teenage affair! What a brilliant and morally sound idea that will certainly end well for everyone involved.* I didn't yet know that being alone is far better than being with someone who relegates you to being their dirty secret, their sidepiece for uncomfortable, sweaty teenage hookups. And it was such a cruelty to someone who, before dating Shane, had been my friend. I wish I had loved her better than that. I wish I had loved myself better.

Whenever Shane appeared on my doorstep, my mother, displaying an affinity for horrible men and an extreme lack of judgment, would let him in and *offer to cook for him.* He'd graciously take her up on it, eating a bowl of pasta she'd made him before wandering up to my bedroom or sitting on my couch while I sat there half-awake, wondering what I had to do to make him stay.

By now, I'd learned not to complain too much about our arrangement. If I did, he'd disappear for a few weeks. I didn't understand all the ways that people could control you with a narrative about yourself. He'd told me that I was immature and inclined to histrionics. And so I tried to be disaffected and to laugh off shit that would have prompted a sea cucumber with a sliver of self-respect to walk (flop?) away.

He told me I was too possessive and too demanding, and I started to think that maybe I was. When a boy from another school gave me his phone number at an extracurricular event, Shane snatched the paper away teasingly and never gave it back. I thought asking for it would make me seem petty or jealous, so I said nothing. His approach was alarmingly effective: I'd started to question my own response to everything. The story he told so, so well was that I was overreacting, overemotional, defensive, difficult, high maintenance. And there was no way I could respond without proving him right.

There was also an unspoken fear, looming in the air, that if word got out, it would likely be my reputation, and only mine, that took the hit. "You know how you could really get me to leave her?" Shane said to me one evening.

"How?" I asked, trying to hide the absolute desperation in my voice.

"If you could cook like your mom," Shane said. Then, he told me, there was no way he'd be able to stay with his girlfriend.

"Oh," I said.

And I don't know if it was because deep down I had already concluded he was full of shit, or because I realized that he didn't deserve that particular part of my soul (even then, cooking for someone seemed more precious than kissing them), but I knew: I would never fucking do *that*.

I finally left for college, and he was unable to show up at my home, unannounced, late at night. I filed him under "Mistakes, teenage," and moved on with my life.

We crossed paths, mostly unexpectedly, once a decade or so, and then years passed without my seeing him, until he showed up at one of my readings for the publication of my first book. He deliberately got at the back of the line, waiting for other people to clear before he approached my table. By then the crowd had thinned; my husband was talking to friends.

"So, *this* is awkward," Shane said.

"No, it's really not," I said, feeling again that same pressure to make sure *he* was comfortable, above all else. I told him how another boy from my past—one I'd dated after Shane—had shown up at one of my events. Someone who had broken my heart years ago had bought my book and had me sign his copy, and it had been fine. Lovely, even. It was possible to forget the past, or at least to leave it in the past. It was possible to grow beyond who we were as shitty teenagers.

Shane rolled his eyes. "I treated you better than *that* guy," he said defensively.

He did not treat me better than that guy. But I was on some sort of weird polite conversation autopilot. And I also was genuinely curious as to how he'd bent his own reality so that he now thought something so utterly untrue.

"Did you?" I asked.

"He didn't even bother turning off the TV when you gave him a blow job," Shane said.

For the record: This is not how to make your case that you were less of a misogynistic asshole than someone else.

There were a lot of ways that I wanted to react, all complicated by the fact that I have zero recollection of the event he was describing. I've imagined all the ways I could have responded differently. His copy of my book was in my hands, and I considered dedicating it with, simply, "Fuck you." But honestly? I wasn't sure if he'd paid for the book yet.

I contemplated calmly telling him to leave. I considered standing up and yelling. But I was also burning with shame, my cheeks flushed at something that I shouldn't have felt shame at. My entire body was screaming "FLEE," and also "Maybe consider starting a new life somewhere far from here, because you've fucked this one up irrevocably." It made no sense that he had the power to make me feel this way. This was a guy who showed up at my house for years, begging me for the same thing he was chastising me for.

There's an expectation that women need to be up for anything, lest we be labeled frigid or a prude (the same high-maintenance and difficult argument but translated to sexual willingness). But the second you *are* up for anything, you're a slut. So you need to be completely willing and competently able to suck a dick. You need to have the enthusiasm of someone who has been walking across the desert for three days and believes that the penis that sits before them will, if stoked properly, spurt cool crystal spring water. But also? You better not have sucked too many dicks. You need to be a dick-sucking prodigy, if you will. A natural at it, despite zero real-life experience. You need to coyly blush and say, "A pee-nis? I have never laid mine virgin eyes on one before. For, you see, Father forbids me to speak to menfolk!" And then you loosen your corset (I forgot to mention: You are wearing a corset) and proceed to go to town on that sucker like a milkmaid whose hands are tied behind her back. The Virgin-Whore Complex isn't new, but no one told us we had to be both at once.

The narrative has been baked in—so early and so deep—that you can't ask for too much, or be too much, or want too much, or make too much of a fuss. Even when someone treats you like garbage. Even long after you've learned that you deserve better. And so I said nothing.

Afterward, I went to a diner with my friends, all of them eager to celebrate my first book, and I barely spoke. No one knew what had happened moments earlier, and I was too ashamed to tell them. When we ordered a giant platter of fries, I wanted a side of ranch dressing with it, a relic of my high school eating habits. But I was too skittish to ask, worried about bothering the server, afraid I'd come across as too demanding.

"Just ask for ranch," my friend Kim said.

"I can't!" I said. "Because twenty years ago I might or might not have engaged in a consensual sex act while a TV was on somewhere in the background. Consequently, I'm a slutty slut-slut who sluts and doesn't deserve food—or really anything."

Just kidding! I didn't say those things. Because I was too ashamed, and deep down I knew that my friends would make me feel better, which I didn't think I deserved (because of all the slutting I'd done). So I just sat there.

It's a hard thing to learn: that we can ask things of other people, that we can order food how we want it. That our bodies deserve to be nourished and loved and fed the way we want them to be. In the end, Kim ordered the dressing for me. I ate my fries, surrounded by people who knew and loved and fed me, and reminded myself that this was not an extraordinary thing.

"I'm proud of you," Kim told me, holding my book in her hands.

She herself is adored by her husband, by her children, by her friends. She is such a picky eater that her spouse lovingly jokes that he needs to create a manual, lest anything ever happen to him. *The Care and Feeding of Kim.* I reminded myself that we can ask this of the world and of ourselves. To be fed, and to be loved, and not made to feel unhinged or overly emotional. This request is not too grand.

Still, sometimes, even now, I hear Billy Crystal's voice echoing in my head from *When Harry Met Sally* . . .

"You're high maintenance, but you think you're low maintenance."

Now I see the biting cruelty of it, of telling a woman who knew what she wanted to eat and what she wanted out of love that she was just too much damn work. But as a teenager, I had only one reasonable response: to lie to myself about what I wanted, for as long as I possibly could, lest I face the unimaginably horrible fate of dying alone. (What's wrong with dying alone, anyway? Do you really want people around as you deliriously mutter the names of old lovers and childhood pets while you empty your bowels?)

I can't entirely blame TV and movies, but I wish they had done a better job. Things have changed in the last few decades. We see female characters who are real, with needs and wants and desires and appetites. *Ocean's 8,* the all-female reboot of *Ocean's 11,* features an entire scene where Sandra Bullock is explaining a plan to her fellow heist member while just *eating.* In an episode of *Shrill,* Annie, played by Aidy Bryant, stands in her kitchen joyously eating pasta by herself, after realizing that, holy hell, she's a *catch.* More and more, women are shown eating, not as a plot point, but simply as something we do, something we are allowed to derive joy from, and not a sign of our neediness or difficulty, or inherent fuckability. We aren't starving for anything—even if we don't end up with anyone.

I'd never realized that was a possibility, not until many

years later. I'm doing my best to unlearn the lessons of my childhood and teen years. Saying my desires and needs out loud, and realizing that doing so doesn't make me demanding or unlovable. Sometimes my husband asks me what I want for dinner, and instead of shrugging my shoulders, I tell him. It's one of the hardest things I've ever had to do—stating exactly what I want. But then it's there, in front of me, this beautiful thing that I asked for.

That's the thing about voicing your needs: The world tells you how bad you'll look if you do it. But no one tells you how great you'll feel.

4

THE BIKINI BODY OF CHRIST

Culinarily speaking, Catholicism is a mixed bag. The entire religion is built around a system of abstinence and denying oneself bodily pleasures, with the occasional pre- and post-Lenten bacchanalia that gave rise to such festivals as Mardi Gras and *MTV Spring Break*. Even on regular Sunday mornings there are moments of brief fasting, which culminate in the symbolic cannibalization of our Lord and Savior, Jesus Christ. We eat his body and drink his blood (*symbolically! Don't yuck our yum God!*), which is, if you think about it, super metal for a religion that considers Billy Joel rock music. My non-Catholic friends have often asked me what the Eucharist—the unleavened bread that is consecrated to become the body of Christ via the process of transubstantiation (*phew*)—tastes like. My answer, unfailingly, is that it's a little like a dry ramen noodle except instead of salt it contains guilt. It's bland and wheaty and not unpleasant, nor could it be described as good. No one has ever said, "You know what I'm jonesing for? A big ol' bowl of the body of Christ." The Communion wafer itself is not going to turn anyone off the religion (Don't worry! We have plenty of stuff that will!), but it wouldn't serve as a recruitment tool, either.

This hasn't stopped some secularists from munching down on the unconsecrated version, out of some sort of perverse novelty, like voluntarily drinking Manischewitz. My friend Doug Mack, a veritable snack expert, notes that selling "stuff that was *almost* communion wafers but literally didn't make the cut" is quite popular in Quebec, where the "host cuttings" can be found bagged up at convenience stores and gas stations. Lightning fatalities don't seem to be higher in that province than elsewhere in Canada, so I'm guessing that higher powers are not paying close attention.

I was baptized when I was a baby. It's the first sacrament of seven of the Catholic Church, a means of washing away all that pesky original sin that your parents got on you when you were conceived and making sure that if you die as a child, your soul doesn't end up in a land full of gambling and drinking and nudity—some sort of afterlife Las Vegas. There are photos of me from that day—bald, drooling, in an absurdly impractical long white lace dress, which I definitely shit in. I am held by an older cousin, who is wearing two-thirds of a rust-red leisure suit (pants and vest) and a dagger point floral shirt underneath. He is one of my two godfathers, no godmother to speak of. It's a deviation from tradition that suggested that maybe my family wasn't made up of true believers, or at the very least they weren't reading the fine print on the contract. My mother claims that both of my older cousins apparently wanted the role, and so she let them have it. In hindsight I have trouble imagining two teenagers fighting over the privilege of being my guides through a lifetime of spiritual development. Just over a decade and a half older than me, neither of them *really* seemed up for the challenge. But one of them offers my husband psychedelics every holiday, which fits the brief.

No one in my family was particularly religious growing up, except for my grandmother, who would sit and pray for hours under her breath at night, almost trancelike. "Are you hungry?" she would ask if we neared her—the call of feeding us was enough to snap her out of it. When we said no—and we always said no, because it was impossible to be hungry, no one was ever hungry, we were constantly fed—she slipped back into it, like a diver come up for air and going down again. I knew I was supposed to love Jesus. I tried to explain to my mother the problem I had with this concept. I was five or six years old, and it was an unfathomable thing to me, I explained, the idea of loving someone I didn't know, that I couldn't touch or hug.

My mother instantly burst into tears. "It's just so beautiful," she said. "That you want to hug Jesus."

This was not at all what I meant. I was having a crisis of conscience because I *didn't* want to hug Jesus, but even at that tender age I figured that maybe I should just be quiet. Letting my mother believe that I was a true believer and aspiring Messiah squeezer seemed to be better for everyone involved. A few of us—my brother, a cousin here and there—received our first Communion, the next sacrament on the checkoff list. We'd rehearse receiving the

Eucharist, the Communion wafer and a sip from a chalice, and I remember all of us in our class giggling if the priest actually tipped the cup far enough for one of us to get a taste of sacramental wine. It was always dry, arid on my tongue, tart to the point of being sour. I'd had wine before. Every day at pranzo—the afternoon meal for Italians, and traditionally the largest one of the day—my grandfather would prepare himself a stein of wine, slicing peeled apples or peaches into the cup and then filling it to the brim from a jug of Carlo Rossi. The flavor was not dissimilar, but at home my grandfather would pull the slices of fruit out, their outsides tinted by the wine, the flavor absorbed into just the outermost layer, and he'd cut me off a bite. Sometimes, I'd get an entire slice. The wine was too strong for me and burned my throat, but the fruit made it edible, and I felt grown up, nibbling on it. Plus, it came without the guilt of knowing that even though Jesus had supposedly died for my sins, if the situation was somehow reversed, I would *not* be returning the favor.

Central Florida didn't let me see much of the world beyond itself. The entire state is flat, and that skews your perception of things. It becomes difficult to see very far. And even when you can, it's just more Florida. But I remember watching television sometime in the early 1990s, when I was maybe ten or eleven, and something caught my attention. A man on the screen, holding a small circle of bread. He explained that bagels contained more complex carbohydrates than cereal. I didn't know what complex carbohydrates were, exactly, but according to the food pyramid of the time I needed to be consuming six to eleven servings of them a day. This seemed an impossible task. But this man could help me. I'd see him again and again on the television—Murray Lender, selling the bagels that bore his name.

I begged my mother to buy me a bag of them. Exhausted by a child whose dietary whims changed with the tide, she obliged, and also bought giant foil-wrapped bricks of cream cheese to spread on top. (I had somehow gleaned from the television that this was how bagels were eaten.) I was enthralled. Bagels felt fancy. Erudite. I was deeply into the Baby-Sitters Club book series, and one of the characters was from New York, a magical place full of bagels and taxicabs (the character in question also had diabetes, which sounded very sophisticated). At the end of one book (The Baby-Sitters Club #18: *Stacey's Mistake*) they ate something called lox, which Ann M. Martin, the author, did not bother explaining at all. It was apparently consumed with bagels. Murray Lender had not informed me of this, which felt like a bit of betrayal (so did the cinnamon raisin variant of his bagels, which my mother mistakenly purchased one time).

I knew I had to get my hands on some lox, whatever it was. My mother was entirely unwilling to spring for it, but when my father came to visit, I mentioned it to him. Perhaps he also realized that buying cured salmon for a notoriously picky child at $15 a pound was a dicey proposition, and so he purchased lox trimmings instead. It was exactly what it sounded like—the scraps that came from cutting the fish for people who were more discerning than me. It was excessively bright in color, and a bit too intense for my taste, but I still ate it happily, and dreamed of taxicabs and living in an apartment and having to take insulin.

When I started dating my now husband, he learned of my affinity for bagels and was somewhat horrified that I'd buy them from the grocery store. Rand promised to take me to New York, where his parents and grandparents were from. He'd get me real East Coast–style bagels, he said, something that was impossible to find in Seattle in the early years of the twenty-first century. I was happy enough with Murray Lender's offerings. I was afraid that if I saw what I was missing, I wouldn't be able to go back. Still, it had been my dream, and it was just another promise Rand made good on, along with loving me and not getting upset when I yelled at him because I was too tired or too hungry or annoyed that I'd worn the wrong pants. That first trip to New York, he took me to Katz's deli for matzo ball soup, to Zabar's for lox and rugelach and black and whites, to H&H, where we picked up bagels. They were chewy and perfect, something that I'd heard was owing to the softness of New York's water. Too many minerals toughened up gluten. That, and the bagels were parboiled before baking, a step that was often skipped in mass-produced bagels. We returned home with a giant plastic bag full of them, which we ate in Seattle, this precious souvenir that we consumed over the next day. Murray Lender might have opened up the world to me, but after that there was no looking back.

"I knew you were going to marry a Jew," my friend Katie said when I told her Rand and I were engaged. She was cackling. "This is all my doing."

"How can you possibly take credit for this?" I asked.

"It's my *influence* on you. It's the closest you can get to marrying me."

Katie had first come into my life in the fifth grade. She was funny and smart and had a quick, dirty sense of humor. She laughed like Edna Krabappel from *The Simpsons*—a sharp, biting "Ha!" She was not my first Jewish friend, but she was the first friend I had who introduced me to the concept of Judaism, and Jewish food. I remember distinctly the afternoon when I was twelve and Katie's mother, Sue, who was constantly feeding me, asked me if I wanted some matzo ball soup. I confessed that I had never tried it. She was apoplectic.

"What do you mean you've never had matzo ball soup?" she said, immediately setting a bowl down in front of me before I even responded. I dug my spoon into one of the little round dumplings. It was miraculously spongy and light and somehow tasted like chicken itself. A notoriously picky eater, I ate the entire bowl. I would later learn that there were two kinds of matzo balls, floaters and sinkers (Sue made floaters), and that people had wildly differing opinions on the matzo balls themselves, on the spelling of the word, on what belonged in the soup, whether you added a pinch of dill or parsley or both, whether you used leeks or onions, actual pieces of chicken or just the broth. A friend of mine and her entire family turned on her stepfather when he added a tomato to the family recipe. In the years since, I have sought out the same soup from various diners and delis across America. I've made my own matzo balls, adding rendered schmaltz—the light yellow chicken fat often used in Jewish cuisine—that I skimmed from the top of my homemade stock. I can't tell you how many bowls of it I've eaten in my life. But that first one, at Katie's house, stayed with me in a way that certain dishes do. When you know that your life is changing, just a little, bite by bite.

Katie was the one who explained to me that the bagels I loved so much were, in fact, Jewish. They were served as part of the catered lunch for her Bat Mitzvah along with a lox schmear that I zeroed in on, happily munching away as I celebrated my friend being called to the Torah, which I understood as something sacred that maybe involved scrolls? During the ceremony itself there was a sort of call-and-response prayer, and I excitedly answered with the congregation the same way I would have during church. A friend stared at me. "Only Jews are supposed to do that," she hissed. I immediately slunk down, my cheeks aflame.

That same year, I became confirmed in the Catholic Church. It was the third sacrament, after baptism and Communion, and supposedly your first as an adult, a way of further committing yourself to the church. In some ways, it was a surprisingly egalitarian affair; the classes were a group of us from my school as well as some kids from other neighboring middle schools, all thrown together. Faced with talking to *literal* strangers, we all clung together, the social strata of middle school temporarily falling away. We sat in a large room—the same one where we occasionally had donuts after church—and listened to different speakers. One came with a giant wooden plank and railroad spikes that he hammered into it, in order to illustrate how Jesus was nailed to the cross.

"The nails probably didn't go through his hands," he

said, "because they'd have torn right through. They'd have gone down here, at his wrists." He also did a lot of Scared Straight talks for our school district, and he didn't bother switching his tone, figuring maybe we could be terrified into being true believers.

Another group of speakers came in for something called "Sexuality Weekend," which, given that this was a Catholic church in central Florida in 1993, was not the open-minded salacious romp the name suggested it was going to be. The more apt name would have been "Abstinence* Weekend— *Because If You Think About Sex, Even a Little Bit, and If You Touch Yourself, or Think About Touching Yourself, or Even Think About Doing Something That You Now Realize, at the Ripe Old Age of Forty-two, Wasn't Actually Wrong, Like Kissing Someone Rather Chastely, YOU ARE GOING TO GET A THOUSAND STDS AND PREGNANT AND DIE AND GO TO HELL FOREVER, WHERE YOU WILL HAVE TO RAISE YOUR BABY ALONE. IN HELL." But no. You'd think an institution that names a building a "rectory" would be more sex positive. We sat through a lecture on the ills of masturbation and how it was just a means of escape (which doesn't sound like a bad thing when you're in middle school), and I giggled and scoffed so much I was branded a "troublemaker" for the first time in my life. Then we watched a *very* graphic video in which a woman gave birth. Those of us with vaginas hadn't seen too many besides our own, and seeing a human come out of one was like a really gooey matryoshka nesting doll.

And then we immediately had lunch.

The closer I got to being confirmed in the Catholic

Church, the less I was sure about the whole thing. Something about it sat hollow in my chest, like when you've told a lie but are in too deep to get out and suddenly you have to fake your own death and move to a country with no extradition treaties. My mother wasn't telling me to do this. There was no familial pressure at all, really. We went to church regularly on Sundays, and without question on Christmas and Easter, and this decree felt as if it were coming from on high. Mom asked me if I was certain this was what I wanted. And I wasn't—not really—but this was what I thought I was supposed to be doing. Everyone was committing themselves to religion in one form or another. I felt peer pressure to take a sweet taste of the body of Christ because all my friends—and hell, all the cool kids—were doing it.

Before you get confirmed, you're supposed to go to confession. You get to learn what it means to have all of your sins forgiven, and atone for them while still feeling really bad about everything, which is the whole point of Catholicism. But somehow . . . I skipped that part. I mean, what was I going to do? Go in and say, "Hey, one time I had a slumber party with a friend and we stripped down to our underwear and training bras and kissed pillows and pretended they were boys from school and it was *extremely horny,* and I only feel bad about it because you're telling me I should? Also maybe all of this"—waves hands around frantically—"is bullshit and there are lots of ways to be a decent person?" What's the bigger sin? To lie *in* confession, or lie *about* going to confession? I just knew I needed to keep eating Jesus along with all my friends. And so I chose the latter.

In hindsight, maybe using subterfuge and outright deceit in order to complete my initiation into the Catholic Church was a bad sign. (We were also supposed to do some volunteer work, which I explicitly did not do.) The joke would be on me in the end: I'd avoided telling a priest my sins, only to end up telling them to everyone, eventually, on the internet. But in the meantime, I was just racing toward a religious finish line, hoping that maybe going through all the motions would lead me to believing in it. It was Fake It Until You Make It: Eternal Soul Edition. I wasn't hurting anyone, I reasoned, and there *was* something beautiful about being a part of all of it. But while I felt a connection to my friends, my family, and my past every time I stepped into a Catholic church and inhaled the incense and heard the chanting of Gregorian monks—which became very popular in the mid-nineties, for whatever reason—the spiritual awakening part didn't happen. I felt myself moving further and further away from the church. Our beliefs differed in ways that couldn't be reconciled. As the years passed, I would describe myself as "having grown up Catholic," and then later as a "recovering Catholic," and then the noncommittal and largely meaningless "spiritual but not religious," which was another lie. I was not spiritual. I didn't really believe in anything.

Before our wedding, I asked Rand what he thought about my converting.

"To what, exactly?" he said. He wasn't practicing. He hadn't even had a Bar Mitzvah himself. His family was, for the most part, secular. He had a few distant relatives who were bothered by the idea that I wasn't Jewish, but Rand's grandmother Pauline shut them down like someone slamming a car door against a cold wind. Pauline was a discerning woman, and she cared about a lot of things. The volume of the music playing in restaurants, the temperature of her coffee, what *The New York Times* had to say about whatever Sondheim revival was currently on Broadway. But she didn't give a damn what god people prayed to, or even if they had one. In the 1930s and 1940s in New York, she was often ostracized in her own community for "not being Jewish enough," something that had nothing to do with her ancestry or her beliefs, but entirely because of assumptions people had made about her. It was as though people had gotten together and decided on a very narrow definition of what Jewish women looked and acted like, and Pauline didn't fit the brief. She'd gone completely gray at nineteen and made extra money as a hair dye model. She was a platinum blonde one week, a crimson redhead the next. It didn't help, she told me, that she couldn't speak Hebrew no matter how hard she tried and that she hated most of the traditional Ashkenazi food her mother would make for her. When Rand's grandfather Seymour took her home to meet his parents, they started yelling that he needed to marry a Jewish girl. (Pauline didn't really understand, because the argument was not in English, but she knew it was about her.) Seymour was so angry he didn't tell them the truth until he and Pauline were nearly married. Years later, she went to register her sons—Rand's father and uncle—for Hebrew school, and the rabbi took one look at her and told her he couldn't accept children whose mother had converted to Judaism. Pauline turned on her heel and walked out. She didn't bother explaining that she wasn't a convert (and in her opinion, it didn't matter, anyway). She'd dealt with this for decades. She was tired of it. And so, she never pressured me about my beliefs one way or another. She made it clear that religion was a deeply personal thing, and only one part of who you were. And also, if you did convert, you were no less entitled to your identity than someone who was born into it. On the contrary, she told me. People who converted had worked very hard for it.

My friends had a relationship with their faith that I envied. Sometimes the symbols of their faith were evident: they wore hijabs or crucifixes or yarmulkes, they had shrines in their homes or restaurants, they bowed their heads, they knelt, they prayed, they made offerings to deities and the dead. Even those inclined to atheism were committed to it more than I was to anything; they were staunch in their nonbelief in a higher power. I loved people who held fast to their beliefs, but I couldn't muster up any of my own. I couldn't even bring myself to take offense when a colleague of my husband's called me a shiksa upon discovering I wasn't a Jew. When Rand and two of my observant Jewish friends found out, they were livid. They had a context for it that I did not, a cultural understanding that the word was ugly. I later learned that it derived from the Hebrew term sheqets, meaning "a detestable thing."

I realized I didn't want to believe in Judaism either, and it began to highlight the core problem that I saw within myself: that it wasn't a matter of finding the right religion. I wanted to convert and then comfortably let my religious tendencies go lax, as I had with Catholicism. I wanted to be a part of my husband's specific type of atheistic Judaism. To not believe, but to still feel tied to all of it, to feel a connection to the food, to the traditions that stretched back to the Old Testament and before. I wanted to believe in something besides the importance of complex carbohydrates, I just didn't want to believe in it *very much.* But to practice a religion half-assed is the privilege afforded to those who are born into something, to those who have never had their faith second-guessed. To convert meant to deal with constantly being under fire by people who had nothing better to do than question someone else's faith. It meant to commit wholeheartedly, to believe it not passively but as a willing adult. It was a choice that required deliberation, not something that I could dismiss as familial tradition I'd simply fallen into. I'd already lied my way into one religion. I wasn't sure I could do it again.

In middle school, Katie would often neglect to do her science homework because she hated our instructor. It was the logic of a thirteen-year-old to spite someone else, when the result served only to stress you out. Now a middle school science teacher, she's doomed herself to a lifetime of the thing she'd avoided. During lunch she would copy my assignments. Sometimes, if she was truly pressed for time, I would grab a sheet of her notebook paper and start transcribing my answers in my best imitation of Katie's handwriting, dragging my hand across the letters after I was done to imitate the smudging that happened due to her left-handedness. It's the sort of counterfeit you commit when you love someone very much. That's what I was posing to Rand. An offer to not believe in the same God he did not believe in. In the end, my lack of faith won out. It always did.

We spent those early days of getting to know each other in kitchens—his, mine, and, finally, ours. The first dinner Rand cooked for me was before we started dating, and I was too young to buy wine, so I showed up with a pineapple. I was nervous to cook for him in return, in my tiny apartment with a kitchen that predated the polio vaccine, but I did anyway. In our first apartment together, he stayed up late the night before my uncle's funeral, helping me assemble a lasagna, my grief pouring out as I stacked the layers. I remember looking up and finding him there, by my side. I hadn't even asked for help. He adopted the dishes I made for him, things that my mother and grandmother had cooked for me, and, Signore, perdonami—he made them better than any of us. "This is why we cook for one another, share food and talk about food and beyond—we just want to be family to one another," Michael Twitty writes in his book *Koshersoul.* This is what Rand and I were doing in each little kitchen we shared: becoming family to each other.

Catholicism itself didn't offer a huge wealth of culinary rules or directives. I couldn't really tell what we did out of religious doctrine and what we did because we were Italian; the two seemed to blend together, a way of putting the Roman in Roman Catholic. We sat around the table for hours. We didn't eat red meat on certain days, and a lot of them seemed to be Fridays. Rand made me steak one year for Christmas Eve—a huge transgression for many Italian Catholics who do not consume red meat before holy days—

and I said nothing. It seemed strange to adhere to traditions based in a religion I no longer believed in. When my very secular family found out, they were scandalized, not because I'd broken a religious rule, but because I'd broken a culinary one. Their practices, the ones they held to with the fervor of fanaticism, I began to realize, were all things that happened around the dinner table. No parmesan on fish pasta, no clearing the table with any expeditiousness, no cappuccino after 10:00 a.m. Culinary and religious tradition became intertwined, and the former always held more sway simply because, well, it was food.

Rand adopted every practice, never questioning it. He was affronted when a recipe for cacio e pepe called for parmesan instead of pecorino, would look pained when he heard about the thousand bastardizations of carbonara that appeared on the Olive Garden menu. It wasn't snobbery for the sake of snobbery. It was, simply, upholding the closest thing to the gospel my family ever knew.

I wanted to return the favor but had nothing to work off of. To future generations, Pauline had passed down an excellent sense of direction and decorum, but not a single family recipe. Not only did she not like the food her mother had made, but she adamantly refused to learn how to prepare it, or any dish, really. I'd never met someone more inept in the kitchen, and I say that with a grudging respect. For her age and demographic, she was an outlier. She used a serrated knife to cut tomatoes, sawing through them as if they'd wronged her. She bought matzo ball soup in jars from the grocery store, the orbs floating in the cloudy liquid like something from a Victorian medical museum. Her latkes were, terrifyingly, made from pureed potatoes she tossed in the blender. They turned a sort of grayish purple due to oxidation, splattered when they hit the oil, and proceeded to soak it up like a sponge. The woman cooked as if every ingredient were a piece of incriminating evidence she needed to render unrecognizable. She didn't eat lunch, revered breakfast, and had a small and sensible evening meal. The family joke was to ask what she was making for dinner. The answer was, invariably, reservations.

Rand's grandfather Seymour has a wealth of opinions on food, and as he's scampered into his nineties, recently widowed and sharp as a new knife, he has not held any of them back.

When I cook for him, it is often the same dishes that his own mother made for him. He will watch me in the kitchen, asking questions that I worry are carrying some hidden judgment. *Do you add this? Do you do that?* He will tell me how his mother did things. How she set aside an entire dish of latkes, covered and hidden in the closet, just for him. How she would grind gefilte fish by hand. Kashrut-observant Jews need two sets of pots, pans, plates, and silverware for meat and dairy, but because his family could afford only one, his mother would soak all the dishes and cookware and cutlery. For holidays, he tells me, she would soak them for three days.

He lets me know when the latkes are too thick, when anything has fallen below the scalding temperature that he prefers his food. He watches me roll matzo balls and asks if I dip my hands in water before doing so. I do, I tell him. It stops the batter from sticking to my palms. He notes that his mother did the same thing. He calls me up to request that I make challah for him. I use a recipe that my friend Sarah swears by, weaving four strands of dough together. The resulting loaf, airy and brioche-like and glossy from a brush of egg wash, is so stunning that Rand stops to stare at it in disbelief.

I keep track of every story he tells me about food, asking him to repeat the same ones again and again. There was a time when I thought I would retell these stories and pass these recipes down to my own children, to help them understand their own history. I saw myself as just someone in a relay race, receiving a baton from one person and passing it on to the next. Now in my forties and without children, I've come to appreciate that the role I play is significant in and of itself. This is what it means to love someone. You cook for them. You help them carry the weight of their own memories.

One Easter weekend, Rand and I were in Rome with our friends Will and Heather and their two children. The city was mobbed by tourists, the crowds so thick that you could barely edge your way through the narrow streets. On Good Friday, we found ourselves in a section of town that had been a Jewish neighborhood prior to World War II. On the ground outside the doorways of homes and buildings are little bronze plaques commemorating the people who once lived there, the dates they were born and the dates they died. Italy has long had trouble reconciling with this chapter of its history, but the rhetoric here does not pull any punches. "Assassinated, Auschwitz," is listed on many of the plaques. One or two say "liberated" or "fate unknown." The names listed are Italian and Jewish—Abramo. Zaccaria. Rachele. I read them out loud, and Will and Heather carefully explained what they meant to their children.

The recent rise of nativist politicians spouting misanthropic rhetoric about who is a real Italian and who is not feels like the past simply repeating itself. In 2011, Pietro Pezzutti, a politician from the right-wing Lega Nord party, passed out bags of polenta—a dish popular in the north of the country—with the message "Yes to polenta, no to couscous." The slogan was an attack on Italy's population of immigrants from North Africa, where couscous originates. For those who are familiar with the country's culinary history, Pezzutti's stunt was as misinformed as it was hateful. The corn from which polenta is made is not indigenous to the country, either. Most Italian food comes from somewhere else. Much of the cuisine in the south borrows from the Arab world (some theorize that nomadic Arabian traders were the first to bring pasta to the Romans). The tomatoes so ubiquitous to many of the dishes are a New World crop.

On that crowded Friday, the six of us ducked into a kosher restaurant in Rome, the city where my family once lived. I translated the menu, traditional Italian dishes prepared according to kosher laws, which Rand explained. A server rushed by and dropped a basket of wood-fired matzo bread on the table, each one shaped like a daffodil. The kids tried matzo for the first time and declared that they loved it, and Rand struggled to explain that this was an exemplary example of the dish, and if they tried the store-bought variant, they should temper their expectations.

"It's not always like this," he said.

I laughed. And as I ate, surrounded by people I loved, it hit me, without a hint of the doubts that plagued me all my life, that this is the only thing I've ever truly believed in.

5

WHAT'S COOKING, AND WHO'S COOKING IT

t's Thanksgiving and I'm standing in my aunt's kitchen—
a claustrophobic box that looks a little like an M. C. Escher
painting (if he had a Costco membership), designed by my
uncle while he was almost certainly drunk. I don't actually
know how I ended up here. I have no recollection of walking
into the kitchen, or putting on the faded apron I'm now wearing. I feel like the guy from *Memento*, but less tattooed and sexy.

Why are we even celebrating this holiday? It's a day dedicated to Puritans and genocide and Tom Brady—three
things my family hates. We came to America in the *1970s*.
It's not as if we were passing down age-old stuffing recipes
from colonial times. (No one in my family can even *make*
stuffing. My aunt just makes a giant meatball, refuses to tell
us what's in it, and insists we eat it with the turkey.)

All of the men in my family conveniently forget how to
cook sometime around November 20. (My brother, who

does most of the cooking in his household, suddenly no longer grasps the complex concept of an onion.) I have somehow been charged with preparing a large portion of this meal. Due to complicated family gender dynamics and the fact that my car is blocked in, I can't seem to escape this obligation. This is an annual occurrence. There are a lot of people I would like to blame for this (whoever the captain of the *Mayflower* was; my family; Tom Brady), but the bulk of the fault goes to myself. I should walk away, but I don't.

I once naïvely thought feminism would be a cheat code to make the right decisions. But sometimes it's just there to make me feel like a hypocrite for not being able to escape my old patterns of thinking, my ingrained habits, the memory of all the shitty, misogynistic things I've done. I know I should know better. That I shouldn't hate myself or other women, because we live in a world where a size 4 Jessica Simpson was once ridiculed for being fat, so we cannot turn on one another. (And what if she *had* been fat? What would have been the big fucking deal? You don't get to ridicule someone's body and demand that they hide it because you don't like how *looking* at them makes you feel.) That men are subject to the same bullshit that women are, and they should be given the space to cry and be held. That the gender binary is oversimplified and outdated and unfair.

Intellectually, I know all of this, but I'm fighting against negative patterns of thought that lurk so deep beneath the surface it's like trying to yell at the bottom of the ocean floor from the beach. It's a cultural toxicity that keeps leaching into my brain—one that swirled all around me from the time I was a kid growing up in America during the Reagan years, when John Hughes was tacitly endorsing rape, and gender roles, while more malleable than before, were still clearly defined. The cultural zeitgeist was that feminism was for women who were cold and humorless and somehow damaged. When *Thelma and Louise* came out in 1991, there was a moral panic that feminists were going to go on murderous crime sprees. It was years before I would learn that feminists simply wanted what *everyone* wanted: to be loved and respected, to spend some quality time with their best friend, and to maybe fuck Brad Pitt in his prime. But it was hard to erase all the other bullshit notions of how I'd been told men and women should behave.

All of this converges with me, standing in a stifling kitchen every fourth Thursday in November because I think it's what I'm supposed to do. (My aunt asks me to add more oregano and garlic powder to her ~~meatball~~ "stuffing." And of course I do because it's not going to make things taste *worse*.)

Growing up, I had plenty of examples of men cooking. My cousins and my uncles and my brother and my dad and even my grandfather—a man who predated the *Titanic*—all did. I grew up believing that everyone should. It was a component of being a grown-up, a signifier that you wouldn't starve when left to your own devices. In my ruthless assessment, when someone could not cook, they'd failed at adulthood. But I found myself judging women slightly more harshly than I judged men when I discovered that they were inept in the kitchen. I simply expected more of them, at least culinarily, which was unfair to everyone.

Imagine my surprise when I left for college and found

that my culinary skills consisted, almost entirely, of slicing up string cheese, arranging it on Wheat Thins, and microwaving it.

I assumed the knowledge of how to feed myself would come to me, that I would eventually figure things out. I cannot describe the abject disappointment that hit me when I reached adulthood and found that it had not. The internet was equally unhelpful during this time. I technically became a legal adult in 1998, and the World Wide Web was, at that point in time, just a weird place where your emails got lost and where the guys from my dorm would wait half an hour for a poorly photoshopped image of a topless Helen Hunt to download. The answers were not forthcoming there. I briefly tried reading those *Chicken Soup for the Soul* books, under the misconception that they were about cooking, but they turned out to be thinly veiled Christian propaganda and kept making me cry. So I just waded through those early years of adulthood on my own, eating mostly movie theater popcorn and french fries and I know memory is an unreliable narrator, but there is a three-year stretch where I cannot remember pooping once.

I met my husband a few years later. I was stunned that he, at the tender age of twenty-two, could actually feed himself. I reasoned that he might be able to feed me, too. He shared his enthusiasm for cooking with me, he took me to restaurants, he fed me vegetables (I pooped!), he took me to Krispy Kreme to buy glazed donuts by the dozen. We picked through recipe books and splurged on copies of *Bon Appétit* and *Saveur* and *Cook's Illustrated.* Friends commented with abject shock. He made me dinner! He cleaned up after himself! This felt like the "ultimate life hack" the internet was always baiting us with: a partner who did roughly half of the household tasks. My gratitude came with a component of guilt: I felt as if I were failing to live up to some outdated standard because I wasn't doing all the cooking or cleaning. But if he left me to do all of it, I would have grown to resent him. There was no winning.

If it felt as if I'd shacked up with a unicorn, it was because I *had*. According to a study published by the Pew Research Center in 2019, among heterosexual couples who cohabitate, women are much more likely to prepare meals than their male partners, and much more likely to grocery shop. This is true of couples with or without children. (Eighty percent of women with children say they are the primary meal prepper, as do 75 percent of women without children. Similar percentages—80 percent and 68 percent—say they do most of the grocery shopping.) Seventy-one percent of mothers said they took on both of these tasks, compared with only 11 percent of dads who did. But the biggest issue is that this discrepancy isn't even perceived by many men: Dads are twice as likely as moms to say that these chores are split evenly. Men believe that they're doing more work around meals and grocery shopping than they actually are.

The early years of the twenty-first century gave rise to something new: the cult of the cool, trash-talking celebrity chef. Rand and I would watch *Iron Chef,* and episode after episode of *No Reservations.* I wanted to be a hip, tattooed, knife-wielding badass, a culinary world traveler who cussed and ate with the locals and drank booze that had drowned reptiles floating in it. But almost everyone I saw doing that on TV was a man. While home cooking remained the domain—and the burden—of women, in the professional culinary world men continued to dominate. In the United States, male head chefs outnumber female head chefs by a ratio of nearly four to one. Worldwide, only about a quarter of chefs are women. And when it comes to being lauded for their efforts, discrepancies are even wider: Since Michelin's current three-star system began in 1931, more than a hundred male chefs have earned the prestigious three-star rating, versus a mere twelve women who have. Only 6 percent of the more than two thousand Michelin-starred restaurants in the world are helmed by women. The James Beard Awards have had a much better track record, though women and people of color have historically been underrepresented among nominees and winners throughout the organization's more than thirty-year history. As of 2023, only eight women have received the organization's honor of "Outstanding Chef." Mashama Bailey would become the first Black woman to win the award—in *2022*. That same year, 36 percent of the nominees for Best Chef were women (rather significant given how relatively few female head chefs there are). The problem isn't in the pipeline. Women are attending culinary school in record numbers. In 2020, 54 percent of the graduates of the Culinary Institute of America were women. The problem is something deeper, about how we regard women and men and where, precisely, each is allowed to cook.

In February 2010, Charlotte Druckman wrote an article asking why there are no great women chefs (a tongue-in-cheek callback to another essay published in the 1970s titled

"Why Have There Been No Great Women Artists?"). The reasoning, Druckman notes, is not that there is a dearth of great female chefs, but rather that women are not allowed to succeed in the existing framework. The parameters for success are set up so that, for the most part, men are allowed to be great chefs. A woman can, at most, succeed at being a great *cook*. But when that cooking extends beyond the realm of the home, we are hesitant to acknowledge her genius. She can prepare a meal as long as she's not awarded, lauded, and, perhaps most important, paid for it. To be a chef requires innovation and entrepreneurialism—attributes that aren't exclusive to men but that men are given the grace and encouragement to cultivate.

I watched as female celebrity chefs were forced into one of two categories: the warm, enveloping mother figure or the voluptuous sex symbol. There were the Ina Gartens and the Lidia Bastianiches, with their strong arms and endless competence, holding platters of food to feed an extended family. And then there were bombshells. Nigella Lawson, who appeared on the cover of *Stylist* magazine sensually dripping in caramel, like a candy-apple version of Carrie. Or Giada De Laurentiis, posing in *People* wearing leather pants and a scarf strategically placed over her naked torso. Male chefs aren't subject to this same bullshit. No one put Bobby Flay naked on a couch with a fruit bowl over his crotch or Rick Bayless slathered in mole. But even if a male chef was considered a sex symbol, it didn't come with the same level of objectification. There were exceptions to the rule, of course.

In Charlotte Druckman's feminist culinary polemic, *Women on Food,* she asks her contributors, "Are there any words or phrases you really wish people would stop using to describe women chefs (or really, women, period)?" Some were obvious—sexist terms like "chick," "bitchy," or "babe," condescending ones like "perky" and "feisty" (terms that no one woman has ever, in the history of words, used to describe herself). The sex symbol/mother figure dichotomy made itself known here as well—words like "gorgeous," "sexy," and "trim" and "nurturing," "caring," and "matriarchal."

One word came up again and again: "badass."

At first blush, it feels almost complimentary (that thing I once aspired to be while watching cooking shows all those years ago), which is part of why it's so problematic. Druckman explained to NPR that the word "is a detonated way to describe a kind of cultural male whiteness—an aggressive, swaggering one." To refer to a woman as a badass was to suggest that she was one of the guys, the archetypical "cool girl," someone to be listened to precisely because of her ability to emulate a specific brand of toxic white masculinity.

"It exalts that bullying, bullish culture at the same time as it puts down the culture of anyone who doesn't follow that model, female, white or otherwise," Druckman said.

In 2013, *Time* magazine published an issue with the headline "The Gods of Food" (the cover of the international edition featured three male chefs: Alex Atala, David Chang, and René Redzepi). The issue highlighted thirteen influential individuals in the food world, and only four women, none of whom were chefs. The editor Howard Chua-Eoan was infuriatingly unapologetic about the piece, saying, "We did not want to fill a quota of a woman chef. We wanted to go with reputation and influence." And he said that the lack of women reflected the "very harsh reality" of the current chefs' world, but it was LITERALLY A REALITY HE HAD THE POWER TO CHANGE.

Mary Blair-Loy, author of *Competing Devotions: Career and Family Among Women Executives,* notes that the prevalence of professional male cooks and female home cooks might be due to something she calls the "family devotion schema"—a cultural model that defines marriage and motherhood as a woman's primary vocation. If a woman chooses to work outside the home, those other obligations of wife and mother don't disappear. She either is overwhelmed by them or delegates them to someone else, violating the schema and seen as a heartless banshee in a pantsuit with, presumably, a womb as frigid as the arctic. (This is hypothetical! I'm just basing this off my Twitter comments!)

And beyond these societal pressures bearing down on her, the notion of becoming a female chef seems like an even more daunting prospect given that professional kitchens have historically sucked for women. A 2011 study found that 37 percent of all sexual harassment cases reported to the federal government involved restaurants. In Anthony Bourdain's *Kitchen Confidential,* he wrote about the bawdy kitchen environments he worked in, recounting a story of a female line cook who came in one day and found her workstation decorated with "hard-core pornography" by a co-worker. Apparently, she just ignored the photos and went to work, after making a single, biting retort, and Bourdain lauded her for this. But what if she had broken down, or stormed out, or just opened her mouth and wailed like a

fire alarm—all of which feel like a completely reasonable reaction to encountering an homage to pegging at *your place
of work*? Would she have been branded as not being able
to hack it in an industry that's historically had a "boys will
be sexual predators" sort of viewpoint? Bourdain praised
the women he worked with for being "tough-as-nails, foul-
mouthed, trash-talking"—able to thrive in an environment
dominated by men through assimilation while failing to acknowledge that the environment was toxic and problematic
to begin with. The only way to survive among the bros was
to become one.

For some, the only solution to making home cooking
more palatable is to make it a dick-punch of masculinity. In
2010, Allrecipes, one of the Web's largest recipe sites,
launched a short-lived site called "ManTestedRecipes." The
premise, according to the initial press release, was that it
would be "a virtual man-cave where men can talk about
food." Because what men really need is a cooking safe space
away from women, where they don't have to deal with us
getting lip gloss and menses all over the counters.

"Our research shows men genuinely enjoy cooking but
have uniquely masculine interests and tastes; they deserve a
dedicated and authentic community to connect with each
other," said Lisa Sharples, the then-president of Allrecipes.
The site was made up of user-generated content; to encourage visitors to submit their "manly recipes" (someone was
paid to write that copy, possibly in American currency but
maybe in beef jerky), they launched the "ManTestedRecipes
Dude Food contest," where the winner would receive $500
and, I'm guessing, a lifetime supply of Cheetos-flavored con-

doms.* (*These don't actually exist.) The format was shockingly similar to the original Allrecipes website, but the backdrop was black with flames—redolent of an open-fire grill, a Harley-Davidson logo, or Guy Fieri's formal wear. While it was live, it had at least 151 entries under the tag "recipes with beer," numerous soups made out of cheese, and an entire top navigation tab dedicated to "chili." It was the Axe body spray of recipe sites, with entries like "Lasagna alla Mike," "Army Chili con Carne," and "Hot as Hell Habanero Sauce." The search bar implored you to "hunt for your next meal." And while it felt as if the editors of *Maxim* magazine had taken over *Food & Wine,* it also wasn't clear whom it was addressing. Did men want to be pandered to in this way? The tagline under chili was "Men dig these pots o' spicy." Which isn't how I'd ever heard men talk about themselves or heard anyone talk about chili.

The site seemed to go defunct in 2013. It's hard to say why. Perhaps someone realized that recipe sites did not need to be separated by gender. Perhaps it's because no one wants a cooking site with a recipe distribution that's more than 85 percent chili. Perhaps it was because the users severely abused the photo submission section, including one gentleman who just posted pictures from his vacation to the town of Dildo, Newfoundland.

It was Rand who reframed my thinking around home cooking. Around the end of 2016, I entered my own personal Blue Period, which overlapped perfectly with my "Reading Twitter All the Time and Sometimes Sobbing" period. I'd just lost my dad, and Hillary had lost the election* (*BIGGEST ASTERISK EVER), and Rand had just lost his job (my fault!). The news kept showing me footage from "rallies," which was actually just a bunch of racists in ill-fitting khakis marching with citronella lawn torches, as if the only thing they hated more than the Jews was mosquitoes. Consequently, I sort of . . . checked out a little bit? I was still technically alive, but I had ceased to function in any sort of meaningful way. I became the human equivalent of a hermit crab. Which I guess is just a hermit.

(Except I was sobbing. Do hermits sob? How would we find out?)

Since I was busy making Victorian widows look chipper by comparison, Rand started cooking more during this time. Prior to then I easily did half the cooking, possibly more, but now I cooked once every few weeks, if that. I would help him out if he needed it, make the occasional side dish, offer to help clean, but for the most part Rand took over the task of feeding us. Initially, I perceived it as a failure on my part, evidence that I was a very bad wife, and bad friend, and maybe just a bad person who should flee society and go live in a swamp. I couldn't yet see it for what it was: someone I loved stepping up and taking care of me when I needed it. He got into the habit of cooking for us, and then, well, he didn't stop.

I've asked Rand about it numerous times. He told me that I did everything else around the house—the laundry, the cleaning, the slow, persistent murdering of houseplants— and that he felt this was something he could do to help out. Besides, he enjoyed it. Of all the tasks that needed to be done, it was one he truly liked doing.

Sometime in 2020, I started posting photos of my husband cooking on social media. I received a slew of positive comments and salivating emojis for the food or just Rand himself. Some were in abject shock at a man doing approximately half the work around the house. "How do you get him to cook for you?" someone asked suspiciously, as though I'd somehow hypnotized him with my nipples. A few bottom-feeders commented on his inherent lack of masculinity. "WTF happened to men?" asked one faceless commenter. "I feel so badly for your soy husband," said another, employing an alt-right insult for men who are perceived as effeminate liberals. "He will leave you for a man eventually," chimed in a third. Because obviously everyone who makes coq au vin also eats cock. *Clearly.*

Did they honestly think that men who cooked at home were less masculine? Did they seriously think Stanley Tucci cooking in his kitchen was not manly? (Had they *seen* Stanley Tucci?) Did they think the second they learned to prepare anything more complex than cereal, their testicles would start shriveling up like the Nazi who drank from the wrong chalice in the third Indiana Jones movie? And while it was easy to dismiss them, they spoke to a long-held truth in American culture and beyond: that a man who cooked at home was doing women's work.

(Grilling was the baffling exception to this because, I don't know, it involved fire, and being outdoors, and large slabs of meat, and aprons that said "Don't Blame Me, I Voted for Titties." Perhaps it is because grilling is seen as a performance rather than an act of service. It tends to happen a few times a year, rather than several times a day. It doesn't involve pans or spoons or whisks, all of which, according to 4chan, exponentially increase your chances of becoming a whiny little baby girl. Whatever the reason, it remains a summertime and holiday exception to the rule, a way that men can cook without worrying that they'll instantly start lactating.)

They are quick to tell me that my husband, who is able to saber a champagne bottle open and makes smash burgers for me upon request, is too sensitive and delicate to protect me in the event of some unspecified emergency. (Admittedly, if a bear attacked us, I would be the most likely target, but that has nothing to do with Rand. Years of being well fed and loved have made me tender and marbled. *I* would eat me first.) But feeding someone and protecting them are not different. To separate the two is to ignore how safe I feel when eating a giant bowl of cacio e pepe. I don't need a bodyguard defending me from nonexistent threats. I need to be fed. Often, and before I start getting so hungry that I get angry about a haircut I had in sixth grade.

If we start accepting that the work women do in the home has value—all the cooking and meal prep and cleaning that is overlooked and devalued—it throws our entire society into chaos a little bit. Our economic system is built on the understanding that women working inside the home (for free, for decades) is a *given*. That historically, in order for society to have functioned at all, women had to quietly and competently and single-handedly do a great deal of invisible labor, and a hell of a lot of that centered on cooking. It was not financially feasible or culturally acceptable to eat out every night, and hiring people to help with these tasks was a privilege offered to only very few. Women by default did all of these things, and as they entered the workforce in greater numbers, that didn't go away; it just added to their responsibilities. Rather than reach some sort of equitable division of labor inside the home, which would have caused a hell-freezing paradigm shift (that keeping a house running is important and hard, that women themselves are just as integral to society as men), people just seemed to dig in their heels further as to what was women's and men's work. Cooking inside the home was still exclusively the responsibility of women, and still considered a uniquely feminine act—an obligation we couldn't free ourselves from, emasculating to any man who dared pick it up. If a woman was also working outside the home—taking on what were perceived as traditionally masculine (that is, paying) jobs—she risked judgment that she was abandoning her family and her duties at home (even if she had absolutely no choice or say in the matter). And she'd be further punished by essentially doubling her workload because all of those obligations remained on her plate. All of this assumes a narrow, heteronormative path of womanhood laid out for us, one inflexible to being queer or transgender or asexual or aromantic or childless or disabled or impoverished or a single parent. If you were a woman, you got married and stayed married to a man, and you cooked and took care of the home for him and your children. Anything else was a deviation from propriety, something for others to shake their heads at, and occasionally pity.

. . .

Mindsets, like tectonic plates, take a long time to shift. But eventually, they do—a series of small movements, until eventually landmasses break apart, new ideas pop up, and koalas are only found in Australia.

I am sitting on my couch, watching *Salt Fat Acid Heat*. On the screen, Samin Nosrat makes focaccia in Genoa, chatting with a local baker in effortless Italian as she dimples the dough with her fingers. She isn't merely making good TV (and good focaccia, as it turns out); she is breaking the archetypes of what a culinary celebrity can be. Nosrat doesn't fit neatly into either of the narrow archetypes female chefs are so often forced into. She is neither a stereotypical maternal figure (she is unmarried and has no children) nor a conventional sex symbol (she wears overalls and sneakers and has an immense smile, dark curls framing her face). She happily shares the spotlight and references her Iranian American roots (two things seldom seen in culinary programming, or on TV, period). Her vibe is more "honor student who wants to be your friend" than "guy who's too cool to talk to you." In the weeks after the show airs, my social media feed will be filled with people making her focaccia recipe. When I try my hand at it, it comes out perfectly golden brown and spongy.

The notion, for a long time, has been that cooking is the domain of some, that it is something that doesn't belong to all of us. That women cannot be professional chefs, that men cannot be home cooks. Gender roles have played out on the culinary landscape. Food has been a battleground, cooking has been an obligation, a game of keep-away, and a burden.

But what if we regarded it differently?

What if making dinner was something we expected not just of women but of everyone? If we shared this immense task of feeding each other (multiple times! Each day!)? Perhaps the resentment and the exhaustion of that task would start to evaporate. What if we acknowledged that a man can cook in places besides a professional kitchen and it doesn't affect his worth? Men are still cooking in the home less than women, but they are cooking in greater numbers than they ever have before. Female professional chefs are being recognized more and more alongside their male peers. The shift is happening slowly, but it is still happening: The awareness that cooking—at home or beyond—is something that belongs to all of us.

In the meantime, I fight these battles on a smaller scale, usually inside my own head. We return home from our Thanksgiving trip, another one in which I spend most of the holiday in the kitchen, swearing that this is the last year (I have lost count of how many last years there have been). I come up with a resolution, the same one I make every year around December 1: Next Thanksgiving will be different. I will add less oregano to the giant meatball. Also, I will not make the meatball. Maybe I won't cook at all. There are a lot of things keeping me in that kitchen (family dynamics, Tom Brady, lack of street parking), but mostly, the biggest thing keeping me in there is me.

I've accepted the feminist notion that women *can* do anything, but the idea that we don't have to do certain things is taking a bit longer to sink in. At home, this place where I have been fortunate enough to build and define a life of my own choosing, it is a little easier. My husband asks me what I want for dinner, and I fight against the feelings of guilt and obligation and see it for what it is: someone who loves me, making a meal for our family.

And sometimes (when he needs me to, when he is overwhelmed, or just when I feel like it) I return the kindness.

6

SECRET AGENTS AND SECRET RECIPES

When my father died, he took a number of secrets with him to the grave, some of them a matter of national security. Among them, less crucial to America's espionage goals during the Cold War, was his recipe for beef Stroganoff.

He was a competent but mediocre cook all at once. Methodical and exact, he was never flustered in the kitchen, wasn't burning multiple dishes simultaneously, like my mother. The results were always the same, middle-of-the-road meals that were easily forgotten soon afterward. Whenever I visited my father, in the small town outside Munich where he'd retired, he would get up early and head to the store and come back with fresh-baked pretzels for me and Rand, or weisswurst—veal and bacon sausage that is boiled and eaten with sweet mustard. His partner did most of the cooking, but every now and then my dad would make one of the only dishes in his repertoire: beef Stroganoff.

Pinpointing the history of beef Stroganoff is a difficult task, because, like my own family history, all of the players involved are long gone, sources are conflicting, and Stalin plays a minor role. There is no one to ask about it, and even if there were, my inability to speak or read Russian or Ukrainian is a hindrance. My father and I spoke roughly ten languages between us, but we only ever overlapped on one. In his later years, when he was too tired, or had too much to drink, he'd slip between German and English and some Slavic language I couldn't quite identify. An old spy is a funny thing. Some of the secrets come out, but when they do, it doesn't really matter. No one can understand, anyway.

Most culinary historians concede that Stroganoff can be traced back to French chefs cooking for the Russian court, but even there the story gets murky. Some claim that the dish was named for Count Pavel Aleksandrovich Stroganoff. If eighteenth-century portraits can be considered reliable (and I think we all know they cannot. Imagine creating a portrait for someone who could easily have you executed. You'd become a human Instagram filter), the count was adorable, big-eyed and round-faced. (He would die of tuberculosis before he was forty-three.) Other stories claim that the dish originated in roughly the same time period, but in Odessa, and identify its namesake as Count Alexander Grigorievich Stroganov. Apparently, Count Stroganov's French chef invented the dish because the elder count had no teeth left and chewing meat was difficult for him—hence the finely chopped morsels of beef. (Count Stroganov would, the story goes, invite people from town to eat the dish at large public tables, an indication of his generosity.) Determining its true country of origin is as difficult as figuring out my father's. People argue that it's Polish, that it's essentially French, that it was technically invented in Odessa, making it Ukrainian.

I remember once asking Dad if he was Russian or Ukrainian, because it was unclear, even after all these decades.

"I wish I knew," he replied. I pulled at my hair.

I try to tell myself that the things I wasn't told right away—his real name, any clear details of his life, and the fact that I didn't know any of his other family members except my brothers (one of whom I didn't meet until I was eleven)—weren't personal. He'd spent his entire career—close to half a century—working for the U.S. Department of Defense (it would be the longest relationship of his life, outlasting all of his marriages). As children, my brother and I were told he was a translator, which was close enough to the truth to explain why he spoke so many languages but boring enough to ensure that no follow-up questions would be asked.

I don't know when Mom figured out about Dad's work. They met when she was working the front desk at a hotel near the American embassy in Rome, where Cold War operatives in dark suits would get drinks. She told me the agents would flirt with her by offering to divulge information they shouldn't. My mother is not the most reliable of narrators, but she has always been beautiful, and she was a decade and a half younger than my dad and his colleagues, and it was Italy in the 1970s. I've seen enough bad Bond films that this feels *extremely* plausible.

Shortly after she and Dad were married, and he'd gotten transferred to Germany, she found a collection of passports and IDs in a drawer while putting away laundry. They were all my father's photo, but the names on each were different. My mother put them back where they were. When she asked about them, he told her they were for work and didn't elaborate. My father didn't lie. He just redacted a lot of details. I was twelve before I learned that "Paul DeRuiter" wasn't the name he was born with. His real name is made of hard consonants and soft, round vowels. Sometimes, when I'm alone, I say it to myself, as if it were a spell, as if I were trying to conjure up something.

Hollywood tends to glamorize espionage. It wants us to think that spies are dashingly cut figures, dripping with savoir faire, the Jeffrey Wrights and Daniel Craigs, the Jessica Chastains and Thandiwe Newtons. But a real spy needs to go unnoticed. My father was short and could blend into a crowd when he needed to. I couldn't tell you if his eyes were blue or green or gray, or what his mustache looked like, when he had one. I can barely put together the features of his face without a photo; given that I've inherited so much of his appearance, I'd consider it an accomplished feat of anonymity. His greatest cover was this: He convinced everyone that he was the most boring man in the world. He was the human equivalent of a tasseled loafer. Practical, and usually seen in the company of middle-aged white men. No one would ever suspect him.

My mother and he were the unlikeliest of couples. My father was rigid and organized, a legacy of joining the armed forces when you are barely sixteen. My mom's personal filing system involves the occasional bucket on which she has written IMPORTANT in black marker. Whenever she calls me, there's at least a 30 percent chance she's going to tell me about a paranormal encounter she's recently had. I've tried hypothesizing the reason behind my parents' marriage (I've done the math—there was no pregnancy expediting it), and the best I can conclude is one of the following scenarios:

1. Some sort of group hypnosis was involved.

2. My mom lost a bet.

3. My father was so deep undercover on a mission that he forgot who he was.

Creatures in captivity manage to produce offspring, despite having nothing in common, and it's odd that we demand more of people. My parents had my brother within a year of their wedding. By the time I was born, four years later, and on another continent, they'd already gone their separate ways. My mother, in an uncharacteristically efficient move, had left my father and Europe in one fell swoop. He stayed in Germany, where he would live for the rest of his life, and she, pregnant with me, went to Seattle, my brother in tow. In total, my parents were married for four years in practice, and another four on paper. It sounds bleak, but I'd say that they did pretty well for two people whose greatest commonality is the hierarchical classification of their species. They never got along, but they never spoke badly about each other. I think they respected each other more than anything else. The older I get, the more tenderness I feel at that realization. It's a lot more than most people get from their parents.

My father was complicated and, I understood as I got older, sad in a way that he couldn't let anyone see. He had an encyclopedic knowledge of history, and my mother said he was the smartest man she'd ever met. He was exceedingly generous. He was polite to people in the service industry, he was an excellent tipper, and he never met a dinner bill that he didn't pick up. But niceness wasn't something he could do. When I tried hugging him as a child, my father would occasionally yell, mock me for my neediness, or simply ask what the hell I was doing.

"When Stalin and Hitler are after you, niceness is not a thing that easily comes," my husband often says, delicately. My father was born outside Kiev, Ukraine, in the 1930s, just before the war began. He was a child through World War II, something that defined who he was but broke him a little bit at the same time. His family was supposed to be sent to the gulags when he was a child, but the day before they were going to be rounded up, Nazis took Kiev. What followed was one of the most horrific massacres of the war, in which thirty-four thousand Jews were slaughtered at Babi Yar. Dad was a few months shy of five years old at the time. He would later make it, with his family (minus my grandfather who was either dead or missing or maybe persona non grata— I don't really know. There are no photos of him; he is an abstraction, a placeholder), out of Ukraine and across Nazi-occupied Europe, and eventually ended up in a displaced persons' camp in Germany. They would live in Germany for a few years after the war before they immigrated to America. Considering how things were going at the time in that part of the world, it could have been infinitely worse. They all came out of the war alive, and with most of their teeth, and Dad possessed the cheery disposition you'd expect from a third grader who narrowly survived genocide.

My dad hated everyone. His favorite person was a dog. But he seemed to genuinely like my husband, as much as he liked anyone. Rand is Jewish; his maternal grandparents were refugees from the war who met in America. His paternal grandparents lived in New York, where my dad eventually landed as a teenager in the 1950s. And so Dad—who referred to humans, collectively, as "a bunch of assholes"—retained a soft spot for my husband, which meant that to untrained eyes he regarded him with what looked like barely veiled contempt.

When he died, he left behind a closet filled with copies of the exact same shirt and a lifetime's worth of unanswered questions. I still don't know where his family was from, despite all my inquiries. I don't know what happened to my paternal grandfather, and I realize that Dad probably didn't, either. Or what happened to my great-grandparents, or any of his cousins or aunts or uncles. My dad tried writing it out for me once, in a letter, when I was working on a family tree project in the sixth grade. I remember the dates of death ended in question marks, and next to a few names my father just wrote "disappeared."

What I've learned about family history has come out slowly and incompletely. My father told me how my grandmother would cook for them on a tiny stove in the back of trains as they moved across the Continent. She was in her mid-twenties (she had my dad at nineteen) and had two small children and her younger sister and mother with her. I guess she cashed in all the favors and luck that life would ever grant her to get them all across Europe during the war. Apparently, Grandma was a force, hell-bent on surviving (possibly just to spite Stalin). She died when I was a baby, so I never knew her. We have the same chin.

Whenever the train stopped, my dad told me how he and my uncle would run out into nearby fields and grab what they could and bring it back to the train car for my grandmother to cook. Kohlrabi or a cabbage—whatever they could steal and carry back with them. I've tried to imagine it: My father must have been a first grader, if my math is correct, his brother maybe four at most. I remember asking him, as a strange anxiety hit me through the decades and somehow threatened my own existence, if he was ever worried that the train was going to leave without them.

"It never did," he said, with a shrug. And as unbelievable as it is, there was the proof: He sat across from me, having grown old against all odds.

My grandmother eventually married a Dutchman who apparently was able to save her life and that of her family, but not his own, before the war was over. My father now had a new name, bestowed upon him by his late stepfather, and it would be the one he went by for the rest of his life. Finding out these things about him and his family has been an effort in patience, a maddening exercise, and on more than one occasion, a result of going through papers that I received as a part of the Freedom of Information Act after his death.

But also: Do you know how hard it was for five-year-old me to convince a man like that that I needed the 1984 Loving You Barbie (with mini stationery set included!) or I would absolutely *die*?

Straight answers weren't my father's forte, something I realize might have been a professional trait. My father wouldn't be rushed, wouldn't tell a story at any pace but his own, wouldn't answer a direct question, no matter how hard pressed. He could reply to a question for hours without saying anything. He once casually mentioned someone who had been angry at him, a fleeting footnote in a story about something banal, and Rand kept asking about it, pulling on a thread, patiently unraveling the story over several hours. What eventually emerged was this: The man in question was angry at my father because Dad had befriended him and bought him a few drinks and then shoved the man in the trunk of a car and drove him across Checkpoint Charlie, from East Berlin into West Berlin. It was there that my father and some of his colleagues interrogated him, in a piece of Cold War espionage that is lost to time and security clearances. Naturally, upon learning my father, a man who regularly fell asleep at the dinner table, had kidnapped someone and driven him from one side of the Berlin Wall to the other, I had a few questions. Dad's response was the same one he always gave.

"It was the assignment," he said flatly.

"You realize," my husband said later, "that your dad was a spy."

"Spies don't wear socks with sandals. Dad was a *translator*."

"A translator who shoved people into the trunk of cars."
I crossed my arms defensively.

"He's not a people person," I said.

Still, it always felt like a strange betrayal, to learn that this man who sported the same crew cut that he had from the time he was sixteen and first enlisted in the air force, this creature of habit and predictability, had lived an endlessly interesting life, and none of us knew. When he wrote to me, which was frequently in my younger years, and then less so as I grew up and he grew older, he filled page after page about the weather. It was like reading a meteorologist's report for a city I did not live in. Sometimes he sent me photos of dogs that were not his that he had seen and liked. He retained some qualities of his teenage years in New York City, a faint accent that tinged his English and made him sound like a Lower East Side native. He would tell me to go to Katz's Delicatessen and get the pastrami sandwich, as though he were revealing something I didn't already know. (I think he'd forgotten what was actually a secret and what wasn't.)

I slowly gathered information about him over the years, as if I were on my own mission.

I once asked my father if his mother had ever made Stroganoff, and he gave me a look of barely contained disgust before he scoffed, "No," as though the answer were obvious. I have spent years wondering what he meant by that, trying to interpret the significance of my grandmother's avoidance of the dish, if it was a sign of her own disdain for the aristocracy, or because she had Ukrainian and not Russian roots. Maybe she just didn't like mustard. One of my great-grandfathers was supposedly killed under accusations of being a tsarist sympathizer, and I wondered if that was part of it. Perhaps it was simply my father's usual reluctance to answer a question at play, creating more questions. It was a common occurrence, for him to have all the answers and be annoyed when people wanted them.

The first recipe for Stroganoff was published in 1871 in the second edition of a tome called *A Gift to Young Housewives,* by Elena Molokhovets. Molokhovets's first edition of the book had come out ten years earlier, in 1861, coinciding with the year that Russia ended serfdom. *Housewives* wasn't merely a cookbook, but a guide to life for the middle class and aristocracy, with advice on how to feed servants and construct a bed for the cook in the kitchen. It feels like a grim read now, knowing the revolution that was on the horizon. Many of her recipes began with the now rather alarming instruction "Send your maid to the cellar." Molokhovets's menus were so extravagant that Chekhov parodied them, listing out course after elaborate course (her recipe for babka supposedly required sixty or seventy eggs). Her book enjoyed stratospheric popularity for more than five decades. But after the fall of the tsar in 1917, in Soviet Russia, where food was often scarce, it felt like an affront, a flaunting of wealth and excess. According to Joyce Toomre, who translated and released an abridged version of *A Gift to Young Housewives* in 1992, Communist ideologues regarded Molokhovets as a symbol of bourgeois decadence.

Molokhovets's recipe for Stroganoff is reproduced in Toomre's book, under the title "Beef Stroganov with Mustard." The beef is cut into small cubes and seasoned only with salt and allspice. A roux is made from butter and flour, and bouillon is added to it, along with prepared mustard. It is, essentially, a classic French mustard sauce over steak—with a dollop of sour cream added at the end, a distinctly Slavic addition. But according to Toomre, by 1912 tomato paste was already being added. Still, Stroganoff would prove to be the ultimate survivor, outlasting the empire that birthed it, the bloody revolution, and multiple world wars. This might have been due to its malleability: The dish would continue to morph over the decades, and by the time it reached its zenith of popularity in the middle of the twentieth century in America, it had dozens of variations, shortcuts born of newfound conveniences like canned cream of mushroom and tomato soup, or ketchup. It can be served over noodles or rice. Mushrooms occasionally make an appearance, as do onions. In 1971, Betty Crocker launched its Hamburger Helper line, which was an instant hit: 27 percent of all U.S. households purchased the product in that first year. Two of the flavors—"Potatoes Stroganoff" and "Beef Noodle"—appear to be loosely influenced by the Slavic dish. The following year James Beard wrote of Stroganoff, in his seminal tome *American Cookery,* that "properly done, this is a dish that is cooked quickly, often at table, and served at once." As grammatically challenging as that sentence is, it's clear that Stroganoff had become a staple for the American home cook.

The problem is that few of the recipes I've found bear any resemblance to the dish my father made. His Stroganoff wasn't particularly creamy, though I have a vague recollection that perhaps sour cream was offered as an accompaniment. He served his over wide, curly egg noodles. There were mushrooms, and tiny slices of gherkin—which seems to be absent from many recipes, though one in *The Moscow Times* insists that the meal be served with a dish of them as a side. His cubes of beef were perfectly cut, and the sauce was tomatoey and salty. I remember once sitting at his dining room table and interrogating him about the dish, trying to get a straight answer out of my father, the near-impossible task that it was. I never got the recipe in full. I have only the pieces that I was able to pull out of him, the bits of information that he released slowly, almost accidentally, the same way I learned anything about him. Our relationship was punctuated by a collection of visits over the decades—not the unbroken line of a father-daughter bond, but a dotted one, the spacing uneven over the years. When I was small, he would try to come every summer or so for a month. But these visits became more infrequent as I grew up and he grew older. I saw him five times between the ages of ten and twenty-five. I didn't see him for five years between the ages of ten and fifteen. When he saw me again, he stared at me and yelled at my mother, "WHEN THE HELL DID THIS HAPPEN?"

"You were gone a long time," my mother replied.

The only through line we had was his letters. I collected them dutifully over the years, even as they became more and more infrequent. That was our relationship—letter after letter, each one pages long but revealing nothing, more than thirty years' worth of them amassed before most were lost in a house fire that my mother accidentally started (more on that later). I still cry when I think of losing those letters, more than I do when I think of actually losing my father. Because I never really had him, but I always had his words, abundant even when he was scarce. That was the closest I came to knowing who he was, struggling to read his penmanship when I was too small to understand cursive (he refused to write in print, even to a second grader). He rarely said he loved me; his response was usually to wave his hand dismissively and say, "Fine." That was my father's way of giving something a ringing endorsement.

"Fine," he'd say.

But he sat down and wrote me letters over the years, page after page, numbered and folded, and mailed to me, wherever I was, his own brand of fatherly devotion. I refuse to think that wasn't a kind of love.

He died in 2016 after a long illness. His long-term partner wanted a funeral and burial immediately, which meant I had four days' notice during the week of Christmas to get from the West Coast of the United States to the Bavarian village where he lived. Logistically and financially, it was impossible, and I accepted that my invitation was merely a courtesy. By the time I was able to visit, a few months later, my father's things had been cleared out, his workshop stripped bare. I had hoped to find something there, but the shelves were empty. When I asked his partner about it, she just shrugged her shoulders and said something to me in German that I didn't understand, but my husband translated it as "It's all gone."

I continue to look for answers. I am convinced I'll somehow find them in these American iterations of something old and classically Russian (or maybe Ukrainian), and no, the symbolism is not lost on me.

The internet offers all things to those who look. It has endless recipes for Stroganoff, a thousand variations on the theme. Russian mustard ordered online arrives at my home a few days later. A FOIA request form, filled out on a .gov site after his death, will yield an envelope full of documents pertaining to my father and a box of military medals. A deep dive into some online World War II database will tell me that Willem DeRuiter—a man with the same name as my father's stepfather—died in a camp in Germany, a Dutch objector to the war. What it does not tell me is if my father used mustard in his Stroganoff, or what was printed on the redacted pages in his file, or if the Willem DeRuiter who died was the same one who fell in love with my grandmother and gave me the last name that you see on the cover of this book. These are not arbitrary questions. The answers are distinct and precise. But the only one who could have told me is gone.

I decide to start with Molokhovets's recipe, or at least the derivative of it, which includes tomato paste. I brown the mushrooms and onions in butter first, before adding some flour to make a roux. It looks . . . well, messy, and not like something my father would tolerate. I can't imagine him purchasing flour. It's too chaotic. I dab out a spoonful of tomato paste next, which hits the bottom of the pot with a splat. I know my father didn't use this, either. I once asked him for the base of his sauce, and he stared at me as if I'd grown a third head. He refused to answer for a long stretch,

getting evasive and annoyed. Finally, exasperated, he re-
trieved a miniature can of V8 vegetable juice—his secret
ingredient—and placed it in front of me. (V8 was invented in
1933—sixty-two years after the first printing of Molokhovets's
recipe. As such, I decide to omit it in some attempt at authenticity.)

He wouldn't allow me in the kitchen while he was cooking, so I have no idea what his process was. I sat in the living
room in his little house in Germany and would watch him
from that distance, his back to me.

I ask Rand to cook the steak separately, in butter, per
Molokhovets's instructions. The recipe tells me to add bouillon to the sauce. I add bone broth, which I figure works just
as well. It thickens almost instantly, turns a sort of brick
red. I stir it. It looks like a pasta sauce, but not quite. The
final additions are a tablespoon of prepared Sarepska mustard, named for the former city of Sarepta, in Russia, and
some sour cream. The result is slightly creamy, rich, and
surprisingly elegant. I toss egg noodles in the sauce and top
it with the steak. The pickles I leave on the side, though my
dad would have cut them and put them directly in. It is not
unlike the dish he made, but also, it is distinctly different.
The way you can sometimes look like your parents and not
at all.

I ask Rand if my father would have liked it.

"Your father wanted things a certain way," he says diplo-
matically. "He didn't like change."

I sigh. I decide to make it a second time.

A brief note of advice: When making a dish that you
hope may offer you a greater understanding of your de-

ceased father, you may want to avoid making it on the eve of the anniversary of his death. Doing otherwise may lead to uncontrollable crying, and inevitably snapping at your husband, who swears he was not being judgmental when he commented that the mushrooms did not brown. *Judgingly.*

That being said, this time around, I don't use a recipe. When your ingredient list includes V8, a recipe is merely a formality, anyway. Rand again cooks the steak for me, in a separate pan. My father didn't do this; he added the beef right into the sauce, which sort of stewed it a little, turned it a brownish gray. (It is dawning on me that my father was not an excellent cook.) I do not ask Rand to do this. I am already subjecting him to a sauce made of mustard and a "delicious" blend of eight fruits and vegetables. There are limits to what you can ask of someone, even in a marriage.

I inch closer to Dad's version; this iteration is less subtle in flavor and texture and tastes oddly sweet in a preprocessed kind of way. It is more familiar, though this in and of itself feels like an empty goal. Without knowing what completely unimaginable tricks Dad used (deglazing the pan with vodka? Interrogating the steak to tenderize it? Locking the noodles in the trunk of an unregistered East German sedan until they soften?), I realize that I can try a thousand times and never get it right. And maybe there's no point. I am trying to re-create the dish only because it was his, not because it was some great culinary feat. (Trust me, it's not.) Maybe the act itself is tribute enough. I make Stroganoff not exactly as my father did but *because* my father did. Some people are unknowable, and what is left is the bits and pieces you try to assemble throughout their life and with a renewed sort of desperation after they are gone. I always thought we'd have more time to figure things out, he and I. You never think the clock will run out, not when there are still questions that need answering. I look at the result. An American dish with old Slavic roots. Something that survived wars, and came through the other side, changed but somehow intact.

It was not quite what I wanted, but it was good enough. As Dad would say, it was *fine*. Sometimes you have to be satisfied with that.

7

THE ONLY THING IN MY OVEN

I am in my forties, and I do not have children. This is by design, though occasionally I let people think that it is perhaps due to factors that are beyond my control. This deliberate obfuscation of the truth feels like a betrayal of some feminist doctrine I thought I believed in, and yet the indisputable fact is this: People are a lot kinder about me not having children when they think it wasn't something I chose.

Even now, as the window closes (is it a window? I don't know. There are many analogies about the end of fertility, none of them good. They involve clocks grinding to a halt, or flowers withering, or reaching for an egg carton and finding out they're all gone, or maybe there's one egg left, but it's a little weird looking, and the shell is all rippled and strange and it's probably from some sort of lizard), I am hesitant to say those words: that I don't want to be a mother. It sounds like a cold and calculated thing, something a comic supervillain would say before she starts up her penis-shrinking laser.

I try to come up with successful women who don't have children, and all I can think of are Cruella de Vil, fashionista puppy eater, and Edna Mode, the designer who made costumes for the superheroes in *The Incredibles.* I suppose it could be worse, really. I'm going to be extremely stylish and have lots of money. Don't ask me to dog sit.

I am occasionally asked if I have children—usually in bad faith, by men on the internet with whom I argue about issues that have nothing to do with whether I have children. It is a means of undercutting my credibility, a sucker punch I don't see coming, even though I should expect it by now. No children, no opinion. Which would make sense if we thought the world actually listened to women who do have children.

I asked my husband if this line of interrogation ever happens to him.

"Literally never," he tells me.

Sometimes I get called a cool wine aunt, which is supposed to be an insult. While I don't drink wine, I am an aunt, and a pretty damn cool one. I teach the niblings to swear in multiple languages, I play with Lego, and their college tuition is *covered.* Do you want to insult me for that, faceless internet dude whose wages are garnished because you owe child support to three women in Idaho? Go for it.

Oh, and I make the best chocolate chip cookies, ever. I make them for my nieces. I make them for my nephews. I deliver them to my friends and watch as their children get smudges of chocolate smeared across their faces. I make them for my husband. And when the house is empty, and I am alone in the quiet stillness of it, I make them for myself.

A lot of people I've talked to have told me that they knew they wanted to be parents from the time they were children. They'd play house and feed their baby dolls and knew that they wanted to be a mom. Part of it, I'm sure, is just how they are hardwired, and part of it is how young girls are socialized. I don't know that people often ask little boys if one day they want to be a daddy.

I was given dozens of baby dolls as a kid, which I insisted were my younger sisters. I never played house or dressed up as a bride. My Barbies, it is apparent in hindsight, lived in a very happy child-free lesbian commune with the occasional dramatic visit from Ken and my brother's Mr. Kotter doll. I never thought about being a mom, one way or the other. I figured the urge would come, that adulthood would cause some sort of seismic shift inside me that would draw me to things I presently had no interest in, like having children and eating blue cheese and paying taxes. But when I think about desires, about deep-seated instinctual wants, the thing that hits me again and again is this: I wanted to *bake*.

It was so overwhelming that I'd go around the house stirring an imaginary bowl when I was little.

The women in my family—my aunts and my grandmother, all of them mothers—did not bake. My mother insists that my grandmother used to make zeppole, which are technically fried, but I have zero recollection of this. The rest of the women who surrounded me when I was small are (and please note that I'm being generous here in my assessment) some of the worst bakers to have ever lived.

My aunt once made a pie that can best be described as cursed, pulling out a piecrust from the freezer that was old enough to remember where it was when JFK died. She proceeded to fill it with apples that she had inexplicably microwaved (I am still unclear on why. I think she was mad at them) and smothered them with baking soda because she thought it was cornstarch. I made her aware of the error (the concoction started hissing and fizzling, not unlike the witch in *The Wizard of Oz,* whom, I should note, you also probably shouldn't eat) and felt a wave of relief because she was *obviously* going to throw the whole thing away. Instead, she proceeded to wash the cooked apples off in a colander, which caused them to more or less disintegrate, and dumped them into the crust again. (I tried to leave before she fed it to me, but she, at a whopping ninety pounds and five feet tall, blocked the exits like a linebacker and demanded I eat.)

The runner-up to this pie is one my mother made, which tasted like corn syrup and was simultaneously over- and undercooked, the crust turning into dust when you touched it with your fork. When I asked her what was in it, she refused to give me a direct answer and said, alternatingly, "I don't know" and "Fruit, probably" and "What's Rand allergic to, again?" and became very, very defensive in that specific way people are when they're poisoning you. I pulled a foot-and-a-half-long hair from one of the slices, which cut through the crust like a fault line.

"You could have just eaten the hair," my mother said, somehow affronted.

So I remained an outsider to baking, this harbinger of American femininity, of warm nurturing motherhood, served hot out of the oven. When my classmates showed up at school with cookies and cakes that were homemade, I couldn't fathom the alchemy behind it.

"My mom made this," they'd say, without fail, biting into a brownie roughly the size of a textbook. I unwrapped my Little Debbie snack cake, a soulless corporate substitute. I needed to harness this power for myself. There was a problem, of course: I had no idea where to begin. I assumed it was innate, like motherhood itself. You were creating, after all. Not life, but a dessert, which, honestly, was close enough. How could you need instructions for something like that? I'd never seen anyone in my family use a recipe, ever, except for my aunt Pia. She scribbled down recipes for desserts that she would later completely disregard ("It says a cup of cocoa, but I put two teaspoons of ground cloves").

And so I soldiered on confidently, despite having no clue what I was doing, sans recipes, sans proper ingredients, sans measuring instruments, and probably, if I'm being honest with myself, sans washing my hands.

I mixed flour with margarine and cooking oil (Did we have butter? Who's to say?). I'd throw in some sugar, sometimes adding a hefty spoonful of baking soda because it had "baking" right in the name. I'd occasionally add a touch of vinegar for reasons that remain a mystery to me even now. If I remembered eggs, or could persuade my grandmother to give me some, I'd throw them in (I removed the shells, mostly). If I could procure sprinkles, I would put these on top. If I could not, I would simply add whatever I found in the spice drawer. The concoctions were somewhat like a rubbery, greasy pancake, edible in only the technical sense, the way crayons are. Sometimes they were tinged gray. To this day, I have no explanation for that.

I once made a batch of these—let's just call them cookies (and acknowledge that the word is doing some *extremely* heavy lifting in this sentence)—for my brother when he was sick. My mother, seeing the effort I went through, insisted he eat them.

"What's the green stuff?" he asked warily.

"Dried parsley," I replied.

I've been told regularly for the last twenty years that I would eventually want children. That the urge would hit me, uncontrollable and overwhelming. There was comfort in this: the awareness that something primal would take over, that my decisions would be made not by conscious choice but by some ancient instinctual longing, the same one that has overtaken humans for centuries. A feeling so strong that it compels half of the population to make more humans emerge from our bodies, even if it may literally kill us.

And sometimes, a glimmer of it would hit me. The idea of holding a small person who was mine. I was curious about it. But I didn't need it, the way I needed air, or water, or lemon pound cake with icing. I was happy with the life I had. When I thought about what it truly meant to have a child, I was indifferent. And I don't know if parents should be that. I think a prerequisite to being a parent is that you should want to be one. And there's a long diatribe here that I could go on about, but simply: Parenthood should always be a choice.

But baking didn't feel like a decision. It was a calling, the way salmon are drawn to the same waters in which they spawned, or pigeons in a city take flight and aim directly for my face. The combining of disparate ingredients, the transformational power of heating them in an oven. The time-lapse videos of cakes rising that I'd seen on commercials, the incredible way the tops would dome up and sink back down just a little. How cookies tore apart, chocolate ribboning out. The way you could press the top of a cake, and it would bounce back ever so slightly to indicate doneness. TV and magazines gave me a vague understanding of how desserts came together, something I was hell-bent on emulating. Was I fascinated with the Easy-Bake Oven? Of course. But I wasn't going to waste a coveted spot on my Christmas wish list on something that I already *technically* had. Our oven was a behemoth; caked with food, vaguely approximating temperatures, it ticked and rattled as it heated up and cooled down, ancient and angry. I stood before it and told myself I was going to tame that fucker—a terrifying prospect, really (I could have easily fit inside the thing, and children's fairy tales suggested this was *extremely* plausible).

Having seen the results of previous baking endeavors,

my family strongly discouraged this pursuit. For years, they tried to steer me in other directions, ones that didn't require them to eat my creativity. For years, I kept wandering back into the kitchen to ineptly make something that resembled a cursed pancake. They couldn't understand the compulsion, and I couldn't explain it to them.

I met my husband a few months after I turned twenty-one, and he was twenty-two, at a time when you are too young to meet the love of your life, and if you do, you are too clueless and busy dyeing your hair and listening to Green Day to realize it. (I was lucky. Eventually, I did.) My husband is the first person with whom I made cookies from scratch, in the tiny fluorescent-lit kitchen of our first apartment. And then I took over, and became excellent at it, a great culinary departure from those greasy gray disks that I claimed were dessert but were actually just haunted dough. I've been told that I would have figured out parenthood, too. Everyone does, at least on a grand scale, enough for humanity to continue. Maybe that's true. Maybe I would have been an okay mother. Maybe I would have been terrible. (The trolls on the internet are clear that I would have been awful, but also I am a soulless monster for not doing it.) It's a hypothetical, something that will never be answered.

As I grew older, I started to wonder if baking and children were, at least in my genetic line, somehow mutually exclusive. That I had no metaphorical buns in my oven, and so there was constantly something baking in my oven. I was not making birthday cakes for my own small humans as I watched them grow. Instead, I made cakes for any reason I saw fit—a random Tuesday, a friend coming to dinner, on

September 23, because that was the day Bruce Springsteen was born. I wondered if there was something irrevocably wrong with me. Something broken and unnatural. I ate a lot of cake and listened to *Born to Run*.

You'll change your mind.

It's a deeply condescending thing, to be told that you don't know yourself. To assume that I haven't gone over this question a thousand times, and nonstop for the week surrounding Mother's Day every year. That I haven't pulled my hair out and questioned whether I'm cold and dead inside (and maybe I am, but that's because I refused to cry during *E.T.,* and not because of *this*). Sometimes I clench my teeth until they hurt, because my husband doesn't get lectured about needing to give me children, but I've been pulled aside and told I'm depriving him of something. I was once having a discussion with a man I knew who snapped at me that I needed to shut up because I didn't have kids. (Someone hand me my penis-shrinking laser.) Somehow, I am blamed for a decision my husband and I both came to. One that he's always been more certain of than I've been.

I'm not telling anyone anything new when I say this: There's not a right answer here. There is a lot of privilege that comes with not having children (including the privilege of having reproductive medical care in the first place), but perhaps the most salient is this: I can tell you that I don't know if I'm making the right decision. I can tell you that the choices I'm making might come back to haunt me after the window has closed and my lizard eggs are all gone. In five years, in ten years, in forty, I may look back at my life and say, I made a mistake. I made the wrong choice.

That is not something that parents get to say.

I don't know that I will. Truthfully, I doubt it. I do the things that people without children are supposed to do. I sleep in every day so that it is no longer sleeping in but me merely rising of my own accord nine hours after I went to sleep in a giant bed next to my husband. He and I travel together—more than thirty countries, on every continent except Antarctica. I regularly make cake at 9:00 p.m., and eat it by 9:30 p.m., knowing that I don't need to set a good example for anyone. If it sounds as if I were trying to justify my life decisions, of course I am. That's all anyone is ever doing. Why do you think so many people want me to have children? Part of it is certainly schadenfreude, because I have laughed at too many diaper blowouts. And part of it is because they want to be assured that they haven't made the wrong choice.

There is no certainty, not one way or the other. I have no idea if this is the right path. It's merely the one I picked.

But baking is an exact science. It is a series of steps, detailed instructions, a list of measurements. It is a sequential thing with a known outcome, provided you are good at following directions, and God, when I want to, I am *good* at following directions. I like the predictability of it. There is no need for improvisation in baking; some recipes specifically discourage it. I can tell the difference now. I know when and where I can make substitutions. I know how many grams are in a cup of all-purpose flour, of white sugar, of cocoa powder (125, 200, 100, respectively). I know there are 14 grams in a tablespoon of butter, and eight tablespoons in a stick of butter, which is—

and here's the tricky part—half a cup. These measurements are a comfort to me. When everything else is uncertain, they remain a constant, an answer to a question I never quite asked. They are real and unwavering.

There are shortcuts. I learned them early. Sometime in my teens, I learned the magic of boxed cake and brownie mixes, of slice-and-bake cookies from a tube, of all the fool-proof ways you can make something reasonably impressive by doing little more than stirring. There's no shame in it. The culinary historian Laura Shapiro, author of *Something from the Oven: Reinventing Dinner in 1950s America,* found that women said they'd made a cake from scratch when they'd used a mix. We've come to regard it as the same thing. If you are insecure about your abilities and want to ensure good results, my long-standing rule has always been this: Make the cake from a mix and make the frosting from scratch. Add a few berries. Everyone will be impressed. Even if you say, "I made it from a box," they do not care.

But I found that I wasn't just concerned about the finished product. I'd been in love with the process. In shortening that, I felt as if I were cheating. I felt cheated. I like taking the long way.

In my twenties, I make Toll House cookies from scratch for the first time.

I've made cookies before. Sliced from a log of dough I bought in a giant squishy tube, next to the eggs. Alongside Rand, constantly sampling ingredients as he followed a recipe, throwing off the proportions ever so imperceptibly. Now I felt the need to do it on my own, to prove to myself that I could make them from nothing. It's as though I were laying claim to something that shouldn't belong to me. Baking, not as part of any familial tradition handed down from generation to generation, but because I *want* to.

First invented by Ruth Wakefield, a restaurateur and chef, the chocolate chip cookie was born of a mistake. Ruth had intended to make an all-chocolate cookie, and was going to use melted baking chocolate to mix into blond cookie batter. But she was short on time, and she had only a sweetened chocolate bar at her disposal. So she hacked it into little pieces with an ice pick as if it had wronged her and mixed it into the batter, intending for the chocolate to disperse throughout. Instead, it remained in chunks, and Wakefield ended up baking history. Her restaurant—the Toll House Inn—now lends its name to the renowned cookie.

The accidental element of the story has long been disputed. Carolyn Wyman, author of *The Great American Chocolate Chip Cookie Book,* writes that Wakefield wouldn't have made such a mistake. She was too precise, too experienced a chef. A promotional booklet for her restaurant described it as having "unruffled perfection" and said that within its walls "confusion is unknown." She was a flawless hostess and rolled with Julia Child. Duncan Hines (who was a real person before he was a cake mix) was an exuberant fan. So it's hard to imagine that those melted bits of chocolate were anything but intentional. Perhaps it's that we refuse to attribute genius to women, even when it is so clearly deserved. Or perhaps it's that we find comfort in the idea that even our mistakes might yield something good.

Several years after she first created her cookie, Wakefield would publish the recipe in a local Boston newspaper, and it would be featured on a radio show hosted by Betty Crocker (again, the person, not the cake mix). Nestlé saw a rise in sales of their semisweet chocolate bars and, realizing the tie to the cookie recipe, began selling the bars pre-scored, in order to make them easier to break apart. They approached Wakefield about obtaining the right to the Toll House name and printing the recipe on their chocolate bars. Eventually, they'd start selling chocolate morsels in bags, with Wakefield's recipe printed on the back.

It's a hell of a legacy. The cookie is iconic. It's also, if you make it, sort of just average.

I have been with Rand for more than twenty years—through almost all of my twenties, the entirety of my thirties, and now into my forties. To be happily coupled with someone for more than two decades means that everyone will ask about your reproductive plans. Friends and relatives and strangers at the airport and people on the internet with anime avatars will all weigh in on our sex life. I've been told many times that I'm barren, as if I were a goddamn field (insert plowing joke here). (Sorry, Mom.)

My friends who met their spouses later in life have told me that they discussed children early, on the first or second date. I know people who had children before they were married, or were pregnant on their wedding day, because they knew they were "running out of time," or simply had kids and decided to figure out the rest later. To be a woman who wants children means you are racing against a countdown timer. This is especially true if you want biological children. Mothers who are too young get judged. Mothers who are too old get judged. You need to be roughly thirty-three, but you have to look twenty-seven. Anything older and you are geriatric, you are infirm, you are past your expiration date. Anything younger and you've wasted your best years.

Cake mixes are generally good for an additional six months to a year past their "best by" date.

My husband and I have had nothing but time. The conversation has come and gone and come and gone, like the tide. We'd have every permutation of it. We've discussed biological children; we've discussed adoption. We've stood outside a train station bathroom in Kyoto and tried to decipher a Japanese pregnancy test, the one time my very predictable period decided to show up nearly two weeks late. We used Google Translate to figure out the results. They were hauntingly poetic.

"You are standing on firm ground," it told me. (The test was negative.)

The immense pressure to do the impossible—to have your cake, and an Instagrammable life, and eat it, too.

Sometimes I eat a piece of cake for breakfast, or lunch, or, if my husband is not home, for dinner. Sometimes all of these nutritional transgressions happen on the same day.

. . .

I don't know what kind of parent I would have been. Anxious, probably. Guilt-ridden. Wondering if I was doing the right thing. The uncertainty would exist either way. But I know I am an excellent baker. I go back to the definitive. A cup of packed brown sugar is 200 grams. If you don't have any, you can make some by adding a tablespoon of molasses to a cup of white sugar.

In my thirties, I find a better version of the Toll House cookie. The *Cook's Illustrated* Perfect Chocolate Chip Cookie recipe. A reworking of the original recipe, with all the same ingredients, in slightly different proportions. The main difference is this: The batter has to rest. The secret, poetically, is time.

I am now in my forties. I am told that time will change my mind. That regret will come. I have waited. And waited. And waited. My lizard eggs are drying up. My cookies are excellent.

I make them for Rand. I bake them for my nephews, and when the oldest reaches for his third predinner cookie, his mother swoops in to stop him. I bake them with my cousin's daughters, girls I watched grow up. Now old enough to do most of the work, they tower over me, laughing. They are beautiful humans. They've been raised so well. Their parents worked so hard. My other cousin visits from across the country, his oldest son in tow, and because I rarely get to see him, I instantly bake him a batch. He is mean the way teenagers are, the way you feel you have to be, steeling yourself against the world. When he reaches for a cookie, I see the cracks in the surface, the kid underneath shining through.

"What?" he says defensively as I smile at him. There is chocolate on his chin.

There are no buns in my oven. There is only this. I don't know if they will remember me when I am old, or when they are old. I don't know if they will ask for any of the recipes I've amassed. I don't need a legacy. Legacies are for other people. Actually, scratch that. I just remembered I offered to pay for their college.

These little shits better remember me until the end of their days.

My mother does not pester me about children. She has two grandchildren already, my brother easing the pressure off me while applying it himself. ("My children need cousins," he told me once. "Talk to your wife's brother," I replied.) She does ask, now and again, if I'm sure. I see it, the fear she has, that I might regret my choices. The same fear all parents have for their children.

I imagine a conversation with my fictional child, as I sometimes do, which is probably weird, but I also give Oscar acceptance speeches in the shower, so don't read too much into it. If they asked me whether they needed to have children, I would tell them, "Of course not. You just need to find what makes you happy."

I think I found mine.

The last time I made chocolate chip cookies, my mother was over at my house. She, a woman who rarely touches dessert, stared at the batch, hot out of the oven, and asked if she could have one.

"Of course," I told her.

She gently picked one up, cradled it in her palm a moment, the way you would something rare and delicate, and took a bite. The chocolate ribboned out, just like in commercials I'd seen as a kid.

"How is it?" I asked her.

"It's perfect," she said.

As far as legacies go, I'll take it.

8

PAYING THE PRICE

f I think back to the dates I went on in my early twenties—an exercise that is painful for a variety of reasons—a familiar scene plays out again and again. As we neared the end of a meal, or even as we reached its midpoint, I started to make calculations of where my purse and, specifically within it, where my wallet was. Sometimes, if I was feeling particularly neurotic, which was almost always, I would simply rest my wallet in my lap (pockets on women's clothing, on the rare occasion they are present at all, are just deep enough to carry exactly three baby teeth). When the bill came, I would have my card or my cash ready, sometimes slapping down payment with such a frenzy that in this recollection the breeze created by this motion would blow back my date's hair, knock menus and plates off the table, and send one petite server careening back as though they were in a hurricane. This is artistic license, but still: I put my money down with the panicked hurry of someone trying to pay for their soul.

I remember being at a Greek café that I loved with a young man whom I was entirely indifferent to. I can barely remember him, or his face. Ask me his name and the only one that comes to mind is Peter Billingsley, who was the kid who played Ralphie in *A Christmas Story*. (It was not him.) More than twenty years later, I just remember the circumstances of our date, which I hadn't realized was a date until I was on it. I had thought that we were just hanging out and seeing a play (a requirement for a drama class I was taking). He suggested dinner beforehand, and suddenly I found myself confused and unsure how to politely escape, which is how people end up buying time shares. I don't remember if I liked him; I don't even think I entertained the thought. I was just blindsided by the situation, terrified by what I'd gotten myself into, and now, as we sat eating, I knew: I could not let him pay for dinner.

We were still blissfully in the nebulous gray area of two people who didn't know each other very well sharing a meal, and whether that coalesced into something awkward where he mistakenly thought I was romantically interested, or something equally awkward where he realized I was *not,* would be determined by what happened when the check came. It was Schrodinger's dinner; I didn't owe him anything, but this only seemed to hold true *as long as we split the bill.*

I understood the concept of consent, but somehow it felt as if I were giving it (carte blanche for the rest of the evening) if I allowed my date to pay for the meal. I fully understand how outdated and ridiculous this notion is; it was antiquated back in the 1990s, when this was happening. I didn't have to do a damn thing if he bought me dinner—

obviously—but I couldn't shake the years of baggage associated with someone else picking up the check. I felt as if I were agreeing to some sort of unspoken carnal contract that limited my later options. I didn't want to back myself into a corner where the only way out was lots and lots of sex because someone bought me a grilled cheese sandwich.

"Why did you let him buy you dinner?" felt on par with "Why did you go up to his hotel room?" I am acutely aware of how messed up this all is! This is Victim Blaming 101. The rape culture was coming from inside the house, or in this case, my own head. A study in 2010 found that when college students were presented with fictional date rape scenarios, the male students assigned less blame to the male perpetrators of sexual assault when they were the ones who paid for dinner versus when the check was split. Even if I didn't think I owed my date anything just because they paid for a meal, I couldn't be sure that *they* wouldn't think that. My motivations were born out of fear more than any kind of egalitarian thinking. And it was so strong I started to question my own motivations; I couldn't trust *myself*. Any physical interactions that followed dinner were suspect. Were they happening because I liked the person in question or because I'd convinced myself that I'd agreed to it when they paid for souvlaki? Was I doing this because I thought I couldn't say no? It was too fraught a question. And so my wallet was on my lap. I was *ready*. Especially if I liked him.

This is why, on my first date with my now husband, I tried to snag the entire bill. Because I was going to positively *pounce* on him (consensually!) the second we were out of this restaurant, and I was a particular sort of early twenties disaster of a human who needed to be absolutely sure of her intentions. I didn't want there to be any confusion in my own head as to why I was doing what I was doing. So when he excused himself to the bathroom, I flagged down a server and asked to pay the check. I figured if I paid for all of it, I would know for sure that I didn't owe my date anything. (I never thought for a second that the inverse of the situation might be true—that he might feel obligated to put out because I bought him dinner. Asking him about it years later, he answered truthfully: It never would have occurred to him.)

But the server *refused to give me the check*. I was a patron at his restaurant, trying to exchange money for goods and services rendered, which is THE WHOLE POINT OF RESTAURANTS, and I was not allowed to do that. It was too much, he insisted, and so he wasn't going to give me the bill. I stared at him, baffled. He was Italian—the restaurant was, too—and since I spoke the language, I began to insist, in his native language, that he let me pay. He continued to refuse, stalling long enough that Rand returned to find me in a heated discussion with our server in a foreign language that involved a lot of hand gestures.

This neurosis doesn't seem to exist solely in me. There's a weird catch-22 in place. A 2017 survey found that most heterosexual individuals polled—nearly 80 percent—believed that men should pay for the first date. I'm not saying that everyone agrees with it (I sure as hell don't), but it's the prevailing belief I was fighting against. In 2018, a female contestant on a British dating show was accused of emasculating her male date because of her insistence on splitting the bill.

And wrapped within that was yet another antiquated idea: that if a man did pay for a meal, he might be granted certain "privileges" later. Some men have gone so far as to demand repayment from women for dates that didn't end in sex. The situation is arguably less fraught in the queer community: A 2016 survey found that 62 percent of single people in the LGBTQIA+ community felt that the person who initiated the date should pay, an idea echoed in the book *Steven Petrow's Complete Gay & Lesbian Manners.* "The rule about who pays on a first date is comparatively easy," Petrow writes. "You invite; you pay." Anna Pulley, who writes an advice column on sex, etiquette, relationships, and queerness for the *Chicago Tribune,* noted that when she asked people in the LGBTQIA+ community about picking up a check on a first date, the responses were less heated than when she asked heterosexual singles (one person responded, "Know what? I've never thought of it before!"). But there was still baggage: A few respondents said that they were worried splitting a check on a first date would give the impression they just wanted to be friends.

Within heteronormative dynamics, the idea is that the man should pay, even though doing so comes at a steep cost to both parties. I discussed this with a friend one evening while out to dinner at La Pergola, the only three-star Michelin restaurant in Rome. He felt the weight of gender constructs not just around the bill, he explained to me, but in ordering in general. As a man, he felt an odd societal pressure to not order things like salad or certain cocktails that were considered too feminine, even though sometimes he wanted those things. They were delicious, but they felt off-limits to him.

"I don't always want to eat a steak or a burger because I'm a guy," he said. These antiquated constructs of masculinity were even detrimental to the group that they had been designed to champion in the first place: straight white men.

Also worth noting: That night, I accidentally ordered $54 worth of bottled water because MY MENU DID NOT HAVE PRICES. And while spending an obscene amount of money on something that *literally fell from the sky* was new and horrifying to me, menus without prices weren't.

The first time I encounter a menu without prices is at another Michelin-starred restaurant, this time in Piedmont, Italy. It is the middle of truffle season, and the air in every restaurant we walk into is thick with the smell of them, of earth and grass, the heavy scent of damp woods. It will follow us long after we leave, clinging to our clothes and hair.

Rand and I are with our friends Oli and Nicole on their first trip to Italy. The waiter hands us our menus and I immediately scan mine looking for prices, because I cannot separate the excitement a meal brings me from what I'm paying for it. The two are inexorably tied. The more you pay for something, the greater the pressure to enjoy it. I know there is more that goes into a restaurant meal. We pay not just for raw ingredients but for the labor, for the service, for the linens and the lighting and the curation of music and the way the chairs align with the tables. These things do not go unnoticed by me, but also: I need to know just how much I'm being charged per shrimp. Sometimes I curse myself when I swallow too quickly because that bite just cost me $3.75 and I should have savored it a little more or at least taken a video of me chewing for Instagram. There are times when I would just rather eat at home, where the stakes are lower and the price of steak is lower. It's not to say that great food isn't or shouldn't be expensive. It's just that...my God, the *anxiety* of it all. This never happens when you get your dinner from a gas station.

But this menu has no prices. Maybe they are listed somewhere—hidden at the bottom of the page in minuscule font in Sanskrit, like every email unsubscribe button ever, but I keep looking and find nothing. I remember how my mother would scrutinize prices when I was a child, her endless analysis at the grocery store, her worries about money, about food, about the world, and the words she repeated again and again, as constant as waves against the shore: "This is all too expensive." Is this all too expensive? I don't know. I wonder if this is an "If you have to ask, you can't afford it" sort of place, which worries me. Because I very much do have to ask.

"The prices are really reasonable," Rand says, as though answering my unspoken question. "The surcharge for adding truffles is not bad."

"I saw that," Oli says.

"What are you talking about? Where are you seeing prices?" I demand.

"Uhhh, on the menu."

"WHERE?"

"I don't see them either," Nicole says.

"It's printed right next to the dishes," Rand tells us.

I glance again at my menu, squinting as though trying to decipher a Magic Eye poster at the mall. There are no prices listed. There is no dinosaur on a skateboard either.

"THIS IS GASLIGHTING," I yell.

Rand gives me a look of subtle annoyance, the one that is a preamble to being right about something. "It's right th—" He stops, his hand hovering over my menu, before his brow furrows.

"Why doesn't your menu have prices?" he asks.

"I TOLD YOU," I shout back at him. (I am a good date.) He shows me his menu. Prices listed for every dish, and an optional surcharge—€15—for truffles.

"What the hell?" Nicole says, peering over at Oli's menu. The maître d', seeing our confusion, walks over.

"The women's menus don't have prices," he explains. "Because women don't want to think about money."

We all look meaningfully at one another for a few moments, before Nicole and Oli and Rand and I wordlessly trade menus. As I peruse the numbers next to the dishes, the world slowly falls into place again.

"This is so unsettling," Rand says, staring at the price-less menu.

I pat his knee sympathetically.

"Try not thinking about money," I say.

Restaurants aren't a new concept. It seems that shortly after people mastered the power of fire, and cooking food over fire, someone was like, "Ugghhh, I don't feel like doing that tonight." In sixth-century BC Egypt, when the pyramids were a mere two thousand years old, people could dine out at a public eatery. Ordering was an easy matter, because there was only one dish available: a mix of cereal, onion, and wild fowl. In the ruins of Pompeii, the remains of a thermopolium—a snack bar—were found dating back to AD 79 (the year Vesuvius buried the city). You could order a soupy mixture of fish, snails, and sheep, or wine with fava beans (the fava beans were actually *in* the wine). In the last two thousand years, chunky bean chianti has thankfully fallen out of fashion, but having someone else do the cooking hasn't. In twelfth-century China, during the Song dynasty, you could go out for dim sum or noodles, choosing from any number of pre-plated demonstration dishes, which would then be prepared for you and presented dramatically by a cadre of highly skilled waiters who sang, even if it wasn't your birthday. Across the globe and across history, humans have sat on whatever their equivalent of a couch was, looked at one another, and said, "I don't know, what do *you* feel like eating?"

But presumably, in all of these places, people knew how much their meal was going to cost them. So how—and why— did I end up with a menu with no prices on it? And why had I never seen one like this before?

It turns out that I'd received something called a ladies' menu—one in which the prices aren't listed, because it's presumed that the person reading it isn't going to pay for the meal. If you've ever gone to a fancy-pants wedding or a catered lunch, you've probably encountered one—just a list of dishes that are about to be served to you. But receiving one at a restaurant is an extremely rare occurrence. And in the United States, it's unheard of, thanks to legendary lawyer Gloria Allred (who was personal lawyer to Norma McCorvey—the "Jane Roe" in *Roe v. Wade,* years after the landmark case).

By the late twentieth century, ladies' menus were already largely obsolete in America—a relic of a bygone era. But some restaurants held on to the practice, like the upscale French eatery L'Orangerie in Los Angeles, run by Virginie and Gérard Ferry. Originally from Paris, the two hoped to bring a bit of old-world elegance to Southern California with their opulent menu. When one reads the dishes now, they feel decadent, the sorts of things best eaten while wearing shoulder pads and a little cocaine mustache. According to Natasha Frost reporting for *Atlas Obscura,* the fish of the day was apparently flown in from France every morning. The veal medallion came with three different mustard sauces and cost $26 (nearly $100 today). Two of the nine appetizers contained caviar.

In July 1980, Kathleen Bick wanted to treat her business partner, Larry Becker, to a celebratory dinner at L'Orangerie. When the two arrived, Bick was given a different-colored menu, one that lacked prices.

Women don't want to think about money.

It would be frustrating anywhere, but given how much a meal cost at L'Orangerie, the act bordered on criminal.

Or civil, to be precise. Bick and Becker immediately left without ordering dinner, and Allred would represent them as they filed suit against the restaurant, alleging that it had violated California's Unruh Civil Rights Act. They sued the restaurant for $250 in damages.

As Allred told *Time* magazine in 1980, the ladies' menu implied "that women will always be taken care of if they're with a man, and that we shouldn't be bothering our pretty little heads about the price of dinner." Allred would call L'Orangerie and ask why the restaurant gave women menus sans prices.

"Because a woman is a woman is a woman," Virginie Ferry said. More than being deeply confusing and wildly unhelpful, the statement suggests that there is something inherently unfeminine in picking up the check. Or in being anything less than entirely ignorant of the prices of what we consume. Challenging the existing rules makes you less of a woman.

The case would ultimately be tried in the court of public opinion. Allred set up a dining table outside the restaurant in protest, garnering the attention of the national press. The public sided with Bick and Becker, who eventually dropped their case; L'Orangerie abandoned the ladies' menus. And the fear of public backlash and similar lawsuits meant that other restaurants across the country followed suit. It was why I hadn't seen a menu without prices until I was almost forty, dining in a mountain town in Italy.

There was a time when handing a woman a menu without any prices on it wasn't such a ridiculous concept. European-style fine dining restaurants started to gain popularity in the United States in the nineteenth century. Delmonico's claimed to be the first, opening in Manhattan in 1827. The

Nineteenth Amendment was nearly a century away; the tampon wouldn't be patented until 1933. If a woman went out unescorted, especially to eat, it was positively scandalous. It was believed that she was most probably a woman of "loose morals"—parlance for being a sex worker.

Actually, I should clarify that. It was scandalous for a *white* woman to go out unescorted. It was literally impossible, illegal, and even deadly for a woman who wasn't white to go out unescorted, if at all. White women might have had fewer rights than their white male counterparts, but they had more than any other group of women and most men.

Still, in the 1830s, many establishments excluded women entirely, particularly during the crunch of lunchtime. (Time was sparse, and it was believed that men had important things to discuss during mealtime, whereas women would gossip and languish around the table.) Restaurant patrons were often exclusively white men who thought they knew better than everyone else. Walking into a dining room was like watching C-SPAN coverage of the GOP discussing reproductive rights.

Some restaurants allowed women to dine in their main dining rooms, provided that they were in the company of a male companion (a rare few had private dining halls reserved specifically for women). Social constructs of the day assumed that the man in the party would pay for the meal, and so the women's menu came—drumroll please—*sans* prices. Women couldn't exist as independent economic entities in most states until the early twentieth century anyway; they were unable to claim inheritances or accrue money on their own, yet they were somehow liable for their husband's debts. So it's not as if a woman paying the bill were even possible, much less in anyone's purview.

The logic of keeping women out of certain parts of the dining halls was supposedly to protect them from unpleasantness, from smoking, from harassment, from—and this is truly a baffling argument—exposure to other, non-respectable women (who were also not allowed in those areas!). This supposed fragility and delicacy of white women has historically been used not only to restrict their rights but to justify violence against people of color since forever.

However, by the turn of the century, restaurants realized the advantage of catering to female clientele. Women were entering the workforce, were legally allowed to have their own bank accounts and even (clutches pearls) their *own property*. Within this world, tearooms gained popularity.

Often run and staffed entirely by women, they focused on, yes, tea, which served to distinguish them from saloons or taverns (which were considered distinctly masculine spaces). Tearooms served food as well (often lighter bites for more "delicate constitutions") and are believed to have pioneered the children's menu. Sometimes they were located in department stores, or adjacent to them, so that women could "refuel" while out shopping or running errands. These menus had prices. And while these establishments weren't off-limits to men, it would be rare to find a man there on his own; most often if he was courting a woman, he would bring her to a tearoom, because it was a respectable place for a date.

By the early twentieth century, tearooms were popping up throughout America. But even as dining establishments began to welcome and specifically cater to women, they remained distinctly segregated. Sex-segregated dining declined by the 1920s and 1930s, but Jim Crow remained, and tearooms served white and Black communities separately. Angela Jill Cooley notes in her book *To Live and Dine in Dixie: The Evolution of Urban Food Culture in the Jim Crow South,* this segregation represented "the privileging of whiteness in the consumer space." As she told *Scientific American* in 2016, "This was not about separation, it was about creating status. . . . African Americans were cooking the food that white diners were consuming in the white dining room and they were physically close to African Americans who were often serving them or bussing tables while they were eating. They just were not physically close to other black diners."

Cooley notes her work was inspired by that of Grace Elizabeth Hale, author of *Making Whiteness: The Culture of Segregation in the South, 1890–1940.* Hale writes that eating establishments presented a specific kind of intimacy—one that involved the "touching of the product to the lips." Previously, slavery had created the hierarchical structure that preserved white supremacy—meaning no further separation was necessary. But with its abolition, segregation would be integral for a white population attempting to establish dominance over the Black community. To eat next to someone of another race—using the same utensils—is deeply egalitarian, a figurative, if not literal, breaking of bread. It's by design that so many of the most significant and enduring images from the Civil Rights Movement occurred at lunch counters. Desegregated dining rooms were a direct threat to those trying to uphold the vestiges of slavery and white supremacy.

The *Green Book* was first published in 1936, outlining establishments and businesses that were safe for Black motorists traveling across the country. Because many of the restaurants listed in the guide were smaller, and often operated out of people's homes, there wasn't space for separate dining halls for men and women, and so these spaces were coed, family-friendly affairs. In 1945, St. Clair Drake and Horace R. Cayton wrote of the dangers of dining while Black in their book *Black Metropolis: A Study of Negro Life in a Northern City*. Discrimination, they noted, was prevalent along the margins of the Black Belt and in places where restaurant owners wanted to maintain an "exclusive" atmosphere. One white bartender boasted that he served Mickey Finns (drinks laced with incapacitating drugs—hence the phrase "slipped him a Mickey") to Black patrons in order to discourage them from coming in. Two Black schoolteachers were seated at a table with the rest of their white party, but ignored by the staff (and told that they would be served only in the kitchen).

As people of color and white women fought for more rights within a white patriarchal system, restaurants played a pivotal role. These places, intimate and integral to everyday life, had for so long been the domain of white people, and specifically of white men. (While white women had fewer rights than their white male counterparts, many were—and are—invested in preserving the existing racist hierarchy. Doing so kept them on a higher rung than most everyone else and meant that their spouses remained in unchecked positions of power. Even those who embraced feminism often failed to do so intersectionally, and were unwilling to acknowledge their inherent white privilege.) The Civil Rights Act would legally if not effectively end segregation in restaurants in the 1960s. Gender segregation in restaurants was still *technically* legal, but by the 1970s many restaurants that served only men had started to fall to changing sociopolitical and cultural pressure. McSorley's Old Ale House (which is still in operation today) in New York City started to admit women only in 1970, after losing a suit in federal court. This is not to say it was all smooth sailing: The bartender subsequently refused to serve the vice president of the National Organization for Women, and a patron dumped an entire stein of beer on her head.

By the 1980s, Allred's lawsuit was the death knell for the ladies' menu in America. It can still be found in some corners of the country, under the guise of exclusivity, at restaurants like the Harbour Room at the Boston College Club and Michael's Gourmet Room in Las Vegas. And so I would encounter it for the first time at a fine dining restaurant in Europe.

And for the second time at a fine dining restaurant in Europe.

And for the third time at a fine dining restaurant in Europe.

Still, I hesitate to complain about receiving a menu without prices. I've basically won a privilege lottery. I am white and cis and healthy and have plenty of money to spend on travel and meals in beautiful restaurants where people bring me food on little dishes with edible flowers tossed all over the place as if someone in the back of the house were a tiny woodland fairy. In the grand scheme of things, it feels like an immensely small problem to not be told how much my food costs and *to have it not really matter,* financially speaking. I should consider myself immensely lucky. And I *do*. But this particular kind of culinary chivalry has an ugly history. It carries with it an idea that this place I am occupying is one where I am a transgressor. I am here only by the largesse and permissiveness of white men. If I, with all my layers of privilege, feel unwelcome, what does that mean for everyone else?

Women don't want to think about money? In America, women make on average eighty-two cents for every dollar a white man makes. And those numbers only get worse when you specifically look at populations of women of color. Black women make sixty cents per dollar, and Hispanic women make fifty-five cents per dollar. Maybe it's more that people don't want women thinking about money, because if we do, we might start burning shit to the ground, and nothing kills the fine dining atmosphere like a gallon of gasoline, a match, and a feminist agenda. It's a recurring theme I've found: The entire notion of fine dining service, and the proper behaviors expected from such an environment, rest on these antiquated gender roles. And to challenge these concepts— which are supposedly indications of polite, genteel society— is to risk coming across as unfeminine, difficult, and rude.

The restaurant critic Tracey MacLeod noted that when a female friend of hers attempted to take her own husband out to dinner at the now shuttered La Tante Claire in London, she "was foiled at every turn. Even though she'd made the booking, the staff treated her as the little lady guest. She got the menu with no prices. He got the wine to taste. She requested the bill. He was given it to pay." When she addressed this with the manager as they were leaving, he simply smiled at her husband and said, "Lucky fella!"

It seems like an innocuous, small thing, but by not giving women the courtesy of knowing how much a meal costs, by not endeavoring to imagine that they might be the ones picking up the bill, the staff is not regarding them as legitimate patrons of the restaurant. They are there as accessories for the male guests. Given the transactional role that a man buying a woman dinner has historically carried in Western society, the entire situation becomes even more fraught.

But the trend is finally starting to change, even at fine dining restaurants. The concept of "ladies first" is giving way to gender-neutral service. At Tied House in Chicago, servers simply serve the dishes clockwise according to seat number. Phrases like "ladies and gentlemen" and handing the bill to the male-presenting patron are seen as antiquated relics of a bygone era. And for good reason: I don't want to guess my way through menus. I do not want to accidentally order $54 worth of bottled water. I don't want men to feel as if they can't order salad. I don't want women to feel a cold sweat of anxiety if they can't wrestle the check away on a first date. And I don't want anyone to have their identity disrespected because restaurants have an outdated view of what gender is.

On that first dinner out with my eventual husband, when he returned to the table, the waiter and I were still arguing in Italian over the check.

"What's going on?" he asked.

"I'm trying to buy you dinner," I said, feeling oddly ashamed.

"Why don't we split it," he offered. And that night, we did. Since then it's a race between us to see who can put their card down the fastest. It's theatrics; we've shared finances for nearly two decades. But every time we've been to a place where I've received a ladies' menu, he doesn't fight me when I reach for the bill.

9

LIKE A HOUSE ON FIRE

In the summer of 2018, my mother's house burned down. That's how she says it: "My house burned down." She uses the passive voice, as though it happened on its own. Which is a little like Brutus saying, "When Caesar was stabbed in the back." Like a baleen whale saying, "When all those plankton were eaten." Like eighteenth-century Parisian revolutionaries saying, "When the Bastille was stormed." Technically accurate, but we need to assign credit where it is due. The house did not decide to suddenly erupt into flames of its own accord, like the baby in *The Incredibles*.

I was in Los Angeles at the time, visiting my brother for a few days, and I was at that inevitable part of any time spent with a sibling where we (I) needed a bit of space from each other (him) so that we could continue to enjoy each other's company (I was gonna stab him in the neck). So I'd spent the day with my friend Bill, who looks a little like a young Giancarlo Esposito, which I am telling you because Bill is an actor, which means he needs work, and I'm sure we can all agree that Giancarlo Esposito is one of the most handsome people on the planet. Anyway, we took his cousin (Bill's! Not Giancarlo Esposito's!) to the beach so he could see the Pacific for the first time. That's mostly what I remember: The day my mother's house burned down (passive voice), Bill's cousin saw the ocean for the first time. I find something poetic in that.

I took an Uber back to my brother's after hanging out with Bill and his cousin, and it occurred to me I hadn't checked my phone the entire time, the sign of someone happily distracted by friends. When I looked, I had somewhere in the vicinity of twenty-seven missed calls, which is never a good thing. Even if someone wins the lottery or has a baby, they are not going to call you twenty-seven times to let you know. People only try to get ahold of you that desperately if the news is extremely bad and they want company.

There was also a good number of texts.

And a few emails.

At this point, my first instinct was to roll down the window and toss out my phone. I was fairly certain that someone had died while I was at Urth Caffé eating a fancy grain bowl with roasted vegetables and a poached egg on top and catching up with an old friend. I felt that weird variety of retroactive guilt that comes from knowing you were enjoying your life while, unbeknownst to you, awful things were simultaneously happening. And now I was having a harsh reentry into reality and trying to piece together what I'd missed.

My first immediate thought was my mom. You'd think it's a function of my age, that something bad happens, and I assume it's happened to my mom. But truthfully, it's always been like this. I've spent my entire life worrying that she's going to die.

I don't remember the first message I checked. I know there was one from my mother's real estate agent, Joseph. She'd been in the process of selling her house.

"Please call me right away," Joseph said. "I . . . I don't want to tell you what happened over voicemail." Saying this was actually much worse than telling me what happened over voicemail.

I didn't call Joseph back. (I also had roughly a dozen calls from my aunt, I'd noticed.) Instead, my brain fixated on an email from my mother's insurance office, with the very calming all-caps subject line of "PLEASE CONTACT OUR OFFICE ASAP." The text of the email contained a phone number and reiterated the message to call them because it was "very important."

At this point, I had not yet abandoned the idea of jettisoning my phone from the window of the late-model Prius I was riding in. Maybe these problems could be ignored (perhaps indefinitely!) if no one could find me? Is this why people sometimes disappear from society? Why you hear about people who go missing in 1984 and their families assume the worst but then someone tracks them down and they're living a completely innocuous life in, like, Des Moines, Iowa (I've never been, but it sounds innocuous)? It's not as though they went to live a life of intrigue and suspense somewhere glamorous like Rio de Janeiro or Paris or even the Paris casino in Vegas—no! They just went someplace excessively normal and sort of started over again. This always baffled me, but in that moment, with a driver and credit card at my disposal and bad news waiting for me in the form of fifty-four missed voicemails (it doubled in size as time passed! Like a ball of dough proofed by pure anxiety!), I suddenly understood. Sometimes everything is so overwhelming that you want to shake the heck out of that Etch A Sketch to clear it. And then throw the Etch A Sketch out the window of a moving car. And move to Des Moines.

I called my mother's insurance office. Of course I did. No offense to Iowa (I'm too claustrophobic to live in a land-locked state). Besides, and I'm sure this is hardly news to anyone, you can never outrun your problems. Definitely not in L.A. traffic.

Pam, the receptionist, answered the phone.

"I just want you to know that no one is hurt and everyone is okay," she said as soon as she heard it was me, which I guess is an objectively good thing to tell someone. The only problem is that if someone tells you that, unprovoked, you know that the conversation is going to be all downhill from there. It is the absolute zenith of your interaction. "There was a small fire at your mom's house," she said.

"Oh," I replied, surprisingly calm. I think it's because, and keep in mind that I'm not a doctor but this *sounds* accurate, I could barely hear her over the sound of all of my major organs vibrating.

"But don't worry! The fire department is there."

"Well, that's good," I said. Though I wasn't certain it

was my voice that was speaking. It sounded as if it were coming from somewhere else, as if someone were playing a tape recorder and, goodness, the voice on it sounded *just like me.* Which was okay, because if the *real* me started talking I couldn't be sure that I wouldn't make a weird undulating sound like a European ambulance siren.

"And they've boarded up the windows and gotten everyone out."

I wanted to point out that this did not sound like a small fire. In the years since, it's occurred to me that Pam had probably dealt with a *lot* of fires, so maybe in the grand scheme of things, like, say, compared with the El Dorado fire in California, which burned more than 22,000 acres of land, this was not big.

"Okay," was all I managed to say.

The fire department couldn't let my mom back into the house, because it was obviously unsafe and she couldn't spend the night there, Pam went on, but they'd gotten her purse for her. But she couldn't call me, because her phone was melted. But she was fine! My mother wanted me to know that. She was *fine.* Some of the firefighters remembered her from another incident several years earlier in which my mom got pinned under several hundred pounds of drywall (that incident was more than twenty years ago, but I need you to know that as I was writing this, I had to gently put my head down for a few moments and just breathe). This, for the record, is not an ideal situation: when first responders see your mom and are like, "Oh, hey, you again!"

"Thank you," I said to Pam. I repeated that a few times, unsure of what else to say. We ended the call, and I held my phone on my lap for a long time, staring out the window.

"It was a pie," my mother says. I think it's easier to tell yourself that you left something in the oven—where things are supposed to be left unattended—than to admit that you left something on the stove and just forgot. Some people from the city had knocked on her front door; they'd arrived to clear some trees, and my mother *walked out of the house to discuss it with them.* While a pan was on the stove. As the city inspectors talked trees with my mom, one of them noticed that smoke was billowing out of the back of the house. My mom tried to run back in. They had to hold her back.

Nero played the fiddle while Rome burned. My mother was discussing trees.

The very kind inspector from the insurance company was also named Bil, but spelled with only one L, as though the second one fell off somewhere and he hadn't bothered replacing it. He said, without any hesitation, that the fire started *there,* pointing to a back burner with his flashlight.

"It wasn't the oven?" I asked, trying not to sound too desperate.

"Nope," he said definitively.

He and I walked through the charred interior of my mom's house several weeks after I had that first call with Pam. There was no electricity, so the house was dark, and the smell was intense, of creosote and smoke, something toxic, not like a wood fire, even though so much of my mother's home had been made of wood. The floor was covered with debris an inch deep, glass shards and bits of wood, and all the unidentifiable flotsam of her life, making a sound like broken chimes as I stepped over it. I paused to look at something in the laundry room, which was adjacent to the kitchen. The object was suspended from the ceiling. It was long and beautiful, cream colored, like a sort of giant droplet, backlit from the window behind it. After a minute I recognized it as the light fixture that hung from the ceiling. The heat had distorted it, melting it into this giant Daliesque shape. The temperature at which glass starts to slump is roughly a thousand degrees.

The kitchen was unrecognizable.

I asked Bil if it was okay if I went upstairs. He nodded.

"Be careful," he said. I think I laughed.

I crept up the stairs, charred but still somehow structurally sound. Bil had told me that if enough smoke permeated the house, the rivets and lines of the drywall would become visible through the paint and plaster. This would be a sign that the smoke damage was too excessive and the house would be a complete loss. I walked down the hall toward an attic room, one that had no windows. The only exit was onto the hall where I was now standing. Three weeks before the fire, my mother had entertained houseguests, family from out of state, and had given up her own bedroom.

"Where are you going to sleep?" I'd asked.

"I'll sleep in the attic," she'd told me.

"Mom, you *can't*. What if there's a fire? There's no way out."

"Oh, God, Geral*diiine*," she said, dragging out the last

syllable of my name, as she often did when she was annoyed. "There won't be a fire."

The hot air had risen, Bil told me, essentially turning the second floor into an oven. I could see the rivets and outlines of the drywall along the vaulted ceiling. The house would be a total loss.

There's an expression for when two people instantly click. "They get on like a house on fire," it's said. As you can imagine, I am less inclined to use this phrase than I once was. But I know that for some people, this is how they feel about their moms. From the day they met, it just seemed to work. They will post, on Mother's Day, or their mother's birthday, a lengthy missive dedicated to "their favorite person," which I will scrutinize like a detective, looking for a clue as to how it's possible, and if it's too late to re-create this alchemy in my own life. A small, petty part of me hopes that they're secretly lying, keeping up appearances for social media. I've described my mother in similar terms approximately twice in my life: in a dramatic performance I dedicated to her when I was four, and again immediately following my brain surgery when I had to remove a tumor and I was *extremely* high on drugs.

Except for those rare stretches of time, possible only because of either childhood illiteracy or medically sanctioned opioid use, I have been consumed with terror that my mother's own bad judgment was going to kill her. As time goes on, this has proven less and less irrational. The fear of any parent is that they will outlive their children. The fear of any anxious child is that they will outlive their parents.

Unattended cooking is the leading cause of home fires. This is bad news for those of us with easily distracted parents who are avid home cooks. When I told my brother what had happened, arriving at his home after that interminable Uber ride, he yelled, "WHAT WHAT WHAT . . . okay, you know what, we knew this would happen," going from shock to acceptance in roughly fifteen seconds.

"I'm so sorry," my sister-in-law said when she arrived home from work, shrugging out of her coat. "But we knew this would happen one day."

No one was *that* surprised.

"What's she done now?" my therapist will regularly ask, with the tone of someone trying to co-parent a problematic teen.

My mother is like a tiny, loud, leopard-print-clad carnival, bursting through the front door and talking at the speed of a Gilmore Girl. This wasn't the first time we found ourselves trying to put out a fire she had set. There was the time she tried to take a miniature hiking pickax with her on a domestic flight. The time she gave my nephew a stuffed animal and the filling was inexplicably infested with grain weevils. The time when she brought a grenade (inert, but to be fair, she did not know that) to Easter dinner. We'd gotten used to the flames. We just took for granted that they would remain figurative.

When I was small, she made nearly every meal we ate. She was an efficient, lightning-fast cook. Dishes would be made concurrently, never using a recipe, all the burners going, like a restaurant during a busy dinner rush. She did not prepare things and "keep them warm" (with the exception of Thanksgiving). She was performing her own balancing act, an intricate circus of remembering what was where and precisely how done it was, before pulling it out at roughly the exact same time and putting it on the table. The sacrificial lamb was usually her garlic bread. She would turn the broiler on to toast it at the end and would inevitably forget it, charring it, though she claimed it was not beyond salvation. For my mother, neither food nor people are past redemption. Cut off a burnt bit, add another can of tomatoes, give him another chance even if he called you a fucking bitch.

Her cooking became a too obvious allegory for her approach to life. I couldn't help her in the kitchen any more than I could in anything else. She'd warn me that I would get burned, as though it were an inevitability, and so I would stand in the doorway, watching her as if she were a trapeze artist without a net. Sometimes my chest would feel tight, and I'd think that she was going to die, and I would watch it happen, unable to stop it. It was a response to being raised by someone who had all the burners—and the smoke alarm—going at once.

At night, when I was small, I remember her going to the stove and double-checking the knobs. "Off, off, off, off," she'd mutter to herself. I'd seen her be cautious. I knew she was capable of it. The eventual burning down of her house (passive voice!) felt like a betrayal.

My mother is, unsurprisingly, a recurring character when

I speak to my therapist. I am loath to admit this; to be a woman and have a complicated relationship with your mother is just so *unimaginative*. I feel like a cliché, a failure, a character in a shoddily written play. I imagine someone walking in and seeing me losing my patience with her over something small. An injury she's sustained because she fell down an escalator while carrying her suitcase, a bill that arrives past due, in a yellow envelope, demanding that you pay attention, because she forgot to pay it. She keeps reminding me of her own mortality, and I'm so angry at her for it. What child ever really forgives their parent for not living forever? Onlookers don't understand: This is a chapter in a long book, one with an ending that I do not want to read, that I am trying to stave off as long as possible.

I vow to be different. Orderly and on top of things. In college, alone in the kitchen of my studio, I finally learn to cook. I am the opposite of my mother. Slow, methodical. (I use *recipes*.) But the further and faster you run from your parents, the greater the likelihood you end up right in front of them again. Being a reaction to someone doesn't mean that you are free from them. I am reminded of this as I am slicing a cucumber in my kitchen one day.

I set a pot to cook and turn away from it for just a moment to cut some vegetables. I pride myself on being focused—so unlike my mother. I am so focused I forget about the pot.

"You didn't forget you have something on the stove, did you?" Rand asks gently.

"No," I snap. (Yes.)

Another time, I find the edge of the sleeve of my robe—

the one I wear when I make breakfast—singed. I do not know when it happened. I didn't even notice. I wonder if her chaos is contagious. Could I have absorbed it by osmosis? And if so, what else could I have absorbed? What if the same propensity for burning shit down (active voice) exists in me, and I've been fighting against it the entire time?

I examine my childhood—the avocation of any writer with time on their hands. I'd always felt as if she loved us, sure, but perhaps . . . not . . . quite . . . enough? That if she had, she could have pulled it together a little bit more. That she'd have gotten rid of the abusive boyfriend and wouldn't have needed me to wake her up to drive me to school. I wouldn't have been a third grader with panic attacks.

But now, upon reflection, it hits me that she *had* been pulling it together, as best as she could. She fed us three times a day, which is more than she ever did herself. She cooked dutifully and made our lunches and did the dishes, and the next day she did it again. And, it is worth noting, nothing ever caught fire (passive voice). There are days when it feels as if it were not enough. There are days when I wish she'd loved us better, and then I realize that what I really want—what I've always wanted—was for her to have loved herself a little bit better.

There is, I've found, no fixing that.

In the wake of her burning down her house (let's-just-call-it-what-it-is voice), I briefly became a skittish cook, terrified of the burners in my own home. (My mother ambled on, undeterred. One of the first things she did when she arrived at our house was ask for a clothing iron and a space heater. When my husband learned of her request, he stood up, wordlessly, and exited the room.) Had my entire past been a series of near misses? I remembered the time a dish towel had accidentally caught fire because it was too close to the burner. The time I'd melted a colander because it had hit the edge of a hot pan. Our exhaust fan had an elaborate grease trap system above our stove, and while I cleaned it regularly (okay, *not regularly* but definitely more often than most people, probably, maybe?), it felt as if the whole thing were basically a powder keg. Humanity had mastered fire, which was ostensibly a good thing, but what made us think we should bring it *inside our very flammable homes with our very flammable families*? How was this anything but sheer hubris?

In the weeks after the fire, my doctor ordered an EKG because my heart felt as if it were doing somersaults. She told me that everything looked normal.

"Is there anything that could be causing you stress?" she asked. I responded by laughing like a Batman villain.

I want to tell you that the fear goes away, but honestly I think I just got used to it. I am now at the age where my friends have started to worry about their parents the way I've always worried about mine. It's new to them, whereas I've feared the danger that my mother invited into her life by her bad judgment since time immemorial. But in recent years, that fear is less nebulous. I can put words to it in a way I could not when I was young: I am desperately afraid of my mother dying. I've been desperately afraid my entire life.

So much of our existence is prescriptive, rules put in place from the time we're small to help us navigate the bevy of horrible hypothetical situations that might pop up. If you catch on fire, you stop, drop, and roll. Even grief supposedly manifests itself in cycles that you can move through, eventually landing on acceptance. I found that in practice none of it was actually true, or at the very least none of it is helpful when the world is suddenly aflame.

Losing my mother's house—and realizing how close I could have come to losing my mother—hit me in a similar way. I thought I was handling it fairly well. Here she was: alive and well and shouting into her new unmelted cellphone. Still, the fear came out of nowhere and blindsided me. It always will.

After the fire, she stays with us for a stretch of time. One afternoon, Rand and I come home to a sulfuric smell. She has, for reasons clear only to her, purchased and hard-boiled two dozen eggs. My husband is a good son-in-law, choosing to scream only with his eyes as my mother meanders through the kitchen, standing directly in front of whatever cabinet he needs to open, or near the stove, her long hair too close to the dancing gas flames. He uses an Italian caffettiera—a stove-top percolating coffeemaker, the kind I grew up with—to make her espresso every morning. He asks her to pick out a pasta for the sauce he's made, more a privilege than a chore, one we bestowed on family members and trusted dinner guests when I was young. I feel the strange, anachronistic wholeness that comes from having your spouse and your parent under the same roof. Your past and your future compressed into the home you've made for yourself. I feel a thousand years old. Somehow my mother seems younger than I am; this has felt true since I was roughly twenty-five. It makes her inevitable mortality—the thing that has kept me up at night for four decades—seem like an abstract, a hypothetical. One day she's going to make good on her decades-long promise to die, and I don't think I'll ever forgive her for it. Then what will I do with myself? I don't have an irresponsible teenage daughter to take her place. I'll be so lost.

It is late at night. I stand up and walk to the kitchen. Before I turn out the light, I stop by the stove, my eyes scanning over each of the dials.

"Off, off, off, off," I repeat to myself, somewhere between a prayer and a spell, an incantation that we might both live forever.

10

GENDER ROLES AND CINNAMON ROLLS

I n late December 2017, the celebrity chef Mario Batali sent out a newsletter, something that his marketing team had done countless times before. But this installment was a deviation from previous iterations. It was sent during the apex of the MeToo movement, and some of us were on a dizzying high from the idea that terrible men might actually be held accountable for the awful things they'd done, mostly to women. Batali had been accused of sexual misconduct and harassment, and in his newsletter he addressed and apologized for his actions. It contained the same sanitized, vague terminology that every missive of this nature included, something crafted by a PR and legal team to sound remorseful without being an admission of guilt. Batali's was so scrubbed clean it became meaningless. He was sorry, he wrote, that his "past behavior" "disappointed" his friends and his family and his team. He went on that it was an honor to share Italian food and traditions with people, a strangely irrelevant digression that made me bristle. Batali had Italian ancestry but was born in Seattle. His food and traditions were *my* food and traditions. He concluded with a message about how he was going to work to regain everyone's trust and respect. And then, at the very end, he wrote, "In case you're searching for a holiday-inspired breakfast, these Pizza Dough Cinnamon Rolls are a fan favorite."

It felt like a record scratch moment, the entire culinary community wondering exactly what the hell was going on. They were livid at the inclusion of the recipe, at the idea that a man who didn't understand consent could determine what was or wasn't a fan favorite. *Here. Sit. Make cinnamon rolls. People love them, you know! Oh, by the way, everyone is saying I'm a sexual deviant. More icing?* My anger had, during that strange epoch of time, felt untethered and hard to grasp, like a current running through the air. And, suddenly, it became focused, channeled at Batali's insipid and completely ill-advised recipe.

If we were to travel back in time, wind whipping in our now graying hair, to a decade earlier, and locate me, this is what we would find: a white woman in her late twenties who'd recently been laid off and spent her days just oozing ennui all over the furniture.

Obviously, I started a blog. I had so much *wisdom* to share.

The Everywhereist has ebbed and flowed since I started it in 2009, a reflection of my own difficulties writing consistently, my doubts about my career, my inability to focus, something akin to writer's block but less romantic that I attribute to laziness. Some years I've written 250 posts. Some years I've written roughly ten. I have wondered if I should abandon it altogether. Sometimes I do, for months at a time. But I always come back.

When allegations against Batali came out, I'd hit a personal and professional malaise that involved wearing a lot of pajamas out in public. I hadn't written anything of substance in months. I considered pitching my essay idea to some food magazines, but I'd always felt like an outsider in that world. Without fail, I got rejections. And that was when they bothered to respond. Most of the time they never replied. Instead, I posted it on my own site. I knew I wouldn't get rejected. I knew whatever anger came bubbling up would be channeled directly onto the page, for everyone to see.

Last night, I made cinnamon rolls. I'm not a huge fan of cinnamon rolls, per se, but this recipe was included in Mario Batali's sexual misconduct apology letter, and so I feel compelled to make them. Batali is not the first powerful man to request forgiveness for "inappropriate actions" toward his co-workers and employees. He is not the most high profile, and he is ostensibly not even the worst offender. But he is the only one who included a recipe.

And of course, the glaring question is why? Was his PR team drunk? Is life suddenly a really long, depressing *SNL* sketch? Do these cinnamon rolls somehow destroy the patriarchy? Does the icing advocate for equal pay?

I figure the only way to answer these questions is to make the damn rolls.

I bake a lot. Never one to pass up on a pun, my husband doesn't bring me flowers, but flours. I've become skilled to the point that I can make a dessert from virtually anything, that I can have a small cake made from start to finish—including baking time—on the table in about half an hour.

Good baking, I've been told, comes from love, and treacly as that sounds, I find some truth in it. Good baking means being able to roll with setbacks and mistakes and ovens that for some reason run twenty degrees hot but only on Sundays, a metaphor so aligned with loving someone that it feels almost too obvious. Good baking requires an attention to detail and care that is hard to muster when you just don't give a shit or you are distracted by your own rage.

Good baking means you have to trust yourself.

I find myself fluctuating between apathy and anger as I try to follow Batali's recipe, which is sparse on details. The base of the rolls is pizza dough. Batali notes that you can either buy it or use his recipe to make your own.

I make my own, because I'm a woman, and for us there are no fucking shortcuts. We spend twenty-five years working our asses off to be the most qualified presidential candidate in U.S. history and we get beaten out by a sexual deviant who likely needs to call the front desk for help when he's trying to order pornos in his hotel room.

Donald Trump is president, so I'm making the

goddamn dough from scratch. I punch down the dough because, according to Twitter, I hate men.

I use Batali's recipe that he's linked to, which I've made before, and I'm already hesitant. Pizza dough is chewy and crispy, not tender; the latter is what you'd hope cinnamon rolls would be. It's a savory recipe—incorporating white wine and a generous amount of salt—and I feel like he's shoehorning it into a dessert where it doesn't belong. He's cutting corners because he gets to cut corners.

I roll out the dough. Batali specifies a thickness, but no dimensions, which is strange if you're making a rolled dessert. There are pieces missing here, and I'm trying to fill in the gaps. The result will be subpar because he hasn't provided all the information, and I will blame myself.

I baste a layer of melted butter over the dough.

A guy on Twitter tells me that I'm a vile man-hater. His feed contains a photo of my very alive husband wearing a feminist T-shirt. Underneath he's written the message "RIP."

I sprinkle the sugar and cinnamon over the top.

I think about the time that I was an intern at a local news station and assigned to hand out cake while celebrating some milestone (it had to do with the Salt Lake City Winter Olympics). One of the producers I'd been working closely with walked up to the table.

"Do you want a piece?" I asked.

"Yeah," he said, looking me up and down. "Oh,

you mean of cake? No thanks." He and another male
staff member laughed while I stood, holding a piece
of cake in each hand, dumbstruck.

Batali does not specify how tightly to roll the
dough. I do so too tightly because fuck everything.

I remember the time another producer walked his
fingers across my lap while I was typing at a computer. I turned to stare at him, and he grabbed my
badge, which was clipped to my waist.

"I wanted to see how your last name was spelled."

I think I've used too much dough.

I think about how the last conversation I had
about compensation resulted in someone who made
more yearly than I ever will telling me I was holding
them "emotionally hostage" and then demanding to
know, over and over again, why I needed the money.

"Just tell me," they demanded. "Tell me why you
need it." Over and over until it broke me.

If they are edible, I will eat every single one of
these fucking rolls myself.

Batali says to cut them in slices roughly three
inches thick, which is too wide. The rolls should not
be that thick. I know this is wrong, but I do it anyway
because that is what the recipe says. (I am not following my gut and cutting them thinner. If I had, I
suspect the results would have been better. But for
most of us, going off book isn't an option.) There is
no estimation of how many rolls the recipe should
yield. Batali says to place the rolls in a small cake pan,
but again, there are no dimensions.

My husband hovers close by, doing a little excited jig. Few things delight him like elaborate desserts made for no apparent reason on a weeknight. But he soon links the pieces together and stops dancing.

"Oh, God," he says. "These are *those* cinnamon rolls, aren't they?"

I nod.

I put them in the oven. I think about how Michelle Williams made less than $1,000 for a reshoot of a movie for which Mark Wahlberg made $1.5 million.

Because I've rolled them too tightly, the middle pops up and out of one of the rolls.

One of the cinnamon rolls has a fucking *erection*.

The recipe calls for too much icing, and the result is that the rolls are drenched in it. We've reached the "ARE YOU FUCKING KIDDING ME" portion of the recipe.

The pizza dough does not mix well with the sweetness. The icing is sickly sweet, the rolls themselves oddly savory. I was right about the texture; the dough is too tough. I hate them, but I keep eating them. Like I'm somehow destroying Batali's shitty sexist horcrux in every bite.

I remind myself that is not how recipes work. That isn't even how dark magic works.

I know that in the court of the internet, any output that is less than perfect will be blamed on me, and not on a hastily written, untested recipe. I've made flaky piecrusts in the kitchens of Airbnbs using warped cutting boards and a bottle of wine as a rolling pin, but this won't matter. *I've* fucked up the recipe.

Most women don't even need to hear the shitty comments made to us anymore. We've heard them so many times we can create our own.

Maybe if you spent less time whining about men who want to fuck you (which you should take as a compliment because who the hell would want to fuck you, anyway) and more time in the kitchen, this wouldn't happen.

I throw the rest of the cinnamon rolls in the trash. (Okay, fine, I eat two more.)

Of course you did. Jesus fucking Christ, you're disgusting and your husband does not love you.

Batali's another drop in the bucket. He's not the first, he certainly won't be the last (he already isn't). The misogyny runs so deep that the calls now come from inside our heads. We blame ourselves. We hate ourselves. We wonder if our skirts are too short, if our bodies are too noticeable. If we're asking for too much, or not enough. We don't trust ourselves, even when we should.

We try to follow a half-written recipe and think it's our fault when it doesn't work.

We need to undo an entire humanity's history worth of hate against women. Apologies are a good start.

Just skip the goddamn recipe.

My piece was shared by a few people, who shared it with a few more, until friends were emailing me because Martha

Stewart had tweeted about it. Pete Wells, the restaurant critic for *The New York Times,* wrote, "When I mentioned Mario's cinnamon roll recipe recently I was haunted by the sense that I hadn't fully conveyed its absurdity. I was right, I hadn't. This piece does." My essay was mentioned in Sam Sifton's column on the paper's website, with the notation that the language was salty but that my writing was "dark and hilarious." In a few days, more than a million people had visited the blog, which crashed from the sheer volume of traffic.

Virality is an impossible thing to predict, and an even harder thing to describe. It's strange enough to think that with all the things floating around online, a huge swath of people in your orbit are reading the same thing. It's even stranger to think that it might be something you wrote. It makes the internet feel oddly small and intimate but still, somehow, just as terrifying and full of awful people.

As with any piece that gets a lot of attention, there were people who said wonderful things, and there were people who told me that I needed to die, immediately, of some painful disease that focused primarily on my vagina or possibly my eyes. "Food is what pays you to write about it," one commenter noted, in a statement that was as grammatically confusing as it was inaccurate, and he went on to tell me that I was ungrateful (to . . . the cinnamon rolls? That I had made?). Someone else told me that the rolls were wonderful, which they were able to figure out with their very powerful ability to taste things through the internet using just their eyeballs, I guess, and that I was just a hateful bitch. I got called the c-word so many times it started to lose all meaning, and Rand found me repeating it to myself just to see if I felt anything. There were a handful of death threats thrown in, a few people who said transphobic and anti-Semitic things because they were confused as to my own identity and just stabbing blindly at whatever they could find in *The Misogynistic Bigoted Fuckhead's Handbook* (foreword by Alex Jones!). A couple people started using the comment section to share Hillary Clinton conspiracy theories. I got Instagram messages telling me that I should "be afraid." I was put on a hit list of prominent Jews in media, which gave me a twinge of impostor syndrome because everyone else was more famous than me, and shouldn't they be hating someone more qualified? (Also, I'm not Jewish, but it seemed weird to point that out to a bunch of anti-Semites, because they might think I was somehow okay with them hating actual Jews.) There wasn't a single platform on which I wasn't getting threatened or harassed. By the time my Twitter account was hacked, forty-eight hours later, a small part of me hoped that I wouldn't be able to get it back.

I curled up into a ball and resolutely panicked. After I managed to get access to my Twitter account again, in a rather questionable state of judgment, I did the one thing everyone says you are not supposed to do. I started talking to them.

For the record, I do not recommend this.

Like, at *all.*

I mean, if you are, for even a brief second, thinking about doing this, don't. Seriously. I wish I could tell you that I had some sort of breakthrough with these people—that I reached out to them and they understood that I was a person with feelings and they apologized and it was a beautiful moment. That we found common ground and ended up smoking weed and talking about our shared love of Willie Nelson. But none of that happened. Nope. I realize that it sometimes *does* happen—that Patton Oswalt and Sarah Silverman and a bunch of other celebrities who are far more magnanimous than I am have connected with people harassing them online and even gotten an apology, usually after paying off their outstanding medical bills. But I am not successful or charming or magnanimous. And while I do think that no one should pay for healthcare, I am not inclined to start paying bills for strangers who have called me a fucking cunt.

Still, I'm a reasonably . . . okay person? I . . . recycle? I'm nice to my husband and at least six other people. I don't talk to my neighbors, but I make them cookies. I think dogs are cute and that their owners should pick up after them and not put the bagged poop in my trash can. The idea that someone could hate me—truly hate me to my core—was a terrifying prospect. Dislike me, sure. Not want to travel across Europe with me by railway, okay, fine. But *hate* me because of what I'd written online (and not because they knew me in high school)? So much that they'd tell me I should die (in extremely creative and graphic ways)? No. I refused to accept it.

I'm *adorable* and fun, damn it.

And so when the hateful abyss yelled at me, I answered back. I asked one guy why he bothered following me on Twitter if he found my work so detestable. I figured I'd open up the conversation, and then we'd go from there.

"Because I need to remind myself that people like you exist," he wrote back. "And you shouldn't." I later found an interview of him in which he said that liberal journalists needed "to be exterminated."

Talking to my harassers just made them realize that their attacks had landed; they had a live one on the line. What ensued was a fire hose of pure hate. I couldn't have paid off their medical bills if I wanted to (I really, *really* didn't want to). It didn't change the scope or magnitude of their hate—it was always there, frothing over, consuming them— but now that they knew I was paying attention, they had somewhere to aim. They insulted me according to their value system, their attacks following the same misogynistic ethos that they believed. How fuckable or unfuckable I was, that if I had children I'd be less of a bitch, that I was bitter because I was supposedly barren, that I had turned to feminism because no man would love me, that my husband was an inferior beta male. (Yawn. Seriously, misogynists: Please, I beg you, get some new material, or better yet, stop hating women.)

I asked them directly if they thought they were being abusive to me—or any woman—online. The response was a resounding no. It was exhausting, like fighting with a Turing machine that was set to "asshole."

The same arguments came up again and again as they defended themselves. They were just "executing free speech," they said (even though telling a woman to shove a cheese wheel into her vagina is not explicitly protected under the First Amendment). Nearly every single one of them accused *me* of harassing them with my line of questioning. Dozens of them brought up an argument that I'd heard before but had never previously questioned: that men are harassed online more than women.

I finally looked up the source of that information. It turned out to be a Pew Research Center report from 2017 in which people *self-reported* harassment. And that methodology in and of itself is problematic, given how many of the abusers I'd talked to claimed that *they* were the victims. Online harassment is *extremely* subjective. Twenty-eight percent of those who had experienced what the report defined as "severe" harassment did not consider their experience to be online harassment (another 21 percent said they were unsure). At the same time, 32 percent of those who had experienced what the report considered "mild" harassment (name-calling or embarrassment—things men were more likely to experience)—*did* consider their experiences to be online harassment.

Also of note is the way in which men and women are harassed differently online. According to the Women's Media Center, a nonprofit dedicated to how women are represented in media, when women experience abuse online, it is more likely to be "gendered, sustained, sexualized and linked to off-line violence." Women are more likely to be targeted with "rape videos, extortion, doxing with the intent to harm," and are more likely to become victims of nonconsensual pornography and stalking.

The Pew report didn't take into account race or sexual orientation, either. According to a study by Amnesty International, women of color were disproportionately harassed more than white women on Twitter (with Black women get-

ting the most hate—roughly one of every ten tweets they received being abusive in some way). A study by GLSEN (the
Gay, Lesbian, and Straight Education Network) found that
LGBTQIA+ youth were harassed online up to four times
more than their cis straight counterparts. As a response to
this harassment, many Americans self-censor—avoiding top-
ics or expressing opinions that might make them a target.
And the group most likely to self-censor in response to abuse
was people of color. Those groups were also most likely to
leave platforms as a result of being abused. So online abuse—
this supposed expression of free speech—was actually silenc-
ing the most vulnerable groups online.

"It's just the internet," I've been told time and again. "It
doesn't really count." In the months that followed, I was a
nervous wreck. There is no line of demarcation between online harassment and "real-life" harassment. Because the internet *is* real life. It's where we do our work, where we
communicate with friends, where we book tickets, and
where we pay our bills. They claimed that what happened
on the internet didn't count, but they weren't emailing ad-
missions of crimes to law enforcement officers; they weren't
posting their Social Security numbers online. Because what
we did on the internet *did* count. They just didn't want it to
count for them. I cried in my car. I didn't sleep. I contemplated backing out of several public appearances because
someone with a history of violence who knew where I lived
had threatened to burn down our home.

And still, as far as online harassment went, I was getting
off pretty easy.

The experiences of my friends who were journalists,

those who were public political faces, who combated hate and disinformation, or who dared write about issues that were deemed less feminine (like gaming or science or technology), experienced it at a magnitude that I could scarcely fathom, on a regular basis. While I have had moments where I glimpsed how awful the internet could be, their experiences are constant, magnified if they are trans, or disabled, or people of color. I've watched them get bullied off social media platforms, flee from their own homes after doxings, or answer the front door to FBI agents following up on credible death threats against them. Their children, their parents, their spouse's lives, have been threatened. They've moved, sometimes to different cities or states or even countries, changed their appearances, tried in vain to get restraining orders against faceless people on the internet. They've had some of the most wonderful moments of their lives—the births of their children, the publication of books, the acquisition of their companies—enveloped by the pall of people who didn't know them but who wished them harm. Those who argued that they could simply switch careers and avoid the harassment weren't simply being insulting; they were being disingenuous as well. Sometimes, even I fell into the trap of this thinking. I wondered if I'd brought all of this upon myself. During the worst of it, I wondered if perhaps I shouldn't have written the blog post at all.

"It just occurred to me," a friend of mine said, laughing, "that Mario Batali probably *hates* you." The idea of possibly running into him in our shared hometown beset me with a sort of simmering anxiety. Oddly, it was the perennial nature of online abuse that caused me to stop blaming myself.

Because even when I wrote a scarcely read travel blog, one that just contained photos of me and Rand, kissing in front of waterfalls and eating cupcakes, I received messages that I deserved to be raped and murdered, my body disposed of where no one would find it. There was literally nothing that any of us could do to stop it. We were treated this way because we existed. If men were being abused online even more than this, then that was an argument to care about the issue twice as much.

I'd experienced it enough firsthand to know now there was absolutely no difference between how we are harassed, whether it was online or off. The narrative is always the same. It is about how fuckable or unfuckable we are. Professional interactions are rife with sexual harassment. (A guy once sent me questions about my brain surgery, explaining that he wanted to have a character in one of his novels undergo a similar experience. When he asked how he could thank me, I joked that he could name a minor character after me. He did. The book turned out to be terribly written erotica. I will not be sharing what my namesake did, but it involved the motif of "sexy baby.") You have to navigate it carefully, because you don't know who will turn hostile on a dime. The ways in which it escalates are lightning fast, threatening your livelihood and your very existence. Victims blame themselves, are accused of lying, exaggeration, or just advancing their own careers. It is all part of the same ugly conversation.

It is hard to classify exactly what Twitter meant if you're a writer. It was simultaneously the worst and the best place in the world. I once received hate messages for *weeks* because I tweeted that the Joker should have been a woman who went mad because too many men told her to smile. (This made a lot of people understandably mad because I said a woman should have an interesting character arc in a comic book, which is just a slippery slope to seeing us as human.) I took a photo of myself with a bunch of packages of maxi pads on my bookshelves and noted that if I stored menstrual hygiene products the way Lauren Boebert stored guns, conservatives would freak out. And then a bunch of conservatives freaked out (way to prove me right, dipshits!).

But Twitter was also one of the most amazing and transformative platforms for the arc of my career and my life. In early 2019, with a few hours to go before the deadline for applications, Max Falkowitz, who has written about food and travel for *The New York Times* and *Food & Wine,* tweeted the following at me:

apropos of tomorrow's beard journalism award deadline,
if @everywhereist's cinnamon roll piece doesn't win at
least one category I say we revolt.

I laughed it off, but my friend Naomi Tomky, another food and travel writing luminary, jumped in and said that I had to apply, and sent me the link to do so. I did, because Naomi literally kept texting me to make sure I followed through, and because, well, she's terrifying when she's being encouraging. A few months later, in my office, via Twitter, I found out that I had been nominated for a James Beard Award for my essay.

I figured that would be the end of it, something Rand and I both kind of accepted. He believed in me more than anyone, but it was the James Beard Awards. Known colloquially as the Oscars of the food world. I wasn't going to win a food Oscar. I grew up in *Florida*. I've eaten fried gator meat in the back of a moving pickup truck. And I definitely used the word "porno" in the essay.

I told myself that it was an honor just to have been nominated, which is something people say when they know they're going to lose. The foundation sent me an official invite for the awards, but I'd already agreed to speak at a conference about online harassment that weekend in Canada. I felt that was the proof of the work I'd been doing and I couldn't just abandon it.

Besides, as my friend Laura said to me, "If you lose, you'll feel silly having flown all that way for nothing. And if you win . . . well, you won't really care where you are."

She was right, as it turned out. I was standing outside a café in Victoria when the winners were announced. My name was tweeted out by the foundation's official account, but I was convinced they were simply listing the names of nominees.

"I lost," I said to Rand.

"But they tweeted out your name."

"They're tweeting out everyone's name," I said, waving my hands as if I were swatting away flies.

"What? No." He shook his head, staring at his phone. "I think you won."

A tiny little icon of an award sat next to my name. And then my phone started to buzz. Congratulations started pouring in, so persistent that my phone would run out of battery from the exertion of it in the next few hours. My blog, which had been nominated alongside writers from *The New York Times* and *The Atlantic,* had won a James Beard Award, for an essay about cinnamon rolls and sexual harassment. That year, Batali would finally sell off the portion of the restaurant empire he owned with his partner Joe Bastianich, along with his minority interest in the Italian gourmet supermarket and restaurant chain Eataly. He would be sued by two separate women for sexual assault; he and Bastianich would be sued by more than twenty employees who were sexually harassed at their restaurants; and he would be charged with indecent assault and battery of a woman he had allegedly groped against her will in one of his restaurants in 2017.

Had I single-handedly solved the problem of systemic misogyny in the food world? I mean . . . yeah? I was basically the Gloria Steinem of culinary blogging. I made myself a pair of wings out of feathers and frosting and flew directly toward the sun.

This high-flying and blissful delusion was short-lived and had the inevitable denouement of any Icarian tale. The lawsuits were resolved without much fanfare (the two women reached settlements that were not released to the public; the twenty employees were awarded $600,000 total). Batali would ultimately be found not guilty of the criminal charges against him. Batali's lawyer portrayed his accuser as a liar, claiming she fabricated the story "for money and for fun." Countless other allegations of abuse, assault, and harassment were floating around, but beyond some sort of public admonishment for it there was no real consequence. He was free to go on with his life, rich and happy.

I sighed and went back to spending too much time on social media. I hadn't checked my Facebook for a long time and found a bevy of unread messages. One of them included a threat from a man I didn't know. Underneath it, he'd typed out my home address.

11

IN CASE OF EMERGENCY: BREAK FAST

I am an anxious person.

Frankly, I think it would be polite if people reacted with a *little* more surprise to that admission instead of nodding their heads and saying things like "Ah yes, that makes sense, you're like the test subject of an experiment where scientists are trying to see if someone can die from worrying about what to pack for a trip."

My hand washing is so excessive that I get cracks in my skin. (Rand and I took a cooking class once, and the instructor commented, with a measure of pride, on how thorough I was with my hand washing. Cue me turning to stare directly at an invisible cameraman and widening my eyes like Jim from *The Office*.) My fear of germs is all-consuming, shakes me to my core, makes me feel as if something were crawling all over me that I need to scrape off. A dinner guest once spilled something on my floor and then reached for a dish towel to clean it up, and I might have screamed for three solid minutes, because WHY WOULD YOU CLEAN THE FLOOR WITH A DISH TOWEL, ADAM? It extends beyond germs to a strange sort of general panic about all the things I need to control. I check my alarm clock thirty or forty times, to make sure it's set properly because what if I oversleep and miss my flight? (I will die, that's what.) If I am late somewhere, it is because I was going to be on time, I was out the door, I was driving, I was well on my damn way, and then I had to turn around and drive back home because I was hit with the overwhelming fear that I'd left the iron on. And it wasn't. But you can bet it was on until I turned around and made sure.

The way in which my brain is broken is there, for everyone to see.

I blame my family, obviously. In an immigrant family that seemed to produce only boys, I was the first girl born in three decades. The older generation felt an obligation to teach me all the ways that America was going to kill me. My mother told me not to walk too close to hedges or bushes that lined sidewalks. "Someone could be waiting to grab and murder you," she said.

This was a foundational memory, cemented in my brain before I could even properly dissect what was being said, at a time in my own personal history when everything uttered by an adult was unequivocal gospel. The only reasonable response was to become afraid of hedges, bushes, walking on sidewalks, spending the night at my friends' houses, and—for an unfortunate stretch of time—toilets. This was necessary to survive, which I believed, at the ripe old age of a single digit number, was very much in my control.

In the years since, I discovered that my family's concerns, though ostensibly from a good place (they didn't want me murdered! So thoughtful! Thanks, Mom!), weren't actually grounded in any sort of fact. The legacy of this, decades later, is that my body and brain are locked in an eternal conflict. I realize that at any given moment I'm probably *not* about to die. But sometimes, right as I close my eyes in my comfortable bed, in my home with a reliable security system, my body does not seem to get this message, and it decides, either as a fun prank it's playing on my brain or just as a test of the Emergency Broadcast Adrenal System, to react as though we were being chased by wolves. Part of my brain logically says, "No, we are not being chased by wolves. We are trying to sleep on high-thread-count sheets," and another, deeper, less articulate part of my brain is screaming and periodically sounding an air horn.

The fear of the unknown remained, the idea that I was going to be killed by something nebulous and unpredictable, like a flash flood or a flash mob. At some point, I reasoned that amassing food—specifically a small- to medium-sized apocalyptic cache of it—would protect me, and possibly even stave off said apocalypse. (The logic is not that different from the idea that bringing an umbrella prevents rain, something that is also true and reasonable and based in scientific fact.) I suppose every human, holding the belief, erroneous or not, that they are under some sort of strange elemental peril that threatens their very being, comes to that same conclusion. It's why Costco exists. A five-gallon barrel of tartar sauce gives you the illusion that your own mortality is in your control.

My favorite part of any survival story is the acquisition of food and water. Give me a protagonist thrown into some sort of apocalyptic scenario, and I am deeply, deeply invested in their next meal. I don't care what happens next: I know for a fleeting moment things are going to be okay. I know that they are doing the most important thing they can possibly be doing. I love when they befriend a dog, which people in disaster stories almost always do, because it adds dimension to the story, but also because dogs are edible! People are horrified by this idea, but honestly, when the chips are down, and you've eaten the last of your chips, I feel that it's good to have a dog or two available. In 1912, Roald Amundsen, the legendary Norwegian explorer, and his crew ran low on rations as they traversed Antarctica in their quest to become the first (documented, white) people to reach the South Pole, and ended up shooting and eating their dogs. Amundsen later said it was delicious, noting that it was "anything but a real hardship to eat dog flesh."

(Some of you are reading this and are probably deeply worried that in times of desperation I would eat your pets. And I want you to know that yes, I absolutely would. I *told* you not to let me pet sit. Also, before you judge me or Amundsen too harshly, please note that the famed Australian explorer Sir Douglas Mawson might have intentionally starved and later eaten his human comrade during an Antarctic expedition during this same period of time. So.)

In Emily St. John Mandel's novel *Station Eleven*, a virus sweeps through the world, decimating most of humanity. It is one of my favorite books—heartbreaking and beautiful—and one that highlights the role that art and our families (the ones we choose, and the ones we are born into) play in our lives. But my favorite part, without question, is a throwaway scene where Jeevan, one of the protagonists, goes to the grocery store and buys roughly a thousand dollars' worth of food in preparation for the end of the world. It is so calculated and neurotic and for me, at least, so relatable. He piles seven shopping carts high in the middle of the night, tethers them together, and wheels them over to his brother's apartment. The vast majority of the population basically dies over the next few days and weeks, but for a second everything is okay, because Jeevan and his brother have Cheetos and canned soup and bottled water.

In *The Hunger Games,* Katniss is desperately hunting for food as she struggles to stay alive. Sure, there are other things going on (I want to say there are . . . murder wasps? Also, jinkies! Two boys like her at once!), but the book is called *The Hunger Games.* It's basically about food. She's even named after an edible tuber that grows in marshes! The girl is walking around a death arena while named "swamp potato." Of *course* it became a bestseller. And then there's Rumaan Alam's elaborate descriptions of the meals eaten in his haunting novel, *Leave the World Behind.* An unspecified apocalyptic disaster is unfolding, and a white family is stuck in a house they rented in the Hamptons with no cell reception. The Black owners show up to take refuge in what is rightfully their own home, and it becomes an exceedingly discomfiting look at race and class. There are a bunch of high-tension meals, made even more fraught by the fact that each one could potentially be the characters' last. In one scene, the characters make a cake from a mix and add sprinkles on top. I think about that often: how everything is falling apart, and they are making dessert from a mix, the apex of efficient home baking. And then they add sprinkles. Entirely superfluous (and, ideally, rainbow colored), but somehow essential to maintaining the illusion that everything is okay. The moral: Sprinkles are a necessity at the end of the world. (I have eight types in my pantry.)

As a kid, I remember our teacher reading us *My Side of the Mountain,* and the most resonant thing that I took away from a survivalist fairy tale about a kid running off into the Catskills by himself was that he'd somehow learned to make pancakes from acorn flour. It seemed like such a miraculous thing, that in the face of loneliness and death and the elements you could find a way to feed yourself.

My fear of death, or something nebulous and undefined but somehow worse than death, followed me into adulthood. Those with anxiety know: It creeps in so deep inside you that there's no getting it out. It's like how after a particularly brutal wildfire season, smoke can permeate nearby wine grapes, seeping through the skins and binding with sugar molecules inside. Most people aren't able to detect it right away if they eat the grape fresh off the vine. But it comes through later when the grapes are being pressed into wine. The enzymes produced during fermentation release noxious compounds. The wine, as a result, tastes bitter and acrid.

· · ·

To be able to prepare for an emergency is, by its very nature, an act of privilege. To be ready in a disaster means that you have money and time and mental energy. That you can afford days if not weeks of shelf-stable food. The ability to plan for your own future survival is not accessible to everyone, especially those who are concerned about their everyday survival. You cannot think about your future safety unless you are safe now.

I have spent my entire life in Florida and Washington, two states that are plagued by very different weather patterns. In my youth in central Florida, we'd get a hurricane scare at least once a summer, a terrifying prospect for our town, built up on a tiny barrier island that stuck off the mainland like a hangnail. It seemed as if it would take very little to wash us all away. I remember putting a frozen pot pie in the oven just as the power got knocked out. Hours later, when it came back on, I wanted to eat it, but my mother was worried about how long it had remained at room temperature. I walked it to the trash like a funeral procession.

My brother and I often complained that there was nothing to eat, which meant that there was nothing to eat right now and *also* in the event of an apocalypse. Food in our house was something that needed preparation. There were plenty of meals that could be cooked for us; my mother was ready to go through a shockingly long list of dinner options, things she could make at the ready, digging through the pantry or chipping away at the contents of the freezer. But I wanted ready-to-eat things. An endless pantry of snacks, of individually packaged chips and cookies and granola bars with real chocolate chips inside them. I needed these things in case the power went out or we needed to outrun a horde. Whatever we did have that fit those criteria was destined for our lunches. My brother and I never touched these; to eat them now would mean to go without them later at school. You didn't make trouble for your future self. That's the whole point. So we'd fill pots up with water and put the remaining empty ones under the leaky spots in the ceiling. I would occasionally open the pantry and take inventory of the canned goods there in case the power didn't come back on. Beans and tomato sauce, mostly, things that you could eat cold if we really needed to, farting our way through the storm.

Seattle, where I live now, is different. We are woefully ill-equipped for most weather that isn't between thirty-five and sixty degrees and raining. Whenever snow hits, which is usually a dusting, as if someone were gently tapping powdered sugar over the entire city, everything shuts down. (Seattle has exactly one snowplow, and it's actually just a shovel duct-taped to the front of someone's Subaru.) But in the days leading up to it, the grocery stores will be packed with shoppers and the shelves will be cleared, as though everyone were planning on hosting a massive Thanksgiving that mostly consisted of peanut butter sandwiches.

But the parameters of these theoretical disasters have always felt well defined. A storm has a beginning and an end. They didn't match my own anxiety, the buzzing that was happening just under my skin. What I feared was harder to pinpoint—more vague, more terrifying.

In 2015, Kathryn Schulz wrote an article for *The New Yorker* that would later go on to win her the Pulitzer. "The Really Big One" details the earthquake that will eventually destroy the coastal Northwest, and the town where I, and my husband, and my mother, and most of the people I love now live. The article paints a graphic picture of what will happen when the Cascadia subduction zone (a fault line that makes the San Andreas look like a hairline fracture) finally decides to kill us all.

> Anything indoors and unsecured will lurch across the floor or come crashing down: bookshelves, lamps, computers, cannisters of flour in the pantry. Refrigerators will walk out of kitchens, unplugging themselves and toppling over. Water heaters will fall and smash interior gas lines. Houses that are not bolted to their foundations will slide off—or, rather, they will stay put, obeying inertia, while the foundations, together with the rest of the Northwest, jolt westward. Unmoored on the undulating ground, the homes will begin to collapse.

It was an excellent piece of journalism, and I don't think those of us who live here will ever quite forgive her for it. In the week following its publication, it was all anyone could talk about, as we buttoned-up northwesterners uncharacteristically freaked the fuck out. "*New Yorker* scares the bejesus out of NW," the *Seattle Post-Intelligencer* wrote. My night terrors now had a whole new storyline to latch onto. Worse, there was no time frame for it. The Big One could happen in the next ten or fifty years. Or it might not happen in the next thousand. It was something large and looming that could strike without warning, the kind of terror that hummed in the background for so long that you sometimes forgot it was there, and then it would hit you anew. Schulz, perhaps realizing that she'd caused existential panic across our entire FEMA district, wrote a follow-up to the article a few weeks later, one that essentially answered the question, "Okay, so now what?"

The truth was, we could plan for it, sort of. Her view on preparedness was that "the perfect is the enemy of the good: don't choose to stock nothing because you can't stock everything." If you had money and space to spare, she advised people to fill a shelf with water and nonperishable goods. I had money. And I had space. And I had a shit ton of anxiety. Kathryn Schulz had no idea what she'd unleashed.

Comfort food is too often dismissed. The unfussy dishes we ate in the halcyon days of youth. The foods we cooked for ourselves when what we ate had virtually no consequence: melting cheese onto whatever we could find; microwave meals that were a feat of physics, as hot as the sun on the edges but still icy in the center; the buckets of take-out fried chicken; a cannery worth of salty soups. The dishes that our parents or grandparents made for us, tethers to places that our families left behind. The endless parade of casseroles that march through when a baby is born or someone has died.

I didn't have comfort foods; I had an entire comfort pantry. In the wake of Schulz's essay, I amassed shelves and shelves of canned and dry goods. Jars of nut butters, packages of pretzels and crackers, cans of garbanzo beans and artichoke hearts. Protein bars by the boxful; salted nuts; a dozen varieties of cereal; case after case of fizzy water (I read that aluminum cans last far longer than plastic. You can drink them even after the water's gone flat). On some level, I suppose I knew that in the event of a complete societal breakdown these things would likely not save me. I do not know how long one can survive on salt and pepper pistachios and dry ramen noodles. But I could imagine what I would eat first if my world was in ruins, and it brings me a strange measure of peace. The race to the grocery, and that frantic acquisition of food as if I were a rodent preparing for a harsh winter. What was I doing in those moments if not comforting myself?

But no matter how many times you try to prepare for the unexpected, you're never quite ready for the real thing. That's one of the main features of emergencies, I guess. You don't see them coming.

Seattle was one of the first cities in America to shut down due to COVID. Microsoft and Amazon announced in early March 2020 that they'd be switching to remote work, and Seattle public schools closed shortly after. I woke up early one morning, just after the announcement that schools would be closed for two weeks (I remember my friends who are parents groaning, and I feel such a deep tenderness for them, for all of us, not knowing what the world held in store for us). I went to Trader Joe's. The store was packed and no one was wearing masks, because that was not yet a thing we were told to do (I distinctly remember being told *not* to buy masks, because we needed to keep them available for healthcare professionals). When I think about it, my brain starts to overheat, and a montage starts playing in my head, as I fabricate near misses of my life, the times I've almost died, but somehow didn't. It's a blooper reel from a horror movie, set to "Yakety Sax."

There were no parameters to this disaster. It was the embodiment of my anxiety itself—nebulous and hazy and spreading over everything. People responded as if a storm were coming. "It was very similar to what you'd see during a hurricane, except it was happening all over the United States," Brent Minner, a marketing director for Hometown Food Company, told *The Atlantic* in May 2020. In those unsettling early months, I'd like to think we were all logical, at least at first. We stripped the shelves of hand sanitizer and disinfecting wipes and bleach and toilet paper, as if we were all going to have either the world's worst or the world's best sex party. After that, we went off the rails, playing a strange game of apocalypse follow-the-leader, watching what other people were doing for clues. I have a vague recollection of seeing someone buy powdered bouillon, and thinking, "That is a great idea, I should buy powdered bouillon!"—the first time in history anyone has ever felt that passionate about cubes of chicken-flavored dust. And then everyone started signing up for grocery delivery, paying to have other people do the dangerous task of going out into the world for us because we were specifically told not to go out ourselves. It made me cringe a little even as I did it because I am fairly certain that people stormed the Bastille for less. I don't remember when we all collectively turned our frantic eyes toward flour. But suddenly it was as if we were in a British war drama, talking about where we might be able to find some.

But I had flour. I HAD FLOUR. It was in my pantry,

along with seventy-two rolls of toilet paper that were there before the pandemic began, because that's *just how many I had down there, on a regular Tuesday afternoon.* Everyone's instincts were the same: to stock up, to fill our larders, to make sure our families had enough to get through this strange disaster, however long it might be. I had done that; I had been preparing for it, or some unspecified awful event like it, for years. I had a basement full of food and a bathroom cabinet full of toiletries; I had bandages and medicine.

And for a little while, it seemed as if maybe everything would be okay. Even as things felt bleak and uncertain, my social media turned into an endless stream of photos of everyone's homemade bread loaves. There was something strangely communal about so many of us sequestered in our homes, baking away. (And also, if I'm honest, I had a feeling of superiority within this. I had a pandemic baking holy grail: a small brown glass jar of Fleischmann's active dry yeast in my fridge, with a yellow and maroon label. I didn't need to resort to making a flatulent sourdough starter. It was inherent proof of my preparedness! I would survive whatever lay ahead *thanks to my yeast!** (*Comments not to be taken out of context.)

My neighbor and I had a history of baking for each other. We'd found that it was what we both did to relieve stress, and though we rarely talked, we often texted and left things for each other on our porches. When the city shut down, she left an entire focaccia on my porch. I made her kouign-amann, a complex laminated Breton pastry, and dropped it off with a note. We never saw each other, but even so, I wondered if this was too dangerous—if the plastic

wrap around our baked goods was harboring some dangerous virus. If we would somehow make each other sick because of our insistence on bringing the other baked goods.
But I didn't want to give this up, too.

In a particular lonely and deranged moment, I started
regrowing my green onions in water. After many long days
I trimmed them and showed Rand. He stared at my bounty,
enough to conservatively garnish a single baked potato.

"You realize that green onions are like sixty-nine cents a
bunch, right?" he said.

"I AM PROVIDING FOR OUR FAMILY," I yelled.

I thought when disaster struck, I knew exactly what I'd
do. I expected something to happen to subtly indicate we'd
moved from "Before Times" to Cormac McCarthy's *The
Road,* like a push alert on my phone or a handful of spectral
horsemen riding across a flaming sky. As Helen Rosner
writes in *The New Yorker,* a klaxon firing, letting us know that
it was time to finally eat our emergency beans. But that
wasn't what happened. It was a slow shift and then a fast
one, until nothing was recognizable and everyone was making sourdough. I wondered if Amundsen received a definitive sign that made him say, "Today, I eat my dogs." But I
doubt it. I suspect he just found himself nibbling on one of
his huskies one day and thinking, "This is delicious." (His
words! No judgment! Don't yuck his yum!) Slowly, I found
my reserves waning, the rolls of toilet paper and bags of
pasta dwindling. I didn't replenish them, because I felt
guilty doing so in a time when everyone was struggling to
find more and also because, if I was honest with myself, I
couldn't find any either. In the absence of these things, what

would protect me, late at night, when I was too tired after a day spent fighting my own thoughts?

I told myself that if I had enough on my shelves, I would be able to handle anything. But it wasn't making me feel any better.

I'd gotten confused—assumed that these things that I'd stored away in the event of an emergency would somehow stop the emergency from happening in the first place. That when disaster *did* strike, I could somehow protect everyone I loved behind a barrier of instant ramen and peanut-butter-stuffed pretzels. Perhaps I should have known better than to entrust my mental well-being to something that came with an expiration date. The contents of my pantry would not stop my father from getting cancer, would not prevent my mother from forgetting a pot on the stove and burning down the house where she had lived for twenty-five years. I was ignoring the first precious word in the phrase "comfort food"—that in order to comfort, the grief and pain have already arrived. The casserole delivered in the wake of a tragedy does not reach back and undo the devastation. But it meets a basic need that we may not be able to address ourselves. It reminds us, at a time when we so desperately need it, that we are loved.

Maybe that's what I'd been doing all along. Not controlling the uncontrollable but caring for my future self. So that when my world did fall apart, I could rest an arm across my own shoulders and ask that all-important question: "When was the last time you ate?"

12

BROS'

The food world is rife with impostors. The false morel possesses plenty of similarities to its edible counterpart, but contains toxins that, if ingested, can cause death. The horse chestnut has a different casing from the sweet variant, but if eaten causes severe gastrointestinal distress. The manchineel is one of the most toxic trees in the world. The fruit looks like a small, unripe apple, so much so that it is called manzanilla de la muerte in Spanish—little apple of death.

Not all culinary frauds are so malicious. The concept of the tastyfake—food disguised as other food—has enjoyed a triumphant renaissance as people share videos of themselves cutting into bags of Doritos that are actually cake. The famed Dominique Ansel Bakery in New York offers pastries that look like hot dogs (passion fruit curd stands in for mustard) and everything bagels (the schmear is actually cheesecake mousse). A Japanese TV show called *Candy or*

Not Candy has celebrities putting random objects in their mouths to see if they are actually chocolate.

I wasn't sure how to categorize my own impostor syndrome—if it was innocuous or something more insidious. People now largely considered me a food writer, an authority on the subject. They emailed me impossible culinary riddles about where they should go eat, what they should make for dinner, how to cook an artichoke, things I was wildly unqualified to answer. I saw myself as I always was: the person who had just been caught dipping pretzels directly into a jar of peanut butter while standing in her kitchen, in her pajamas, at 1:00 p.m.

(When my husband asked what I was doing, I replied, "Cooking.")

Sometimes when I wrote, no one noticed, and other times a great number of people did, and I couldn't quite figure out why or how that was. It was a peculiar duality, a sign of how I felt in my career. The same pattern would repeat itself again and again: I would write. Sometimes, a piece would blow up. With the positive praise came the hate, the threats, the same accusations again and again: that I was ill-informed and unqualified to write about food, that I was either too ignorant or too snobbish to appreciate what was before me. That I was ugly and old, that I was deserving of violence. That I was, ultimately, a fraud. So much of this echoed my own fears. And so when people described me as a food writer, I vehemently disagreed.

. . .

By the time Rand and I left for Italy in October 2021, our first trip to Europe in two long, uncertain years, it felt as if the fog of the pandemic was starting to lift. Just a few months earlier, Seattleites were racing to get vaccinated with the zeal you'd expect from science-loving liberals receiving long-awaited free healthcare. By the summer we thought that the world might return to normal, a sort of naïveté that I look back on now with painful tenderness, the way you do when children talk about growing up to marry the neighbor's hamster.

Our last trip to Italy had been scheduled for March 2020, understandably canceled as the country shut down and borders closed. We watched the news coming out of Bergamo, a little mountaintop town we'd visited years earlier, that would become an early epicenter of COVID in Italy. I wondered how bad it was in Milan, where my cousins were, in the villages where my aunts and uncles lived. There was a fear that neither Rand nor I breathed aloud until now that we were heading back: We had thought that we would never see so many people we loved ever again. And that this was true for so many people.

But on a warm night in the fall, we landed in Milan, and we stepped out onto the balcony of our hotel, overlooking the rooftops on the narrow street we found ourselves on. Below, a crowd of young people shouted in Italian. We went out for pasta, and over a perfect plate of pappardelle, I cried. We attempted to make up for lost time; my cousin's baby was now a toddler. She told me how he had spent the first year and a half of his life indoors, how the first time she took him outside, he was afraid of grass. My great-aunt was miraculously still on this earth. I sat with her in the tiny hilltop village where all my aunts and uncles were born, where my namesake aunt is buried. We darted around the country, seeing all the people we loved, all the things that I had taken for granted because they'd started to feel too much like home. What is more overlooked than the familiar?

In Lecce, a town located at the tip of the heel of Italy's boot, filled with Baroque buildings the color of sand, we met up with friends who'd flown in from different parts of Europe, and we flung off our masks and hugged with tearful trepidation. I had not been around this many people in years. We spent a week together, eating and exploring and plunging in a glacially cold rooftop pool. My husband is a planner, and he meticulously looked up restaurants and sites that we needed to visit. We ate oozing burrata and salty-sweet prosciutto, we dipped our toes in the Adriatic, I screamed when my friend Lisa cut her spaghetti with a knife. We ate beautiful, delicious, but relatively forgettable meals—stories that no one wants to hear about. The tale of a fabulous dinner you weren't in attendance for is excruciating to listen to, as satisfying as staring at a painting of a banquet when you're hungry. And yet this was the question I was asked again and again, as a so-called food writer: *Tell me about the best meal you've ever had.*

I often reply, "Let me tell you about the worst meal I've ever had instead." Ask someone about the most disastrous dinner they've ever experienced, and the answers are, without fail, infinitely more satisfying. Bring us your tire fires, your hot messes, your absolute shitshows. Was someone going through a nasty breakup and live tweeting it during appetizers? *Do* tell. Let us vicariously partake in something awful, cringe in empathy while knowing that we didn't miss out on anything. Let us feel blessed that we narrowly avoided death by dysentery. That's where the good stories lay, I'd found, in those accursed meals. I suppose there was some measure of avoidance, of cheating, within that: I felt as if I didn't need to be a food writer to tell those stories. Just someone with a predilection for disaster.

This is the tale of the worst meal I have ever had. And this is when I realized that I was a food writer.

On our last night in Lecce, Rand booked us at a restaurant he'd read about. The chefs had recently won a Michelin star—one of only eleven restaurants in all of Puglia with the distinction. Isabella Potì was one of the youngest female chefs to achieve the honor and had become a sort of celebrity along with her partner (both romantic and professional), Floriano Pellegrino, who had started the restaurant several years earlier with his brother (hence the name Bros'). Their Instagram was full of pictures of them wearing outfits that were made out of . . . I want to say laser-cut leather? They looked chic in a clinically depressed kind of way. Rand filled out a form when he made the reservation, letting them know of his allergies and the dietary restrictions of one of the other diners in our party (*foreshadowing!*), and on our last night together we headed out to Bros'.

What ensued was arguably one of the worst, most bizarre, most expensive meals I have ever had, the story of which I will be dining out on for what I suspect will be the rest of my life. When I got back home, I sat down and wrote this blog post about our dinner there:

There is something to be said about a truly disastrous meal, a meal forever indelible in your memory because it's so uniquely bad it can only be deemed an *achievement*. The sort of meal where everyone involved was definitely *trying* to do something; it's just not entirely clear what.

I'm not talking about a meal that's poorly cooked, or a server who might be planning your murder; that sort of thing happens in the fat lump of the bell curve of bad. Instead, I'm talking about the long tail stuff—the sorts of meals that make you feel as though the fabric of reality were unraveling. The ones that cause you to reassess the fundamentals of capitalism, and whether or not you're living in a simulation in which someone failed to properly program this particular restaurant. The ones where you just know somebody's going to lift a metal dome off a tray and reveal a single blue or red pill.

I'm talking about *those* meals.

At some point, the only way to regard that sort of experience—without going mad—is as some sort of community improv theater. You sit in the audience, shouting suggestions like "A restaurant!" and "Eating something that resembles food!" and "The exchange of money for goods, and in this instance the goods are a *goddamn meal!*" All of these suggestions go completely ignored.

That is how I've come to regard our dinner at Bros', Lecce's only Michelin-starred restaurant, as a means of preserving what's left of my sanity. It wasn't dinner. It was just dinner theater.

No, scratch that. Because dinner was not involved. I mean, dinner played a role, the same way Godot played a role in Beckett's eponymous play. The entire evening was about it, and guess what? IT NEVER SHOWED. So no, we can't call it dinner theater. Instead, we will say it was just theater.

Very, very expensive theater.

I realize that not everyone is willing or able to afford a ticket to *Waiting for Gâteau* and so this post exists, to spare you our torment. We had plenty of beautiful meals in Lecce that were not this one, and if you want a lovely meal out, I'll compile a list shortly.

But for now, let us rehash whatever the hell this was.

We headed to the restaurant with high hopes— eight of us in total, led into a cement cell of a room, Drake pumping through invisible speakers. It was sweltering hot, and no other customers were present. The decor had the chicness of an underground bunker where one would expect to be interrogated for the disappearance of an ambassador's child.

Earlier that day, we'd seen a statue of a bear, chiseled into marble centuries ago, by someone who had never actually seen a bear. The result was a creature that looked like some cross between a mop and the alien Odo from *Deep Space Nine*. (Just google it.)

And this is a perfect allegory for our evening. It's as though someone had read about food and restaurants but had never experienced either, and this was their attempt to re-create it.

What followed was a twenty-seven-course meal (note that "course" and "meal" and "twenty-seven" are being used liberally here) that spanned four and a half hours and made me feel as though I were a character in a Dickensian novel. Because—I cannot impart this enough—there was nothing even close to an actual meal served. Some "courses" were slivers of edible paper. Some shots were glasses of vinegar. Everything tasted like fish, even the non-fish courses. And nearly everything, including the most substantial dish we had (a plate of six noodles in a sauce of . . . I want to say resentment?), was served cold. Amassing two dozen of them together amounted to a meal the same way amassing two dozen toddlers together amounts to one middle-aged adult.

I've checked Tripadvisor. Other people who've eaten at Bros' were served food. Some of them got meat, and ravioli, and more than one slice of bread. Some of them were served things that needed to be eaten with forks and spoons.

We got a tablespoon of crab.

I've tried to come up with hypotheses for what happened. Maybe the staff just ran out of food that night. Maybe they confused our table with that of their ex-lovers'. Maybe they were drunk. But we got twelve kinds of foam, something that I can only describe as "an oyster loaf that tasted like Newark airport," and a teaspoon of savory ice cream that was olive flavored. I'm still not over that, to be honest. I thought it was going to be pistachio.

There is no menu at Bros'. Just a blank newspaper with a QR code linking to a video featuring one of the chefs, presumably, against a black background, talking directly into the camera about things entirely unrelated to food. He occasionally used the name of the restaurant as an adverb, the way a Smurf would. This means that you can't order anything besides the tasting menu, but also that you are at the mercy of the servers to explain to you what the hell is going on.

The servers will not explain to you what the hell is going on.

They will not do this in Italian. They will not do this in English. They will not play Pictionary with you on the blank newspaper as a means of communicating what you are eating. On the rare occasion where they did offer an explanation for a dish, it did not help.

"These are made with rancid ricotta," the server said, a tiny fried cheese ball in front of each of us.

"I'm . . . I'm sorry, did you say rancid? You mean . . . fermented? Aged?"

"No. Rancid."

"Okay," I said in Italian. "But I think that something might be lost in translation. Because it can't be—"

"Rancido," he clarified.

Another course—a citrus foam—was served in a plaster cast of the chef's mouth. Absent utensils, we were told to lick it out of the chef's mouth in a scene that I'm pretty sure was stolen from an eastern European horror film.

For reasons that could fill an entire volume of Time-Life Mysteries of the Unknown, THIS ITEM IS AVAILABLE FOR SALE AT THEIR GIFT SHOP. In case you want to have a restraining order filed against you this holiday season.

Now, at this point, I might have started quietly freaking out. A hierarchical pecking order was being established, and when you're the one desperately slurping sustenance out of the plaster cast of someone else's mouth, it's safe to say you are at the bottom of that pyramid. We'd been beaten into some sort of weird psychological submission. Like the Stanford Prison Experiment but with less prison and more aspic. That's the only reason I have for why we didn't leave during any of these incidents:

- When a member of our party stood up during the lengthy stretch between courses to go have a cigarette outside and was scolded to sit down.
- When one member of our party was served nothing for three consecutive courses, because they couldn't figure out how to accommodate her food allergies.

- When Rand was served food he was allergic to, repeatedly, because they didn't care enough to accommodate his.
- When a server reprimanded me for *eating*. We were served reconstituted orange slices (one per person) as a course. I asked if I could eat the real orange that had been served alongside it (we'd all gotten one, and I, at this point, was extremely hungry). "Yes," the server said, annoyed. "But you aren't really supposed to." He let me have two segments and then whisked the fruit away. (I later found out that other diners of Bros' had tried to do the same thing. They were reprimanded because the fruit was "display only.")

No, we just sat there while the food was portioned out a teaspoon at a time, a persistent and sustained sort of agony, like slowly peeling off a Band-Aid. That's the problem with a tasting menu. With so many courses, you just assume things are going to turn around. Every dish is a chance for redemption. Maybe this meal was like Nic Cage's career: You have to wait a really long time for the good stuff, but there *is* good stuff.

BUT NO. We kept waiting for someone to bring us something—anything!—that resembled dinner. Until the exact moment when we realized: It would never come. It was when our friend Lisa tried to order another bottle of wine.

"Would you like red or white?" the server asked.

"What are we having for the main?" she inquired.

His face blanched.

"The . . . main, madame? Um . . . we're about to move on to dessert."

We sat for a moment, letting this truth settle over us. Because by now it had been hours, and at no point had we been served anything that could be considered dinner. (There was one time when I thought it might happen. The staff placed dishes in front of us and then swirled sauces on the dishes, and I clapped my hands, excitedly waiting for something to be plated atop those beautiful sauces. Instead, someone came by *with an eyedropper and squirted drops of gelée onto our plates.* "We've infused these droplets with meat molecules," the server explained, and left.)

I don't know if our experience was the norm. I've looked at Tripadvisor's photos for Bros', and other people who've gone there seem to have been fed actual food. Like, even this person who was served the same weird meat droplet course at least got it with a triangle of foamy-looking bread. Do you know what it's like to envy someone for a piece of foamy-looking bread? IT'S NOT GREAT.

"There's no . . . main?" Lisa said to us in disbelief after the server had retreated.

"Hey," I said, my hand resting on her arm. She was shaking slightly from low blood sugar. "It's okay."

"They haven't fucking fed us," she said, her eyes wide.

"I know, I know," I said. "But look. We're in this

amazing country. And I don't know about you, but nothing is going to stop me from enjoying tonight."

She nodded.

"Because I'm surrounded by my favorite people," I said, and I squeezed Lisa's hand for emphasis, "and I'm at my favorite restaurant."

Lisa sputtered laughing. No more food was coming, but there was something freeing in that. Because this meal had never been about us to begin with. It sure as hell wasn't about the food. And there is something glorious about finally giving up.

We sat through a few more courses including a marshmallow flavored like cuttlefish and a dish called frozen air that literally melted before you could eat it, which felt like a goddamn metaphor for the night.

And then someone came in and demanded we stand and exit the restaurant. Thinking we were getting kicked out, we gleefully followed. Instead, we were led across the street, to a dark doorway and into the Bros' laboratory. A video of the shirtless kitchen staff doing extreme sports played on a large-screen TV while a chef cut us comically tiny slivers of fake cheese.

Rand was, of course, allergic to it.

The bill arrived. The meal cost more than any other we'd eat during our trip by a magnitude of three. They'd given us balloons with the restaurant's name across it, and Chef Isabella emerged and insisted on posing with us for a Polaroid that we did not ask for. We were finally released into the night, after every other restaurant had closed, ensuring that no food would be consumed that evening.

"That was abhorrent," we all agreed as we shoved the balloons into a dumpster (I'd made everyone take one, with the baffling logic that they'd somehow help offset the cost of the meal). We howled at how ridiculous it was, and how they'd poisoned Rand. How maybe we should have known that a restaurant named Bros' was going to be a disaster.

It was like an awful show that we had front-row tickets to. But wasn't there something glorious about sharing it together, the way that a terrible experience makes you all closer?

"No," someone said, and we laughed even harder.

P.S.: The next day, one of the staff tried contacting the only single female member of our party via Instagram messages. "Hey, I served you last night!" he wrote. She immediately blocked him.

- Bros', Via degli Acaya, 2, 73100 Lecce LE, Italy.
- Cost: a rather mortifying €130–€200 per person.
- Note: The Tripadvisor reviews show a lot of elaborate courses, and these were all way, way more food than anything we ate. I cannot express to you how little we were fed, and I'm not a particularly big eater. Allergy and dietary restrictions were largely ignored.
- Recommendation: Do not eat here. I cannot express this enough. This was single-handedly one

of the worst wastes of money in my entire food and travel writing career bwah ha ha ha ha ha ha oh my God.

My review spread across the internet like a flame during a dry summer. Once again, my blog collapsed from the weight of traffic—more than five million visitors in a week. The Italian press caught wind of it, and I made national headlines across Europe. A colleague told me that he knew I had reached cultural saturation when it started making the rounds in his office *in Romania*. *Late Night with Stephen Colbert* did a segment on my piece, my photo suddenly appearing right next to the man himself, larger than life on my TV.

The day after the post went up, the restaurateurs behind Bros' replied, adding more absurd fuel to the fire. Chef Floriano wrote a three-page "declaration," which he demanded be printed in full on *The Today Show*'s website. Which is a brave move from a guy who doesn't use spell-check. It included three separate renditions of a man on a horse. It stated, *"What is art? What if [sic] food? What is a chef? What is a client? What is good taste? What looks beautiful?*

"What is a man on a horse?"

The argument within all his culinary wankery and pretentious bloviating was that food was art. And so some people—mainly me, whom he referred to as "Mrs. XXX—I don't remember her name"—could not inherently appreciate it.

It's strange to find yourself in the middle of a headline-making culinary incident in which your name is inexorably tied to that of an asshole Italian chef. It is even stranger to find it happening for a second time. To paraphrase Bruce Willis in *Die Hard* and *Die Hard 2 (Die Even Harder?)*: How could the same thing happen to the same person, *twice*? All this time I had thought that chaos was courting me (passive voice), but now I wondered if I was an agent of it. Was I just my mother without realizing it? I immediately checked to see if the burners in my kitchen were off. They were. But I *was* setting fire to culinary bridges across my ancestral homeland. The common denominator here was me. And my writing.

The wave of responses came rushing in, a tsunami of people telling me that I was hilarious and brilliant, that I'd nailed the problem with fine dining. The corollary of that came in as well—messages that I was an ignorant slut, that I should just shove McDonald's into my orifices and shut up, that I was the reason people hated Americans. It was a deluge, of both praise and hate. And within all of it, one message stuck out to me—sent via Instagram, from a woman I didn't know. She'd worked at Bros'.

"Floriano knows only how to do one thing," she wrote. "And that is to rule by fear."

She described to me an allegedly toxic working culture, and told me she witnessed things that shouldn't occur in any workplace, ever. It turned out that Chef Floriano hadn't even written his ridiculous "What If Food" response himself. He'd simply added a few lines about me, but the original piece was fan mail written by some fawning sycophantic guest who couldn't get enough of Bros' nonfood. I wasn't sure what to do; I wasn't an investigative journalist. And even if I was, I was part of this story. The bandwidth required to look into this sort of thing was huge. I asked if she wanted me to pass on her information to several contacts I had. She told me yes. Later, she'd email me to say that a reporter from *The New York Times* was working on the story. I felt a glimmer of relief.

Not long afterward, a different reporter from *The New York Times,* Jason Horowitz, the Rome bureau chief, contacted me. He was working on a story about my meal at Bros'. By then I'd already given countless interviews to everyone from *The Today Show* to CNN to *The Washington Post.* But the tone of his email was different and hard to pinpoint. It felt . . . confrontational. He'd already talked to the chefs at Bros', and it seemed that everything that they said was taken as fact. If I disagreed with their recollection of events, I had to provide evidence. Suddenly I was in a he said/she said for my own account of dinner. Every aspect of my experience was scrutinized. Horowitz asked us for proof that we'd informed the staff of our allergies. He questioned my ability to speak Italian. He told me that the staff had claimed we were rude to the waiters.

"I wanted to confirm that you are a James Beard winning author. You won for your Batali essay correct?"

"Careful," Rand said. It was evidence that could easily be found on the James Beard website. "This guy is baiting you. He's expecting you to go off about how you're a James Beard Award winner. He's going to make you look crazy."

"What are you talking about?" I asked. But everything he said felt plausible.

"He already knows exactly what story he's going to

write. And in this one, you're the villain. The only thing you can do is give him as little ammunition as possible."

The questions continued—badgering, insistent, like a lawyer who'd decided I was a hostile witness. I wanted to ask if he'd spoken to his colleague who was working on a story *right this minute* about how this chef was allegedly abusive. I wanted to ask if he understood that Chef Floriano had everything to gain by claiming I was rude—even though we hadn't even *seen* him that night. That I—we all, frankly—were polite and ate our three hundred calories and tipped graciously because we knew that the front of the house was working their asses off to serve us the physical manifestation of the chef's pure id under the guise of its being edible. That we didn't realize how wildly bizarre the entire evening was until we left. That the only place where my razor edge of anger and snark ever came through was on my blog, because as a woman I couldn't act like that in person without paying a huge price for it. And now I was anyway. Some small part of me did want to go off about being a James Beard Award–winner. It was the accomplishment of my life and he'd reduced it to nothing. I wanted to ask him if he'd asked the chefs at Bros' a comparable question. *"I wanted to confirm you have a Michelin star. You won for making food that looks as if it were inspired by a Hieronymus Bosch painting, correct?"*

But they had everything to gain by making me seem unhinged and I had everything to lose. Instead, I simply asked, off the record, if he had looked into the allegations of abuse against the chef.

"I know that our being thorough can be a pain but

thanks for bearing with me," was the extent of his reply. I stared at my computer, helpless. He already knew the story he wanted to write.

The article came out two days before Christmas, during a slow news week. It appeared at the top of the newspaper's homepage, and in the front section of the print edition—a glowing puff piece about the restaurant. "Of Mouth Molds and Michelin Stars: Chef Finds Fame After Epic Takedown." A huge color photo ran along with it, of Chef Floriano serving food to two diners. I am portrayed as the bullying villain, the eviscerating award-winning food writer who started a global pile on against two talented young Italians. The article mentions Isabella Potì's cheekbones and her beauty ("Isabella has this face"), while Floriano is quoted as saying that my group's "premillennial age" made us "too old-fashioned" to appreciate the food served to us—a revamping of the maiden/crone dynamic playing out on the front page of the paper of record, each of us defined by our appearances rather than our accomplishments. Horowitz notes that "some people" found Floriano's tattoos misogynistic (one of the tattoos in question, not mentioned in the article: a prominent one across his chest that reads "Bros before hos"). I was described as "seizing on the moment" with "social media posts and national media appearances." As though my blog post getting attention has somehow made me an opportunist.

There was no mention that they'd ignored our allergy requests.

Chef Floriano noted that if we had behaved similarly in a trattoria, we would have been kicked in the behind. It was not the only time he'd made a veiled threat of violence; he'd told another publication that had we been in New York, we would have been punched. Compared with other comments I'd received, it was hardly the worst. But I'd always dreamed of having my name in *The New York Times*. Seeing it like this, in an article that tacitly endorsed violence against me, I felt my heart crack, just a little bit.

Shortly after publication, Horowitz emailed me the piece, wanting to make sure that I had seen it.

This was my reply:

Jason,

I read the piece. I was amazed that in a story about the youngest Michelin-starred female chef, and a female blogger, and accusations of abuse from female staff, you managed to ask the most important question possible: How does the man feel?

Anyway, congratulations on virtually ignoring all of the allegations of abuse leveled against Pellegrino, and instead painting him as a misunderstood genius. Then again, I'm in the group of "some people" who find a tattoo that reads "Bros before Hos" to be misogynistic.

Oh, and for the record, I'm 41. So I'm technically on the cusp of being a millennial. Two members of our group were older than me, the rest were significantly younger. How that plays a role in enjoying a meal, I'm still unsure. Anyway, I'm off to take my geriatric tongue to breakfast.

I realize the impracticality of the advice I'm about to dispense, but hear me out: Nothing will cure you of impostor syndrome faster than being torn apart on the homepage of the paper of record. This is counterintuitive. It should have fed into all of my insecurities. There they were, in print, for everyone to see. Chef Floriano's quotations, and Jason Horowitz's framing of them, were just more of the same insults I'd received again and again. That I didn't know what I was talking about. That I was a snob and ignorant all at once. That I was old. That I deserved to be beaten. That I had no place in the world of food. It was just a reflection of everything that I had been dealing with for the last few years, and for the first time I was able to see it clearly for the bullshit that it was. After all, if I was really so unimportant, why spend so much time discrediting me in one of the most important papers in the world?

Not long after the story came out, the chef who'd worked at Bros' under Floriano emailed me again. *The New York Times* had decided not to pursue the story about his alleged abuse. She'd been told that he was not known well enough outside Italy for them to report on it. It didn't have enough widespread appeal, they said. I told her how sorry I was, and that I felt as if I failed her. I read through the other accounts, from other people who worked under him and had sent their affidavits to the reporter, and felt that frustrated sting of helplessness. In the coming months, Chef Floriano would take footage of my face from interviews I'd given and splice it together with sexually explicit content, which he then posted as a reel on the official Bros' Instagram account.

I'd like to think that horrible people are punished in this world for what they do. But when I see Chef Floriano reveling in his bad-boy persona, flipping off the camera, untouched by consequences, that becomes harder and harder to believe. I knew that bad stories got more mileage than good ones; I hadn't considered that the same was true of people. That the jerks and the abusers, the assholes and the arrogant blowhards, tended to get bigger, better press than the ones who really deserved it.

I hated that calling out Floriano's terrible restaurant gave him more notoriety. "Floriano Pellegrino and Isabella Potì are richer and more famous than ever," one Italian paper wrote. I am grateful to him for one thing: Because of him, I did enjoy a wonderful meal, cooked by an incredibly talented chef.

Her name is Jessie Liu.

I first met Jessie months earlier; she was the chef who had worked under Floriano and contacted me via Instagram (she has given me permission to use her name and discuss her experiences in this book, for which I'm grateful). She now worked at an Italian pizza restaurant in Copenhagen called Bæst, which continually ranks as one of the top pizza restaurants in all of Europe. She told me that we should stop by if we were ever in town.

It required very little for me to convince Rand that we needed to go to Denmark *specifically* to meet Jessie and eat some of the best pizza on the Continent. We arrived just as they opened, and a line was already forming. She walked out of the back of the kitchen in her pristine white chef's coat to greet us and shook our hands with a calm confidence.

Jessie is originally from Taiwan, but she's worked all over the world—under Andoni Luis Aduriz in Spain and Dominique Crenn in the United States. Her stint at Bros' had been short but memorable for the scope of how awful it was. Food was deeply important to her; she told me how she wanted to open up her own restaurant one day. At Bæst, she was in charge of making fresh cheese for the pizza—a critical responsibility, because it had to be made day of and there was no opportunity for mistakes, one given to only the best chefs in the kitchen.

"So . . . how do we fix systemic misogyny in the food world?" I asked her.

"I honestly don't know," she said.

The question I posed is wildly unfair. I was asking Jessie to fix a problem that she didn't create, one that she was fighting against, that she was a target of. Jessie's responsibilities—ones she took very seriously—were to make excellent food and be good to her co-workers, things she did very, very well. But we were asking women chefs to do so much more—to fight against sexism, misogyny, and harassment (and women chefs of color to fight against racism on top of that), all while cooking excellent food that would never get the same attention as their male counterparts. Do everything a male chef does, but backward, in clogs.

As we talked about her time at Bros', I asked her if she'd ever considered leaving the food world. No, she said, shaking her head. Even when it was bad, even when she dealt with toxic people, she just loved cooking, and food, too much. As we talked, and ate, over dish after dish, the staff stopped by our table to talk. Jessie wasn't just loved; she was deeply respected. This was what was at risk when toxic chefs were elevated—not merely that they succeeded, but that people like Jessie weren't seen. That, more than anything else, was the true crime of it.

With my spoon, I pierced the cheese she'd made. There is something perversely satisfying about digging into a perfectly white, jiggling orb of fresh mozzarella. In some form or another, the cheese has existed for thousands of years, undulating and soft, as if some delicate piece of the marble statues that surround you everywhere in Italy has suddenly come alive for your consumption. It usually has an extraordinarily simple flavor profile, to the point of being bland (culinary snobs will rear their heads at this assessment; they need to accept it as fact), and it is so revered in Italian cuisine that it will often appear at a table with little if any adornment.

In short: You absolutely cannot afford to screw it up.

Jessie had explained to me that the diet of cows in Denmark was different from that of cows in Italy, so the milk was more acidic, and the resulting cheese they made from it at Bæst was a bit sharper. Just as rich and creamy, but with a little more tang than I was used to, and somehow just as perfect as, if not more perfect than, anything we'd had in Italy.

"If you start a restaurant and you need investors, let us know," Rand said to Jessie. This caught me by surprise. I've been tempted by the idea in the past, but Rand always said that the one thing he never wanted any part in was a restaurant. When Jessie stepped away from the table, I asked him if he meant it.

"Of course," he said. "You know she'd be amazing."

"Yeah," I said, reaching for another bite of fresh mozzarella. She already was.

13

JULIE & JULIA AND ME

Julie Powell was proof that my dreams were not apocryphal. She started a blog and turned it into a bestselling book, ultimately adapted into a film by Nora Ephron. Powell's project was an ambitious one: to make every dish in Julia Child's *Mastering the Art of French Cooking*—524 recipes—in under a year, in a tiny New York City kitchen with no dishwasher (other than, she joked, her husband, Eric). It was a human guinea pig project that people latched onto, turning Powell into a culinary blogging celebrity. In the early years of the new millennium, these were the sorts of miraculous dreams that the internet afforded us; we'd not reached a cultural saturation point of online food stunts. We were so young and new, kittens with their eyes closed; we could not see TikTok's insidious butter boards, or giant charcuterie arrangements inexplicably laid out directly on countertops—these culinary affronts to horizontal surfaces did not yet exist. So much so that in

Amanda Hesser's piece about Powell's project, she explains that "blog" is short for "Web log"—a necessary clarification in 2003.

I could not call myself a Julie Powell hipster; I had not read her blog when she was writing it, did not follow along on her adventures in real time. I was not aware of her, not really, until six long years later. It is October 2009, and I am twenty-nine years old. So is the fictional version of Julie Powell on the screen in front of me. I am somewhere in New Jersey, watching Nora Ephron's latest—and what will ultimately be her last—film, *Julie & Julia*, based off Powell's memoir of the same name.

Afterward, I am buzzing with what I will later identify as something between longing and jealousy. My husband and I go see the film with his grandparents on a sticky fall night shortly after it comes out. I have been blogging for a year and a half, ever since I was laid off the year prior. I have written hundreds of posts, in hopes of giving myself focus as my twenties draw to a close and my contract work proves unfulfilling and hollow. I am in awe of her—played by Amy Adams as the quintessential early twenty-first-century rom-com female lead, messy yet charming and wildly uncomplicated but constantly telling everyone how complicated she is. At twenty-nine, it's easy to draw similarities between myself and Powell's character. This is by design, of course. We *all* see ourselves in her. She is flawed but good, she occasionally cries on the floor of her kitchen, she longs for something more. And then, miraculously, she achieves it, through her sheer love and enthusiasm for something bigger than herself. My ambition, my ennui, my stress, even my tears—it is somehow both validating and reductive to see it given the Ephron treatment. But by the end of the film, we'd diverged: Powell is triumphant, despite a few delicate jabs from Mrs. Child herself ("I've heard of her. I haven't seen any of her stuff," the legendary cookbook writer told *The New York Times* in 2003) and has emerged with publishers and agents fawning over her, a clear literary niche for herself carved out. And I am still me. I slump out of the theater, feeling mopey.

Rand asks us what we thought of it.

"Really good," I say, afraid of admitting much more. The crisis I am having seems insufferable even to me, and besides, he knows so much of it firsthand. "Just keep writing," he tells me, every time I ask him what I'm doing with my life, which is on a near-daily basis. "Good things happen when you write." But I have yet to see any evidence of this. I vacillate between thinking I'm an absolute genius and a worthless pile of trash; between being hell-bent on making it and knowing that I will fail, utterly. It is self-indulgent and torturous. In the years to come, it will hit me: This is just what it means to be an artist.

"I enjoyed the Julia," his grandmother says, with a little laugh. "I could have done with less Julie."

I take a disproportionate amount of offense at this feedback. It feels deeply personal, an attack on me and my ridiculous dreams. I find myself doing simple math equations. Julie Powell's big break comes when she is thirty. I tell myself that I still have a year to go. It is the beginning of something that will continue for years: me, holding Julie Powell up as a benchmark of success.

. . .

The agent on the other end of the line represents a wildly popular culinary and lifestyle blogger. I know this already, of course. But she repeats this to me.

"Yes, I know," I say, trying to convey as much enthusiasm as I can over the phone. It sounds forced. It *is* forced. "The Downhome—"

"The Downhome Gal," she finishes.

"I am a *huge* fan," I say. This is wildly untrue. I am not a huge fan of the Downhome Gal. I find her site a little distracting and hard to navigate and there are a *lot* of butterflies on it. But it is clear, by the cadence of the conversation, that this piece of information was relayed to me in order to establish a sort of hierarchy, and I am attempting to acknowledge that. This lie, I hope, helps me do so—a kissing of the literary ring. The Downhome Gal, she tells me, is relatable. Relatable and *real.*

"One thing that the Downhome Gal does not do," she says, "is write negative things about her husband. *Ever.*"

I let out an inadvertent snort. (This does not go over well.) I have definitely written negative things about my husband. Several times a day. Often directly to him. Recently I've been doing an unfortunate Pacino impression wherein I affectionately yell obscenities at him.

"Well," I say, trying to keep my voice light, but somehow this makes it sound thin and reedy, "that's, um, that's not me."

"No, it's *not,*" she says.

Rather unsurprisingly, the Downhome Gal's agent does

not wish to become my agent. Which is probably for the best because we may hate each other. But the conversation, the judgment that dripped forth from it, starts seeping inside me, leaving me to wonder if I am a terrible person. I occasionally write about my exasperations with Rand: his eternal optimism, his infuriating calmness, his tendency to dump important documents into a drawer that I never knew existed until one day I would open it and they would rain around me like a ticker tape parade (I picked up the errant pieces of paper. We needed them for our taxes). I was living with a very handsome, wonderful man who occasionally turned into a chaotic Muppet (like Kermit when he flails his arms around with delight, announcing the very next guest on *The Muppet Show*). To not write about that, to not complain, seemed disingenuous. Of course I complain about him. I'm in love with him.

I cuss, too.

The Downhome Gal doesn't cuss. The Downhome Gal also doesn't advertise that the rugged cowboy she married is part of one of the wealthiest landowning families in the country. She's "real and relatable" while hiding the fact that she owns huge swaths of the Great Plains. (Also, she has *amazing* hair.)

I need to neither cuss nor speak ill of the people I loved the most—two of my defining characteristics. And I should probably get better hair somehow. (Theft? eBay?) The path to authenticity feels wildly inauthentic. I am stymied.

People tell me I will get used to the sting of rejection. But that hasn't happened. It feels a little bit more like being attacked by a swarm of bees—where the culmination of it only makes it worse. Where whatever doesn't kill you just comes really close to killing you.

It is 2011. My deadline for landing an agent and having publishers vying for me by my thirtieth birthday (like Julie did!) is now nearly imperceptible in the rearview mirror as time zooms along. I should probably do something else, I think. (I think this a lot.) It is the age of Bourdain, and my contemporaries in the travel world are pushing over one another to try to catch the flaming cigarette that he throws into the crowd like a bouquet, to be anointed the next Anthony. We have yet to learn there will never be another like him. Since I am not as likable as the Downhome Gal, I try to adopt an air of brash coolness in my writing. Since I have been admonished for cussing, I decide to cuss even more. But this doesn't feel right, either. I am not nearly as cool or as irreverent, but also, women are not afforded the same leeway to be these things. If we try, people will label us shrill and a bit bitchy, words no one had ever used to describe Bourdain.

My blog, I am told repeatedly, lacks focus.

"It seems to be mostly about how much you like your husband," one agent tells me in the middle of his rejection.

"I . . . do?" I tell him. I also want to point out that according to the Downhome Gal's agent I barely like my husband at all. (Also, I'm still doing the Pacino impression.)

Another tells me that she has an idea for my book. She wants to take all the stories I have and fictionalize them. Make them bigger and wilder.

"Like the story about your mom—maybe the two of you could end up in jail at the end of it!"

"Mm-hmm, mm-hmm," I say, gently, the way you do when you are having a conversation with someone who has, without warning or provocation, suddenly started sharing conspiracy theories about how environmentalists are purchasing and eating baby koalas via the Zabar's catalog. It is the sound of attempted de-escalation. "But . . . we *didn't* end up in jail," I say, and as soon as the words leave my mouth, I realize we're done.

I don't want to fictionalize my stories. The whole point is that they're ridiculous and true. My mother, Rand, and I had taken a cross-country flight together for the holidays, and she had forgotten the presence of a hiking pickax with retractable switchblade *in her purse.* We narrowly avoided getting strip-searched because one of the TSA agents *thought my mom was cute.* I don't need to add anything to it to make it more ridiculous than it already is.

This agent does not want to work with me, either.

I keep writing anyway. I am not sure what else to do.

I had never met Julie, though it is entirely possible that I could have by now. We have mutual friends; we are both in the food world. But she remains such a luminary to me that even when I see her replying to people in Twitter threads I've been tagged in, I say nothing.

I find myself stunned when the message comes through a mutual friend, bearing news of Julie's death in October 2022. It is the sort of by-proxy loss that feels like a hit-and-run—something sharp and unseen, out of nowhere, that leaves you reeling. I don't feel entitled to actual grief; it feels showy and a little performative, frankly, to cry over a celebrity. Instead, I start diving into her work, as though I were trying to discover evidence of a friendship between us that never existed. My behavior has me slightly concerned. At best I am being obsessive.

I think I'm simply trying to get to know her, far too late.

Her blog no longer exists in its original form on *Slate*. In order to read it, I have to sort through the pages that have been archived on another site. Twenty years later, it feels like a fossil, the way watching movie trailers from the 1960s and 1970s does, the medium having changed so drastically between then and now that this early iteration feels entirely foreign. Some of the entries make me wince a little, how she describes food and fatness (she worries about the weight she will gain as a result of this project and calls Paul Prudhomme—the late, great Cajun chef who occasionally weighed more than a quarter ton—"a martyr to the culinary arts"). It's something I've found on my own site as well: The early installments, stretching back to 2008, are cringeworthy, a sign of how far we've all come, but also just how terrible a stream-of-consciousness blog written by a self-absorbed white girl in her late twenties can be. When your biggest problem in life is that you aren't quite who you want to be yet.

But what is perhaps most surprising is just how, well, *blog-like* it feels. We are used to culinary writers weaving personal stories into recipes. It is the stuff of punch lines, the endless wading through life stories to get to the actual recipe. The dozens of apps that promised to do this task for us, stripping away the human element and leaving us with a staid list of ingredients and instructions. What I fail to see is that this thing, now commonplace to the point of annoyance, was once new. Her name became synonymous with culinary blogging, with putting herself through rigorous trials in the name of personal growth. She inspired a slew of impersonators, people working their ways through cookbooks and blogging about it. For a fleeting moment, as I was trying to find some focus in my own life, I considered my own Powell-esque project: I was going to eat and review every restaurant in the Pike Place Market. The goal was not nearly as lofty, and true to form it centered on consumption of food rather than creation of it. I gave up before I even started; a friend of mine told me it had already been done.

Powell's blog, nearly impossible to navigate in this archived version, illustrates what a novice Powell was in the kitchen even more so than the book based on it. She is not an incompetent cook, but the story about her having never eaten an egg was true. She omits ingredients, she substitutes olive oil for butter, she ignores Child's suggested pairings, she woefully messes things up again and again. But the way that she describes the chaos is infinitely readable and often beautiful. On trying to split a beef bone apart to extract its marrow, she writes,

> The pink stuff begins to drip out. This is somehow not how I imagined beef marrow. It's like guts, kind of. I stick my smallest paring knife into the center of the bone past the hilt, and scrape the stuff out. . . . I'm an inveterate cow eater, but this invasion of a leg bone is rather squirmingly intimate.

And then, slowly, she improves. I read through the entries, following along as she learns to be a better cook, day after day, in real time. She curses, she makes mistakes, she is not always likable. She is a far departure from the sanitized version of her in the film, about which she seemed to have some conflicting feelings. During one interview, she looks self-conscious when someone mentions the movie, giving an awkward smile with the edges of her mouth turned downward: when the world's impression of you is at odds with what you know is true about yourself.

I begin reading *Julie & Julia: My Year of Cooking Dangerously* and her next book, *Cleaving: A Story of Marriage, Meat, and Obsession,* concurrently. Switching between the two is to become unstuck in time, to flit between a marriage that is seemingly happy and one that is falling apart. Even though it's been a decade since its publication, *Cleaving* still feels like a bombshell. Publishers delayed its release until a few months after the film version of *Julie & Julia* came out, a calculated marketing move. Detailing the affair she had in the wake of the Julie/Julia project, Powell's *Cleaving* feels like a betrayal to those of us presumptuous enough to feel as if we knew her through her first book or Adams's portrayal. She describes her transgressions (not just the affair that stretched out for several long years, despite her husband's protestations, but also sex she had with veritable strangers) in aching, almost gory detail, the obsessive, destructive nature of it. It is watching a collision happen in slow motion; there is nothing to be done about it. You turn your head, but through your fingers you keep watching, anyway. Woven within the story is her learning the art of butchering, of cutting down animals into their parts for consumption. There is an obvious symmetry between the two books—one story about putting ingredients together into what we recognize as a meal, the other about cutting a creature apart into something we recognize as ingredients. Even so, I feel jet-lagged as I move between *Cleaving* and *Julie*. There is a moment where I pick up her book and forget where I am in the story; I cannot identify if it is her husband or her lover holding her, if she is in the middle of the Julie/Julia project or dealing with its aftershocks. The persona created in *Julie*, Amy Adams's wide-eyed depiction of her on-screen, was so overarching that I have trouble believing any evidence to the contrary, but there it is, page after page after page of it. I am not the only one who has trouble with this disconnect: Readers revolted; critics were brutal. Linda Holmes (who praised Powell's first book) wrote of *Cleaving* for NPR,

> I found [Powell's] latest book one of the most
> unpleasant reading experiences I've ever had.
> Not uncomfortable, not challenging, not in-your-
> face, not too real. Unpleasant to read, ultimately
> pretty boring except when it's irritating, and a
> book from which I took nothing away at all
> except perhaps a clarification of my own sense of
> what I do and don't want to read.

The response of readers was similarly harsh. They veer into hateful territory—so quickly that it knocks the wind out of me for a second.

She is referred to as a psycho, a "sick stalker," a "slutbag," as fat and ugly in the online reviews for her book. Someone opines that they hope her husband will kill her. It's clear that people didn't merely hate *Cleaving*. They hated Julie. And while it makes sense that the artist and the art are intertwined, particularly in the case of a memoir, it all feels like a little god-damn much. People were angry because they felt that Powell owed them something, that she had dared ruin the impression they had of her, one that she never endorsed. ("How could you?" wrote one reviewer.) Powell addressed this phenomenon directly in a piece she wrote for *Slate* in 2009:

> It's hard for me to remember, sometimes, that for people who know me through the experience of reading my books or, even more discombobulating, watching Amy Adams play me in a romantic comedy and then reading my second book, I must really seem like a fiction, a character in a novel. And the problem with characters in novels is that they have more responsibility than ordinary messy actual people do to make sense.

And I hate to sound like a broken record here, but my God, men in food were not equally castigated for their sins. Their addictions, their cussing, even their extramarital affairs, were regarded differently, as the unfortunate result of being a tortured or brilliant or temperamental soul, one passionately drawn to the culinary arts. Marco Pierre White said women were too emotional to work in kitchens while abusing his staff and allegedly cheating on at least two of three wives and remains a legend in the culinary world. Paul

Hollywood of *The Great British Bake Off* admitted to cheating on his wife of fifteen years, but his affair hasn't stopped him from belittling hobbyist bakers as if it were his job (which ... it might be?). Even Bobby Flay, arrogant bowl of potato salad that he is, has somehow managed to accrue enough goodwill that numerous allegations of marital indiscretion over his three marriages didn't earn him the same scarlet letter as Powell. They could be messy in their personal lives and still be authorities in the world of food. It seemed to give them even more legitimacy, a world-weary edginess to be taken seriously.

But women who cooked didn't seem to have this leeway—to be messy, to be sloppy, to be, occasionally, very bad at cooking. The results needed to be pristine—the Instagram-worthy images, the immaculate blogs, the perfect results. Even Julia Child and Nigella Lawson (whose own private lives have been dissected throughout their careers) joked that you could make mistakes in the kitchen, but their results were always picturesque, and definitely edible. Powell was showing the dirty bits behind all of it. I, a mostly unrepentant meat eater, found myself recoiling through some portions of *Cleaving,* where she describes in excruciating detail how to cut apart animals, how she cuts the cheeks from a pig and runs the band saw through its skull. My view has always been that if I was going to eat meat, I could not be particular about it—no skittishness about eating meat on the bone, no turning up my nose at offal or cartilage or feet or brains or tongue. I have plucked the eyeballs from roast fish and eaten them with just a second of hesitation. Those animals have paid the price for my appetite, and I do not get to pick and choose. It feels as though Powell were showing us the same thing—that we don't get the intimate view of her life without knowing what was really going on. She shows us the truth behind the lovely steaks we see in the counter, and the truth behind the story of her life everyone glommed on to. It feels unfair to turn away in disgust at it.

Rather unsurprisingly, the *Julie & Julia* oeuvre largely glosses over any marital problems Powell might have been having at the time. There is one minor fight between Adams's Powell and Chris Messina (who portrays Powell's husband, Eric, "spot-on" according to the author herself) over the project and its demands, but it feels sudden, wedged in, almost unbelievable. But now, as I read through the book, the way she jokes about sacrificing her marriage in pursuit of her cooking endeavors rings differently to me:

> Risking her marriage, her job, and her cats'
> well-being, she has signed on for a deranged
> assignment. 365 days. 524 recipes.

Another section of the book feels even more telling: Her friend Gwen is contemplating sleeping with a married man and looks to Powell for some sort of absolution. Powell tells her to go for it:

> When did I become poster child for the sanctity
> of marriage? . . . All my single friends seem to
> think I'm some kind of moral authority. I don't
> *do* sanctity.

From the beginning, Powell was not as people saw her, and she was quick to correct them. But we saw what we wanted to see. I sift through the pages looking for additional evidence of some future affair and, macabre detective that I am, evidence of something else—as though her life being cut tragically short by cardiac arrest might somehow be fore-shadowed, as though she were a character in a Shakespear-ean play. I want to have an intervention, to tell her to sleep more, to work and drink less, to stop whatever punitive self-destruction her life has become. I feel as if I have some sort of moral high ground from which to preach advice: I rarely drink; my marriage isn't crumbling. But I'm able to be this sanctimonious only because she's so open with her flaws. I feel as if I were having conversations with Julie—the way she did with Julia, the tone and tenor wildly different. I regard her not in the way one would a friend but something more and less than that. A wayward relative, someone I feel obli-gated to worry about, a measure of exasperation at their behavior. I think of a reply someone left to one of her tweets, several days after she has died. "Oh, Julie," was all they wrote. The sadness and heartache captured in those two words. The intense intimacy of it. The way people laid claim to her and when she fought back, they were angry.

I find myself in the same loop—angry and upset with Powell, a woman whom I did not know, whom I have no right to project these feelings onto. She owed me nothing. I doubt my name ever crossed her lips. And yet I feel as if she's somehow squandered my dreams.

"Do you think," Rand says to me gently, "you're upset because these were *your* dreams, and maybe not hers, and if they don't make her happy, you see it as an indictment of what you hold dear?"

He's not wrong. She repeatedly notes that she never even set out to be a writer (at the start of her first memoir, her aspirations are in acting). She accidentally ended up where I wanted to be, and in doing so highlighted that so many of my goals were no guarantee of happiness. I am angry at her because she hadn't lived up to expectations that I had no right to have, and ended up being flawed and so achingly human. I am angry, because she did something besides live happily ever after.

I remember the first time a blog commenter told me that they were disappointed in me. It sent me into a not-so-quiet rage.

"What fucking right does this person who doesn't even know me have to be disappointed in me?" I yelled at my monitor. ("You tell 'em, baby," Rand said calmly.) This is what happens when you write about your life, the inevitable side effect of being a memoirist. I had been on the other side of it. Strangers expressing disapproval online of my opinions, of my language, of any time my views or values differed from theirs. ("I can't believe you're a liberal," someone said to me, horrified, as though it were a secret I'd kept hidden from them. Really, Deborah? Just what about me screams "conservative"? Tell me so I can tattoo it and make it listen to the Clash and maybe do a semester abroad so it stops this nonsense.) At events I've often had people come up to me and say, "I feel like I know you."

Almost immediately following will be an awkward apology on their part.

"Sorry—that must sound so weird."

"No, no," I say. "It's not weird at all." I'm lying a little bit; it's *kinda* weird, but the weirdness is not their doing. It is something I have cultivated by referring to my blog readers, on more than one occasion, as, literally, "friends." The weirdness comes from the fact that I put myself in this situation intentionally. I have put so much of myself out there—into the blogosphere, in essays and my books, on social media in various forms, that strangers recognize my husband as he goes on walks around Seattle, that people I do not know will come up to me and ask how I am doing in the wake of my brain surgery. These are deeply personal matters, and there are days when this is a deeply jarring thing. But a door like that is almost impossible to close again, even slightly. I have no right to be upset about the circumstances, because I have shared these stories with them voluntarily. This is the pound of flesh I traded to become a writer. And so I tell them that it's not weird at all.

"It means," I say, "that I've done my job."

But there are days when I wonder what the trade-off to all of that is. When strangers make jokes that are too personal and too close and level the sort of judgment against you that you expect only from people close to you—friends or family or long-established enemies. "This post doesn't feel like something you'd write" or "I'm disappointed in you" is a deeply frustrating thing to read from someone who isn't my editor or my parent. They didn't have the right to be disappointed. And despite what they thought, they didn't know me. They knew *about* me. It was a curated impression that I'd created. It wasn't fake, by any means. But it wasn't a complete picture, either. It was like trying to guess a song from one note.

I've made the same mistake. I assumed that I could figure out Julie Powell from her writing, that I could somehow know her from her work.

In 2009, just before the film came out, Powell wrote a piece for *The Atlantic*. It expressed, in delicate, diplomatic terms, her problems with being depicted by Ephron, with the fame, with the fact that people would now know "Julie" but not Julie:

> I've had a movie made about me—or, rather, a
> version of me that's been made up by a very
> famous and accomplished person I've met only a
> handful of times—and I find the whole thing
> thrilling but also occasionally upsetting and hard
> to come to terms with.

Ephron's version of Julie was so complete, so overarching, that when an interviewer sprang the news to Amy Adams that Powell had had an extramarital affair, Adams responded, "*My* Julie Powell would never do that." It must be a maddening thing—to try to write your own story and then feel, a little bit, as if it's been taken from you.

An iteration of Powell's personal blog still exists on Blogspot. The posts stretch from August 2005, just as she wrapped up the manuscript of her first book, to April 2010, a scant six months after her second book was published. It is an unremarkable thing, full of grainy cellphone photos and broken links. But the comments are, as always, telling. The comments section is full of people expressing intense anger at her for *Cleaving,* or starry-eyed fans whose sole exposure to her has been through the movie. There are countless comments from people who say they are now inspired to write their own blogs—dropping links to their own sites. The optimism of it, bordering on naïveté, makes my heart clench a little.

"I want to be just like you!" someone writes.

I remember in the early days of my site just how grueling it was, how I so desperately wanted to be liked. I am graciously learning to give fewer fucks as I've gotten older, but there have been years and years of my second-guessing myself and having a crisis whenever a negative comment did come through. Perhaps I did cuss too much. Maybe I was too sarcastic, cracked too many jokes, and loved my husband too much or too little, depending on whom you asked. I remember there was a very brief window when a television producer asked me to do a travel show. *Can you wear your hair up? Down? Your nose ring... does that come out?* I pulled my hair into a ponytail, curled it, wrenched the hoop out of my nose that had been in there since I was nineteen. It didn't matter; they didn't want me, nor the version of myself I was cobbling together to make them happy.

Someone left a comment on Julie's blog, years ago, that she "seemed like a cunt in the movie." I try to imagine what it's like to take the blows intended for a fictional version of

yourself, one that's not even true to who you are. I kept looking for all the ways in which we were similar, overlooking
the fact that she paved the way for all of us to be ourselves.
She already knew she was going to be a punching bag, no
matter how unfairly, and despite that she kept on showing
her messy, miserable true self. She tore her story out of everyone else's hands and made it her own again, even if that
meant she wasn't the hero of it. When the comments come
in, and the strangers tell me I haven't lived up to their expectations, Julie reminds me of the importance of writing for
myself. It's an act of rebellion, a gift from a woman I will
never know.

14

OLD HAUNTS

When I was a kid, my favorite restaurants were as follows:

- Denny's, where I ordered the popcorn shrimp
- Skippers (a regional seafood fast-food restaurant once ubiquitous across the Pacific Northwest that now has a handful of locations left), where I ordered the popcorn shrimp
- The aforementioned Red Lobster, where I ordered—wait for it—the shrimp scampi (I contain multitudes.) (Multitudes of shrimp.)

And I figured this would never change. That these would be my favorite restaurants for the rest of my life because I honestly couldn't imagine loving anything else.

(My frontal cortex was not fully developed. That feels pertinent to add.)

I assumed that this was how love worked. That the shrimp and restaurants and people I loved would be with me forever. That there was a permanence to everything. When you've graced the planet for only a few years, this achingly naïve logic makes sense—the world has been static in that time. Buildings haven't been torn down, people haven't yet left you, and your heart is so new and unbroken. You go to Denny's and order the popcorn shrimp. Invariably, it is there on the menu. Why wouldn't it be? This is where popcorn shrimp belongs: on a Denny's menu, and in your stomach.

This mindset propels you forward, defines your friendships, causes you to engage in tiny little death pacts with the girls in your class (it is the 1980s—they are usually named Jenny). After an afternoon shrieking across a playground, you are willing to absolutely *die* for them, to offer up a kidney, to maybe let them brush your favorite My Little Pony's hair for fourteen seconds while you viciously micromanage. You are not merely friends, you are *best* friends, and what's more, you are best friends *forever*. This is a concept that you cannot understand fully—what does forever mean when you are seven? Middle school is forever away. Forever, according to this math, is six years. It does not matter; you sign a contract not completely understanding the terms. Friendship bracelets and little charms etched with the words "BEST FRIENDS" (pre-fractured to look as if it had been broken in two) are the grade school equivalent of buying a dual burial plot.

Now, at the ripe old age of "everything hurts, all the

time, because I tried to put on a sock," I have learned that the only constant in life is the impermanence of everything. Buildings come down and new ones go up. Restaurants close their doors. Denny's menu no longer includes their signature popcorn shrimp (they offer a golden fried variety that I will emphatically tell you is not the same). The best friend you had when you were seven will not be the best friend you have when you are twenty-five, because there are limits to how long you can bond over wanting to marry the same Muppet. I had plenty of examples of this over the years but still found it hard to accept. The friends who disappeared like a Polaroid in reverse, the ones who burned our friendship to the ground as if they were collecting insurance on it. The parade of best friends and neighbors and the girl whom I played with for an hour while our moms waited in line at the DMV. The ones who promised to guard my secrets and shared my toys and my clothes and did my makeup and broke my heart and told me it was my fault because I was distant or cold or sarcastic or my mom's number got called before hers did. Usually the problem was inherent; I was *me,* and I kind of sucked, and they found that annoying. Sometimes they would tell me I had changed—an accusation, a charge leveled against me that I didn't know how to refute. Everything else had changed—wasn't I allowed to change as well?

In the throes of rejection, it's so easy to tell yourself that you are better off, that clinging to someone or something that doesn't want you serves no one. There are reasons why relationships fall apart, and those reasons become more apparent under the eagle-eyed vision of hindsight. But there is also the fear that maybe you are now marked, unlovable, and, worse, un–best friendable. When the Romans sieged Carthage, they salted the ground so that nothing else could grow there. You wonder if the same is true of you, as you hide under a pile of blankets crying into a giant tin of caramel cheddar popcorn.

It doesn't change the fact that some days I look across the wreckage and still miss the people who walked out of my life.

Some days, I still miss Denny's popcorn shrimp.

Ask me now, today, if I have a favorite restaurant, and I will shrug noncommittally. I'll tell you I don't have a best friend, either (if you really press me, I'll admit it's my husband, a statement that is simultaneously true and somehow worse than saying your best friend is your mom). These responses are born of self-preservation. I've seen what happens when you love a place or a person and they inevitably break you into teeny tiny pieces. Like any good, emotionally stunted writer, I've found linguistic loopholes to express my emotions while still preserving the labyrinthine collection of walls around my heart.

"This place is fantastic," I will say, which leaves the door open just enough to backtrack later. It offers me an out, a sort of semantic escape hatch in case of emergency. "I want you to meet one of my *oldest* friends," I will throw out when introducing people—avoiding words like "closest," or "best," or "most likely to be called as a character witness" in some inevitable trial. It spares me the absolute agony and squirmy vulnerability of having to admit how much someone means to me. And also, I want everyone to think that not having a best friend is a choice I made because I'm cool and inscrutable, rather than just something that happened to me because I'm whiny and ask too many questions during movies.

Besides, my friends probably already know I care about them deeply, so it's not as if I have to *say it.* This is why Hallmark cards were invented! (Note: I do not buy Hallmark cards. But they exist. And the people I love should know that there is probably one that perfectly encompasses how I feel about them, sitting on the shelf in the drugstore.) Proclamations of love—even platonic—are messy things, to be saved for those moments when you are drunk or think you might die. If I never admit to any soft feelings, I have plausible deniability when things inevitably go awry—when a friend breaks my heart or a beloved restaurant closes or an admired chef turns out to be a walking sex crime. Because nothing is worse than being wronged by someone you *actually* loved.

It's not better to have loved and lost. It's better to deny that you ever loved at all.

Indulge me in a flashback. It is 2003. I am in my early twenties. I have just graduated from college and am working at a purgatorial office job. (The highlight of my day is that the soda machine in the kitchenette is free.) I am faced with the impossible, existential nightmare of trying to figure out what my life is supposed to be just as it is starting. Also, I have cut some very aggressive bangs. (I was going for

Audrey Hepburn from *Roman Holiday,* but the result was more Winona Ryder from *Beetlejuice.*) Every radio station (we still have those!) plays Death Cab for Cutie or the Postal Service or the Shins or the Strokes constantly. All their songs sound exactly the same, and also clinically depressed.

I first meet Robin at a friend's dinner party. I do not know what to do at dinner parties, except hope that no one will ask me what I do (the answer: I sit at a desk and wait to see if enough time has elapsed for me to get another free soda). Robin enters the front door like the lead of some jaunty musical. She's beautiful and boisterous and charming, and, I'm pretty sure, singing? She's in law school, and knows what her life is going to be, and she lays it out for me. I stand holding a glass of wine and try to remember what part of a person's face you're supposed to look at when you're listening to them, and decide on "anywhere but the eyes." I have learned (to pretend) not to fear confident women who have their shit already figured out. I'm not naïve enough to think that it might rub off on me in some way, but rather that if I surround myself with them, it might telegraph to the world that I, too, am confident and have my shit figured out and know what to do when holding a wine-glass and a plate with food on it and you want to get the food into your mouth but can't. (I consider burying my face straight into the plate.) Maybe I can fool everyone if I hide among these women who have bouncy hair and know how to use tampons without looking as if they'd murdered someone and don't eat appetizers face-first, and in this way I can make it through adulthood. I do not need to keep this up forever. Just until I die.

There is no ramp-up to our friendship; it is simply there, in front of me, fully formed from the very start. It is like how horses can run within an hour of being born. I am accustomed to friendships that are built up slowly, like grains of sand on a dune. Anything more than that, and I think I am being set up to be robbed, or recruited into a pyramid scheme where I have to sell vitamin shakes. Baffled, I ask my friend who hosts the dinner party if I am going to wake up in a bathtub of ice, missing a kidney.

"Robin," she says, "becomes your best friend the night you meet her." That is what happens. Within moments of existing, our friendship is up and alive and running.

Years pass. She is there for countless birthdays, mine and Rand's. She tells me that she's happy about the tiny lines that are creeping in around her eyes. ("My face has character now!" she says, laughing.) She almost always wears dresses. She sings a lot. She dresses up for Christmas parties—one year like Mrs. Claus, another year like a tree, with a giant star in her hair. When she is eight months pregnant, my mother asks, "Oh my God, are you having a baby?" and Robin looks down and says, "I hope so." She is effervescent and fun and silly and the life of every party I have. Two decades later, it is difficult for me to admit this. It would be easier to tell you she was awful, that she grabbed babies out of prams and farted on them, that her favorite painter was Hitler, that she subscribed to Dane Cook's newsletter.

The hardest part of reckoning with the people who hurt you is that there was a reason you loved them in the first place.

Officially, things end with the two of us walking around a park a dozen years after that first dinner party, Robin listing all the ways I (and Rand, too, why the hell not) have wronged her, with an eerie sort of calmness. Afterward, I sob uncontrollably (she heads to a pumpkin patch). She leaves my life as abruptly as she comes in: There is no subtle fade-out, no ghosting, no slow drifting apart over years while stalking the other person occasionally on social media (a.k.a. the natural order of things). One day we were friends, and the next we were not. Or maybe I'm kidding myself. Maybe our friendship had been running away from me for a long time. Maybe it was already gone, and I just didn't want to let go, so I just let myself be dragged for a while.

The magic and misery of living in one place for a long time is that it is filled with ghosts of the past: of relationships that have run their course, of now shuttered restaurants, of the person who you once were, spiky banged and insecure. Some days they are bittersweet reminders of the life you've lived. Some days you just feel haunted.

Café Presse is gone now. But there was a time when it was nearly always packed, trendy music and conversation thick in the air, windows fogged from the perpetual dampness of a fourteen-month-long Seattle winter. Robin first introduced me to the unassuming little French bistro in Seattle's Capitol Hill neighborhood. I don't know if this is actually true, but thanks to the imperfection of memory and the permanence of print, now it is. The old adage is wrong: History is not written by the winners, but by the memoirists. Be careful with a writer's heart; in the end, the facts are how we choose to remember them.

I don't recall the first time she told us to meet her there. Café Presse does not have the same defined parameters as Robin did in my life—no clear beginning or end. It was simply there, constantly over the years, helping me bridge that stretch of time across my twenties, where adulthood felt less and less like a costume I was wearing. It hovered perfectly between casual and fancy—the sort of place you could meet someone for a quick lunch or a birthday or an impromptu afternoon wedding on a clear summer day. The food was affordable and unfussy, came out quickly and seamlessly every single time. Smooth pâté with cognac-soaked cherries, chunks of baguette that threw shrapnel of crust into the air when you tore it apart. Piles of golden frites, too hot to touch, Bibb lettuce salad with hazelnuts and sharp shallot vinaigrette, crunchy orbs of falafel, frilly slices of cured ham, a gooey croque madame that we'd order "for the table" and then feign amnesia when it arrived.

It didn't occur to us, as we were trying to survive the mundanity of the every day, that this is what life *is*. This is what we get. A collection of moments, of paying bills and going to work and trying not to stay up too late and walking into a room and forgetting why you went in there in the first place. Of waking up one day no longer twenty, and then no longer thirty, of everything constantly shifting like the floor in that Jamiroquai video. Maybe this is what we speak of when we talk about nostalgia. A longing not for a thing or a place but for a version of ourselves that is now gone, something that slipped through our fingers, piece by piece, day after day after day, without our realizing it.

Robin and I were there for each other as the days

passed, for ordinary and important moments. At dinner parties, at birthdays, sitting on the couch of her condo, eating popcorn. She was there with me in Café Presse countless times, sharing an appetizer, or a crème brûlée, her telling me to get the grilled sardine sandwich. She would visit me in the hospital when I had surgery to remove a brain tumor, a perfect poker face, as if nothing were wrong, as if everything would be okay, even before I knew that it would be. When her son was born, I showed up outside her apartment with a lasagna the size of a briefcase, still warm from the oven. At her wedding, Rand gave a speech and tried not to cry as he told her that she was one of the most important people in his life.

And when I married Rand, Robin was there.

She was there both times.

The second time is the one everyone remembers. Robin officiated, on a scorching-hot day at a winery in southern Oregon. She wore a navy-blue satin shift dress, her blond hair pulled back in 1940s-style victory rolls. She'd pinned a silk flower I'd given her in her hair. Her boyfriend had just returned from Afghanistan, weeks earlier. Standing next to him, she was overjoyed, a smile so big that it looked as if it might fly off her face. I had a photo of the four of us—Rand and me, her and him, all of us looking so, so beautiful, as if nothing could touch us, minutes after the wedding.

I would, eventually, set fire to it in my sink.

But before my long white dress, before the champagne and the bouquets, and the ineffectual pyromaniacal witchcraft I conducted in my kitchen, there was the first time I married Rand. And then, there was only Robin, and the two of us. And the bystanders who happened to be at Café Presse on that sunny September afternoon.

While it would have been absolutely on brand for me to want to get married in the brick-walled back room of a restaurant that smelled like melted cheese and fresh bread, this had not been our initial plan.

We were set to get married the following week, in front of our friends and family, with a band and mediocre food, in southern Oregon. But Jackson County, where we were getting married, stated that officiants needed to be part of a congregation that had a physical location within its borders. (This felt like shockingly high standards from a place that had to disband one of its police forces because the police chief kept getting charged with crimes, including "stealing stairs.") (This is 100 percent true.) Robin had been ordained over the internet, but Jackson County refused to acknowledge the power vested in her by internet Jesus. I panicked, but Robin said she could handle it.

She offered to file the documents in Washington State the week prior; we needed to get together to sign them. She suggested Café Presse, carrying with her a stack of papers. We just needed witnesses. Rand grabbed our server, and told him that he needed his help, and the help of one other person.

"I can probably handle it myself," our server said, affronted but laughing.

When Rand told him that we needed two people to sign

our marriage license, our server burst into happy tears. I never saw him again, but his signature is there, forever.

Robin's is, too.

It gives me a wonderful line, rarely used, because only the three of us were privy to the truth of it: "I loved Rand so much I married him twice."

My brain, looking back, tends to condense the timeline of when and how things went sour.

It smooths it out, reduces the narrative into something easier to digest. In my mind, things fell apart in a matter of months. The truth was that it was slow, stretching out over years. There was always something simmering just below the surface, a sense of unease, a discomfort that I figured couldn't possibly have been from anything she'd done, right? Things I chose to ignore for a long time because they were my feelings, and I didn't want to inconvenience her with them. Our friendship felt impenetrable but fragile all at once, like the underwater glass tunnels at aquariums.

She had an unwavering sense of what she believed to be right and just. She didn't back down from a fight. She was fearless and unapologetic and never questioned herself. I didn't realize the corollary of this. Someone who was staunchly unapologetic would, ultimately, never apologize. If someone always saw themselves as just and right, they would struggle to see where other people were coming from. If they never second-guessed themselves, they would never acknowledge that they'd made a single mistake. It seems obvious now, an old cliché playing out: that the best things about her were also the worst things.

For a long time, I said nothing, convinced these feelings

would go away. But I felt awful when I spent time with her, felt as if she saw through me and talked over me and that I was simply a means to an end. I tried to talk about this with her exactly once. I told her that it felt as though she held all the cards, that she was intransigent, that the only viewpoint she cared about was her own.

This, understandably, was not a viewpoint that she wanted to hear.

I do not make it to Café Presse before its final service. The reservations for its last few days fill up within forty-eight hours of the announcement of its closing. There were plenty of excuses for why I decided not to try. COVID was spiking. A friend of mine offered to meet me and try to get a table, but the wait for lunch was supposedly hours to get in, and even then there were no guarantees. The line, I heard, extended around the block, in the frigid rain of a Seattle February. But the truth was this: It felt too painful. The vulnerability of it, the idea of being turned away, was too much. My pride couldn't take another blow.

Also, I didn't want to put on pants.

Ten days after the doors of Café Presse closed, I meet its co-owner and chef, Jim Drohman, on a bracingly cold and clear morning. Though I'd been here countless times, had seen him before, towering in the back, we'd never spoken. Talking to him now feels like meeting someone for the first time at a mutual friend's funeral. You wonder why it took you so long. And if maybe it's just too late.

The restaurant is dark, and the giant clock that used to hang from the wall is gone. I don't even notice it's missing at first, but once he draws my attention to it, I can't take my eyes off the empty space. It's as if my tongue were working a spot where a tooth is missing. I go back to it again and again.

I don't know what to call this place now. A restaurant is not just the physical space, but the people inside it, the servers and the line cooks and the bussers and the clientele. It is a living thing that moves and hums and shouts and vibrates. Now, stilled and empty, it feels unalive. There is a drabness I never noticed before, the way darkness makes a space feel more run-down than it is.

Jim has owned this place for fifteen years. He is very tall, his words carefully chosen, his delivery undramatic. I am none of these things, and outside this place I wonder what we have in common. I ask him if it's hard to walk away. Barely a half beat passes.

"No," he says definitively.

It's clear that I'm romanticizing this place; maybe it's just that, and nothing more. An empty space, malleable and shifting, taking on the personality of whatever occupies it. We peek into the back dining room, and he asks me at which table I signed my marriage license.

"Right here, I think?" I try to picture it, but I'm afraid to. I know that memories alter the more you revisit them, and I want mine to remain pristine. I want to hold that moment still, as if it were stuck in a snow globe, protected and unchanged even as the world swirls around it. Or maybe I'm just afraid to head back to that point in time. To remember who was with me. He tries to recall the name of the server who signed my marriage license. His co-owner, Joanne Herron, was the other witness.

I don't know which table it was, or even which side of the room. These seemed like such important things at the time, but now the tables are stacked up. The room is just a room. The lights have gone out. I don't even have a picture from that day.

Jim shows me the kitchen at my request. I don't stay for long; I feel as if I were intruding, and I don't want to bother him more than necessary. It feels deeply awkward, as if I were an actor who has missed her cue, as if I were marching out of beat, a solo act after years of being part of something bigger. Garfunkel, or Tennille, or whoever the other guy in Wham! was. (I am very tempted to turn and run out the front door, but I think it's locked.) Whatever I'm saying goodbye to isn't here anymore. The dining rooms of Café Presse were in the front and the back, but the kitchen was smack dab in the middle, the literal heart of the place. There were doorways that opened up into the kitchen that gave you a glimpse inside. I remember countless brunches here, a string of mornings spent in this place, the bustle of food that was ready, the chefs working to get the orders done, the noise and life of it.

Walking inside now feels like seeing the workings of a magic trick I'm not supposed to know about. The room is quiet. The burners are cold and scrubbed clean. The lights are off. The kitchen is long, and even empty it feels a little cramped. The ceilings stretch up so high, and the pots that hang are far out of reach. The air is still—not that of a room freshly vacated, that temporary sleep before it comes alive again. A different sort of stillness. It's done. The life cycle of this restaurant is over. Devoid of people, absent of the food, scrubbed clean of the memories that I can't or won't retrieve. It's just a room.

I ask Jim why he's closing down. I want there to be a reason. Something definitive that I point to. Maybe I can even blame myself. Maybe I didn't come here often enough. I moved to a different neighborhood not long after my friendship ended with Robin and never came back to this restaurant again. I was scared of bumping into her. Maybe this was just another restaurant that I'd assumed would always be there for me, when I was ready to come back. Another thing that I'd taken for granted. "Beloved Neighborhood Eatery Closes" is a headline I've seen a dozen times, and I lament it each time, but how often did I go to those places? I am a food writer. It's entirely feasible that I could have done something here. This is my fault, I decide.

Or COVID. Was it COVID? It must have been COVID. Jim shakes his head.

"It was just time," he says.

Robin began the conversation that ended our friendship by telling me that Rand was bad at his job. At this point in time, she was also Rand's boss (he'd hired her a few years earlier and then decided to make her CEO of his company after he stepped down).

I was confused, because she said she wanted to talk, and now it felt as though I needed to pull our friendship together in order to save Rand's job (spoiler: I did neither!). Robin refocused and told me all the reasons I was a bad friend. That I deflected conflict with jokes (insert slide whistle noise), that I was selfish, that I blamed others for my own shortcomings, that I distanced myself when things got tough, that I always took Rand's side when the two of them disagreed. (Only four-fifths of these were accurate in my opinion.) That I hadn't supported her during the layoffs she'd had to implement a few weeks earlier.

"I'm the scapegoat," she said. "I get it. That's what I am."

I wanted to fight back. I wanted to ask her why the hell she was bringing half of this stuff up when it was too late for me to do anything. I wanted to scream, "ROBIN, WHY ARE YOU TALKING ABOUT RAND'S WORK PER-FORMANCE? DO YOU THINK HE AND I ARE THE SAME PERSON? HAVE YOU GOTTEN US MIXED UP? ALSO, I AM SHOUTING SO YOU CAN HEAR ME OVER THE WRECKAGE OF OUR FRIENDSHIP."

But I was scared that I'd get Rand fired (I did anyway!), and I was afraid of what would happen if she and I were no longer friends. Would our marriage license get revoked? (No! Praise internet Jesus!) Would our wedding photos look strange? (No! But some of them kept catching on fire.) (Be-cause I kept lighting them on fire.)

She told me not to mention our conversation to any of our mutual friends. A request that I kept because I was ashamed. Ashamed that the second I tried to tell her how I truly felt, she didn't want me anymore. Ashamed that when I saw that was the inevitable outcome, I immediately tried to backtrack.

. . .

I was out of practice when it came to breakups. I hadn't been dumped in more than a decade. (I was always the person who got dumped. A lot of people just can't handle a strong, smart woman who cries on the toilet.) But Robin walking out of my life felt worse. To have someone not want to date me made sense! Lots of people didn't want to date me! (I'm horrible!) But to not want to be friends? Where did we even go from here? There was no "let's just be friends" alternative to this. She knew me, and she decided that she didn't want to anymore. I dealt with it as best I knew how. I lay in bed and cried for a month, and then Trump was elected and my father died, at which point I cried a little harder.

After weeks, or perhaps months, or maybe years— honestly, it became hard to tell at this point, the days are an unwashed blur of grief, depression, and pajamas—Rand said to me, "I need you back." The person who loved me and who had lost his job and the company he loved and one of his closest friends and didn't blame me (he didn't blame me!) needed me back.

I needed myself back.

The problem, of course, is that like most things, it's easier said than done. Losing a person—or even a place—so tied to your past feels as if you were losing the last vestiges of the person you once were. You get disoriented. You go through a bit of an existential crisis. Whoever said that time heals all wounds probably died of sepsis. It does not. But in the case of a broken heart, it does soften the edges of the pain a little bit. There was no shortcut, no conversation, no come-to-God realization. It was just days passing, a thousand imperceptible moments. *Life.* Moving on and being beautiful without her, until it didn't hurt the way it used to.

I still existed. I was *fine.* It honestly surprised me at first that I could live without her.

Real estate moves on faster than people do. A good restaurant location in Capitol Hill—where Café Presse once stood—does not stay empty long. Something new has moved in. The space in my heart proves distinctly harder to fill. For a long time, I hold people at arm's length. I am afraid to tell them how much they mean to me. I find my loopholes. "I love you," a friend who is less broken than I am will tell me as they leave my house, pulling me in for a hug.

"Oh, yeah," I often say after a moment's hesitation, along with one of those hugs that's more like a pat. "*Us,* too."

This, I'm told, is incremental progress. A baby step over those times when I deflected and shouted, "WHY?" and everyone laughed. Still, there is an out. A tiny opening to escape through. You never know when you need those.

But sometimes, I look at these people who love me, I squeeze them back, I press my cheek against theirs. I try not to shout into their ears, so close to my lips: "I love you so, so much." I chip away, ever so slightly, at the walls around my heart. The restaurants and relationships that come into our lives are not things that exist spontaneously. They need love to keep them alive. And so I try, but do not always succeed, to tell people how I feel, to visit the cafés and restaurants I love, again and again. To lay my heart and cards on the table, right there next to the napkin dispenser.

No one tells you about the sunk-cost fallacy of friendship: Knowing someone for a long time doesn't guarantee your relationship with them will be better for it. It feels as if because they're tethered to so much of your past—your messy youth, your wedding day(s), a thousand haircuts, good and bad—you can't walk away, even though, honestly, you probably should. You probably should have years ago. Restaurants don't share this same compunction. When it's time to end things, they close, or they take the popcorn shrimp off the menu. It's so simple.

People move through my life, buildings come down and go up again, I grow older. Years later, I am riding in my car with my husband. We stop at a red light, and an empty lot at the corner of an intersection looks familiar. It is fenced off, the two-story building that once stood there gone, whatever was supposed to come next stalled for some unforeseen reason. I point my finger at the square of asphalt and rubble, parts of it turning to mud in the near-constant precipitation of a Seattle fall.

"That's where you took me for our first date," I say, remembering the Italian osteria that was once tucked away in the bottom corner of the first floor. If you had told me, at twenty-one, that he and I would outlast the restaurant we were sitting in, I would never have believed you.

"I'll take you back there for our anniversary," he says, and I sputter a laugh. I try to conjure up an image of the place, candlelit and crowded. The two of us, impossibly young, sitting at a table, trying to figure each other out. The people we were when Robin came into our lives. The way she once fit so inextricably into my world that I could hear the sound of her voice in my head like a song. But before I can steady the picture in my mind, the light changes, and we've already moved on.

15

THE COMMENTS SECTION

I am convinced that if you were to make a topographical map of the internet, it would just be an infinite collection of tiny hills upon which people are willing to die. At some point in recent human history (I'm guessing 2014), the web became almost entirely full of opinions that were:

1. Very angry

2. Extremely inconsequential

3. Written by people who think that there shouldn't be anyone gay in *Star Wars*

Recipe sites are no different, though usually less focused on John Boyega and Oscar Isaac's sexualities (mostly) (JUST LET THEM KISS, J. J. ABRAMS, YOU COWARD). Instead, they demand the person who put pureed peas in guacamole be put to death. These sites bring us together, they tear us apart, and off in some corner of the comments section someone is shouting, "I HATE OLIVES WITH PIMENTOS, THEY LOOK OBSCENE," and we know you do, Diane, but this recipe does not contain olives with pimentos.

I once wrote that if you were swamped during the holiday season, you could buy pumpkin pie instead of making it from scratch. I must give credit where it is due: Usually for a mob to convene like that, it's because a scientist has been stealing body parts and sewing them together into a hideous patchwork monster so that he might feel the power of God in his own hands. But these people were ready to burn my house down because I told them it was okay to buy dessert. Someone replied that if I wasn't willing to make the pie from scratch, I didn't deserve a family. (I think he got the phrase "unwilling to make a pie" and "unwilling to stop eating endangered baby sea turtles" mixed up.) I once had a guy harass me on numerous platforms because I made fun of his girlfriend, Mountain Dew. I've gotten hate mail because I don't like mayonnaise, which apparently Jesus fed to the apostles.

The comments section is basically Thunderdome for people who want to talk about how "chili used to mean something." A large percentage of these people have decided to simultaneously ignore the instructions and get mad at them. They have the collective reading comprehension of a half-eaten bag of Cool Ranch Doritos, and they are ready to blame you for their own mistakes. They're basically first graders, except with unfettered access to the internet. When a recipe called for pizza dough, they used pureed cauliflower. As a result, the pizza they made does not look like a pizza. It looks like a disk of pureed cauliflower, which bears a striking resemblance in both texture and color to cat vomit. They should probably have a juice box and lie down about this setback, but instead it is everyone's fault but their own.

I admire the hubris it takes to be angry about this.

I am a meticulous follower of recipes. Part of this has to do with the fact that I'm very bad at being an adult. And I don't mean in a "Wheee! I'm so fun and carefree" eating-Popsicles-in-the-snow kind of way that men find extremely attractive in characters played by Kirsten Dunst. I have adult *energy* (translation: vaguely constipated), but just not any of the authority or competence. I'm like a very draconian accountant who has never seen the number five before.

This leaves me in a state of perpetual anxiety that I am just . . . being alive wrong. If I am driving down an empty road, I will occasionally be hit with the overwhelming terror that maybe I am heading the wrong way down a one-way street, and I have been for several miles, and maybe I've never actually driven the correct way down any street, ever. Whenever I am at the airport and I'm about to go through TSA, I suddenly become panicked that maybe there is a large quantity of cocaine in my purse, even though I have never even seen cocaine, and I wouldn't even know how to get a large quantity of cocaine (maybe Costco?), and let's be honest, I'm a white woman with TSA PreCheck and expensive shoes, so someone from Delta would be like, "Ma'am, do you need help carrying your cocaine to the gate?" Which is ridiculous because I don't even fly Delta.

But recipes are one of the few times we get instructions for life. And if you follow the instructions very, very closely, not only do you get to eat food, but also the nagging feeling that you are basically the worst person ever to operate a human suit goes away a little bit. Consequently, I carefully follow instructions because I'm absolutely certain that it's going to save my life one day. As though I will be in charge of defusing a bomb (shut up, it could happen) and the person on the other end of the line (it's Pierce Brosnan, circa 1984) will be like, "Cut the red wire." I'm obviously not going to say, "Why don't I just cut the yellow one? It's basically the same thing." AND THAT IS WHY I CANNOT SWAP CANNED ARTICHOKES FOR FROZEN ONES EVEN IF THE RECIPE SAYS, "CANNED ARTICHOKES ARE FINE." BECAUSE WE DO NOT NEED *FINE,* WE NEED TO FOLLOW THE DIRECTIONS OR WE WILL TURN INTO HUMAN CONFETTI, MELISSA.

But *look.* Look at these chaotic goblins, these overconfident ghouls who take a recipe from an expert like Padma Lakshmi on the *New York Times* website or Marcus Samuelsson on Epicurious or "AssFace45" on Allrecipes and defy it so openly. Who are these people who are willing to look directly at the face of God (or at Padma Lakshmi, same thing, basically) and shout, "ORANGE JUICE AND ORANGE SODA ARE BASICALLY THE SAME THING."

What are the rules by which they live their lives? Do the rules even exist? I once bumped into a mannequin at a department store and I *apologized to the mannequin.* And it was not a realistic-looking mannequin (it was one of those headless ones). So, blaming someone else for your obvious, willful mistakes? This is a level of chutzpah I cannot fathom.

"We used Pepsi so I'm not sure if that was why it was a bit too sweet but I think we will use regular soy sauce next time if I don't have a Coke," a brave, possibly drunk woman commented on a recipe for London broil.

"There isn't any Coke or Pepsi in this recipe," the site's author replied, illustrating the restraint of a Franciscan monk. Because—and I feel that this is probably not news for most of you—these are two very different substances. On the Venn diagram of Pepsi and soy sauce, the overlap is very thin (the narrow sliver containing only two haunting words: "brown" and "liquid"). Yet people are forsaking this knowledge and are baffled as to why things do not taste right, something that clearly falls under the categories of "obvious" and "natural consequences" and "are you fucking with me?"

The arrogance is *staggering,* and I'm somehow envious? There is no other scenario where you can get away with swapping one thing for something entirely different and demanding equivalent results. Imagine ordering a Pepsi at a restaurant and the server instead brings you a bottle of Kikkoman and says, "Oh, it's the same thing." Lab rats can differentiate between these substances.

I mean, dear God, I was sent to the principal because *I expected too much from my education* from my third-grade teacher, and here these people are, expecting Pepsi to taste like soy sauce. They literally contain none of the same ingredients. (Unless carbonated water and regular water count as the same ingredient? I don't actually know. This is information my third-grade teacher did not teach me.)

Look—sometimes I get the need to go off book. Yotam Ottolenghi's recipes contain forty ingredients and you have to start making them six months ahead because you have to grow the herbs from scratch or leave your spices out until a full moon and then you have to lure virgins to dance around them until they are all so exhausted that they collapse and that is *a lot* to do for a risotto. But don't be surprised when someone takes a bite and is like, "Hey, listen, I don't want to alarm you, but I don't think any virgins danced around your saffron."

But these people are viciously demanding more, and it's making me wonder if those of us who do follow directions and do everything right and blame ourselves when things go wrong and apologize to mannequins should, I don't know, maybe expect a little more, too? (It is very hard to say this. I still have residual trauma from being sent to the principal thirty-five years later. Seriously, screw you, Mrs. Schmidt.)

Intermixed with those who are swapping cough syrup for maple syrup are individuals who are happy to have found an outlet for their rage now that the guillotine has fallen out of fashion.

"Why the annoying redundancy of calling this challah bread? Challah IS bread. Would you call a baguette baguette bread?" writes a user on Claire Saffitz's recipe for *The New York Times*. And yes, yes, you would. It is literally called "baguette de pain" (baguette of bread).

But I appreciate anyone who is willing to be both pedantic and uninformed. When the world is turning into a smoldering uninhabitable rock, and it feels as if you were powerless to stop it, our anger has to go somewhere. Why not unleash it on the people who *really* deserve it? Those who have committed the unforgivable crime of sharing food recipes for free on the internet.

"This was a yankee dish that's only okay if you are starving," a user opines on a recipe for Sandy's Frito Pie on Allrecipes (the nearest thing to a political comment I found). "My GF and son will get me a cheaper coffin because of this dish."

Wade through enough of them and the appeal of the comments section on a cooking site becomes staggeringly clear. Food is a perfect outlet for our anger, the one thing we can be frothingly opinionated about in a way that is safe, because it is both deeply personal and somehow doesn't make us feel vulnerable. People having different opinions from ours on this topic don't negate our humanity or value or make our safety feel threatened. They are just charlatans with no taste, but they can't hurt us. We can be as passionate as we like, and if we disagree, at the end of the day it's fine. No one is going to outlaw pineapples on pizza or insist we eat turkey bacon or that we stir walnuts into our brownies. This is one place where our bodily autonomy remains secure, where we are still people in the eyes of those who disagree with us, where the crimes committed are against not us but the culinary world.

Gordon Ramsay famously posted a picture of his goopy, electric-yellow carbonara to Twitter, and the responses were venomous. Numerous people equated it to dog food in multiple languages and told Ramsay he should be ashamed, and someone started the hashtag #StopViolenceAgainstPasta.

"Every time you do this, an Italian vomits and risks dying of disgust," one user wrote.

"Ma come cazzo ti viene in mente?" another said. (Loosely translated: "How the fuck did this even enter your mind?") The comments section of a recipe site offers a window into everyone's soul; it is a place not devoid of passion, but largely devoid of politics. Ideas that are held strongly but often hurt no one. I am adamantly sure that peas do not belong in carbonara. I also don't *really* care if Ramsay puts them in his (he will be wrong, and I will tell everyone this. But it also doesn't *matter*).

Many users are eager to report on the disasters that befall them in their kitchens, and sifting through them, I find that I feel less alone. It isn't that my self-doubt dissipates, but that I realize everyone has it. We have all accidentally reached for baking powder instead of baking soda. I am not the only one who has stood in her kitchen and cried and screamed that I suck at everything and blamed the internet and left a scathing one-star review even though it was definitely probably my fault. I am not alone in this. We all make mistakes, we cry and yell and throw a pie on the ground, and we try to teach others what we've learned from eating pie off the ground.

In that tender section of user-generated content beyond the end of a recipe there are also memories, and stories, and occasionally even helpful pieces of advice: the things that emerge whenever people are allowed to talk freely about food.

Rather than allow comments, the *New York Times* Cooking site has a section where readers can add "Cooking Notes." The distinction is important, Sam Sifton, founding editor of *New York Times* Cooking, told *The Ringer*'s Alison Herman in 2019.

"We made the conscious decision not to call them comments. The call to action was to leave a note on the recipe that helps make it better."

Some have heeded this prompt more closely than others.

"A warning to other hypochondriacs," writes a user on Alexa Weibel's vegan cacio e pepe recipe. "Fortified nutritional yeast is high in the vitamin B-12. A common side effect of excessive consumption of B-12 is . . . neon green urine. Thanks to a busy week at work and a dwindling pantry, I made this undeniably delicious pasta recipe 3 times in the last 4 days, becoming perturbed when my normally unremarkable pee transformed into a hue normally found only in glo sticks. Don't be like me and panic. It's just the [yeast]."

While these comments arguably do not improve the recipe themselves, the internet is better for them.

In 2015, a woman named Sydne Newberry left what *The Cut* would regard as "perhaps the greatest recipe comment of all time" on an entry for Katharine Hepburn's brownies (apparently the famed star was very particular about the dessert). In the notes section of the *New York Times* Cooking site, Newberry wrote,

> This has been my go-to brownie recipe for 30 years, even after going to baking school! I agree that using the best cocoa possible makes a

difference. These days, I use Callebaut. In the 80s, an acquaintance in Germany to whom I brought some of the brownies, and who considered herself a great cook, asked for the recipe but was never able to get it to work. She kept asking me what she was doing wrong and I was never able to solve her problem. Eventually, she moved to the US and stole my husband!

It is a story full of intrigue and devastation and ultimately triumph (the other woman never figures out the recipe!). It would eventually end well for Newberry: She would remarry, and she describes her second husband as "the love of her life."

Did Sydne Newberry's note actually make the recipe better? It's usually a foregone conclusion that better cocoa yields better brownies. But the rest of her brief entry—fewer than a hundred words long—offers something we so desperately need from any recipe: a bit of history, a human connection to go along with the dish we are making. The thing that we gossip over. These aren't merely Katharine Hepburn's brownies; they are also, and perhaps even more so, Sydne Newberry's.

My personal favorite comment comes from another brownie recipe, courtesy of Allrecipes. It is for black bean brownies, a dish I will never make. A user named Karen has left the following comment:

I STIRRED EVERYTHING TOGETHER
LEAVING BEANS WHOLE, FANTASTIC!!

BEANS SEEM LIKE CHOCOLATE CHIPS!
WILL MAKE AGAIN!

I have never once, in my many years of eating solid food, thought that black beans seem like chocolate chips. But there is something so earnest and joyous about Karen's comment. About someone writing happily—IN ALL CAPS—about how beans seem like chocolate chips!

There is no pretension in it; she doesn't feel the need to draw parallels of how many desserts use red beans as a sweet filling, that chocolate itself comes from a legume. Because she has nothing to prove to anyone. I can argue with her all I want. But she has a window into the culinary world (of beans) that makes her happy. How is she anything but triumphant?

The notes and comments of a recipe are where I go to first. I pay close attention as they tell me to add a little more flour to my gougères, that there is not nearly enough salt, that beans seem like chocolate chips (you know what, Karen? I kind of get it). Even when everyone disagrees, even when everyone is telling Gordon Ramsay that he should be ashamed and that he has murdered Italian cuisine, there is something uniting all of us. This love, of food, of cooking, of feeding the people you love, of having opinions that are so, so important but also not. It's all there in the comments section. Someone will teach you something. Someone will share something beautiful. And if you listen to what they have to say, things will undoubtedly be better.

16

HANGER MANAGEMENT

I was told as a small child that I had high blood pressure. I don't know quite where or how this myth began. But the second anything annoyed me or started to upset me, some older relative would say, "Stop. You have high blood pressure, you can't get upset like this. It's bad for your heart."

I was a fourth grader who panicked about her salt intake. I conflated my own anger with what I thought were heart problems and became unable to distinguish the two. The more I suppressed the feeling, the more my chest felt as if it were going to explode. I asked my mother to buy potassium chloride, a salt substitute for people who were concerned about sodium and also wanted to incorporate the taste of battery acid into their diets. I lasted a few miserable days, before I went back to my usual habit of sucking on pretzels until they were denuded and soggy. I figured I'd die young, a faint popping sound in my chest cavity as my aorta ruptured.

Years later, despite having spent years trying (and failing) to suppress the desire to rub Cheetos dust on my gums like someone testing cocaine for purity, I found out my blood pressure was astonishingly low. My doctor recommended eating more salt. It was what my body had been screaming at me all along, via an overwhelming desire to suck on bouillon cubes like they were cough drops. I'd just been taught to ignore it, and my anger along with it. I don't know if my family did this on purpose, but I do think it made things easier for them. There was no space for me to be a little girl who got angry, because that would one day mean I would be a woman who got angry (an emotion women in my family did not express well).

This was their collective way of telling me to "smile." I listened, because if I didn't, I thought I would literally die.

As I grew older, I found I wasn't alone in my fear of my own anger, in having never been taught how to voice it properly. Most women I talk to about this (whispered, in code, pretty much exactly like Offred in *The Handmaid's Tale*) want to get angry but have no recourse. They fear being forced into some unflattering or dangerous archetype that the world told them they'd be if they expressed the faintest glimmer of rage. The bitter ex, the stressed-out mom, the bossy exec, the man-hating feminist—the countless racist or sexist clichés that would be tossed at them for getting angry at the systemic injustices of the world (because misogyny has a thousand words for "unhinged bitch" but not a single one for "multiple female orgasm"). So they tamp it down because if they start to let it out they'd get arrested or killed or be told to calm down, which is a surefire way to give someone a rage stroke.

As always, marginalized women were hurt the most by this suppression of emotion.

The author Joshunda Sanders notes that she was raised with the understanding that the onus was on her, as a Black woman, to suppress any outward expression of anger that would be misconstrued and turned against her by a dominant white culture. As she writes for *In These Times,*

> We never want to give white people—who already
> view us as immune to pain, as consistently and
> forever unequal—a reason to think we are irratio-
> nally upset, which is how anger voiced from a
> Black woman is usually construed.

A friend of mine was harassed in a grocery store by another patron, during a spate of attacks against Asian Americans on the East Coast. When the store management removed the man, they asked her why she didn't say anything.

"My name is Karen and I'm *Chinese,*" she said, laughing. In her family system, she was taught not to complain, she explained. And now in recent years, her first name had become synonymous with white women who complained with no justification. Of course she wasn't going to say anything. Even when her own safety was at risk (because it was at risk either way).

As far as anger goes, I'm on the highest rung of the privilege ladder for women who *could* express this emotion. I'm a white cis American woman in my forties; you better believe that if I ask to speak to the manager, I will get a refund or someone will honor a coupon that's so old it's actually a daguerreotype. I can complain without risk of death or arrest or even lifetime banishment. But even I've been socially trained to believe that I need to be nice to the guy from AAA who told me I got my flat tire because I was a bad driver even though the car was parked in my driveway at the time. And so while I wanted to shout "FUCK YOU, MIKE FROM MIKE'S FRIENDLY TOWING, I HOPE YOUR DICK IS CHEWED OFF BY SQUIRRELS," I tipped him. Because I didn't want him to think I was a bad driver *and* a bitch.

This isn't new. There are literally ancient Greek myths about how an angry woman is an affront to nature. It's the whole story of Medea! She gets completely jilted by Jason (after Medea saves his life and helps him get the Golden Fleece and flat out gets exiled so he can be a hero, he runs off with a young princess—the fourth-century BC equivalent of a midlife crisis). And the allegory here is that if a woman gets pissed off at her husband, she will straight up become unhinged and *murder her own children.* Because we can be a lot of things, but we can't be angry (or president, apparently. Or have bodily autonomy in, like, thirty states).

But men are entitled to their anger. It is entertaining, and masculine, and somehow heroic and a sign that they are good fathers even if (and maybe because!) they kill a few people. It's the root of every superhero or action film ever. A man, up against the odds, and deeply *pissed off.* Arnold

Schwarzenegger and Liam Neeson hunted down their daughters' kidnappers. Denzel Washington and Jackie Chan hunted down the kidnappers of the girls they were hired to protect. Sylvester Stallone arm wrestled for custody of his son in *Over the Top* (this movie is very bad, I have seen it many times). There are a thousand men who are fed up and not going to take it anymore, giving very moving monologues about justice and then dropping someone off a building.

The culinary world is an even worse reflection of it. There's Gordon Ramsay, who by 2014 was screaming on approximately two dozen different TV shows across various cable networks. And then later, out of the kitchen, surrounded by his peers, he'd seem perfectly calm and collected. If Ramsay was anything but a white guy with a pompadour of blond hair sitting atop his head like a tuft of cotton candy, this ersatz homage to Jekyll and Hyde would probably result in his experiencing any of the following:

- Having someone gently pat his arm and stage-whisper "calm down" at him
- Only being allowed to cook in a kitchen with plastic spoons for knives and lightbulbs for heat
- A court order that would require him to wear one of those Hannibal Lecter masks around his children
- Forced hysterectomy
- Death

Ramsay is just parroting the culinary environment he was trained in. His mentor was the legendary Marco Pierre

White, who controlled and trained his chefs using what he described as a "theater of cruelty"—in short, straight-up abuse and assault. He would curse and scream, slash their chef whites with knives, throw pots, hang people up by their aprons and throw them in trash cans. He is rumored to have made Ramsay himself cry—a favor Ramsay returned for a new generation of chefs. It isn't just that men (and almost always, specifically white men) are the only ones allowed to get angry; it's that anger is one of the only socially acceptable emotions we allow men to demonstrably feel. Anger is what is considered a secondary emotion—meaning there is another emotion lying underneath. For men, the underlying emotion behind anger is often, according to numerous psychologists, fear. Given the volatile environments of professional kitchens, it makes sense that this fear would be ingrained in generation after generation of chefs, manifesting as rage.

According to the psychologist Sandra Thomas, a leading researcher in the field of gender and anger, anger is often perceived as a distinctly masculine trait. To be overtly enraged and even violent is frequently viewed as an expression of manliness. In that same vein, women are taught that anger is unfeminine, and to suppress it, until one day we drop dead from a lifetime of biting our own tongues.

Because tamping down your emotions is wildly unhealthy, your body eventually says "fuck this" and starts eating itself. According to a report in *The Guardian* ("How Women and Minorities Are Claiming Their Right to Rage"), "Suppressed, repressed, diverted and ignored anger is now understood as a factor in many 'women's illnesses,' including . . . disordered eating, autoimmune diseases, chronic fatigue and pain."

And once again, the groups suppressing their emotions the most, because it's most dangerous for them to express them, are the ones who face the most health issues as a result. The researchers A. Antonio González-Prendes and Shirley Thomas note that Black women are faced with the paradox of having to be seen as pillars of strength (suppressing emotions—particularly anger) while simultaneously feeling powerless from a societal standpoint. As they write in "Powerlessness and Anger in African American Women: The Intersection of Race and Gender," this dynamic results in "heightened levels of emotional distress that include frustration, anger, and resentment." And has been associated with hypertension, coronary heart disease, and numerous other health issues.

The stress of keeping all of this bottled up is literally *killing* marginalized women. And yet the prevailing advice from the CDC and the American Heart Association remains to diet and exercise in the face of heart disease, putting much of the onus of surviving racism and sexism on those experiencing it most acutely.

I had always assumed that I had a relatively good relationship with food and my body. But recently I found myself staring at the reflection of my ass in the mirror and I found it unrecognizable, like some hybrid of Dorian Gray and a *Cathy* cartoon character. When a stylist asked me what I loved about my body, I spent a long time puzzling over an answer before I finally said, "My nipples?" I wasn't sure if I actually had a good relationship with my body or with food or if, like my anger, the problems were there, simmering just below the surface, waiting to come out.

The more I wrote about food, the more fraught this became. I had never tied my worth to what I ate, but now how I was perceived, what I was known for, my career—so much of my literal, *actual* worth—was linked to food. The American dream is to do what you love and get paid for it, which in my case is, obliquely, "consume curly fries." I'd always dreamed of being a food writer, of eating in the footsteps of my heroes, and now that I'd done it, there was a slew of strangers telling me that I was disgusting, that I was fat, or that my body was falling apart because of what I put in it. That I was going to end up incontinent, sitting in my own filth with no one to change me because I was unloved (as someone kindly informed me on Facebook). One woman commented on my blog that my kidneys were probably failing from all the sugar I supposedly ate, and that I should check my pee. If it was cloudy, I was dying, she said, and that was good, because I deserved it. I tried to avoid looking, but the next time I went to the bathroom I couldn't help notice that my urine was slightly opalescent, and I knew this was because I hadn't had enough water, but it also planted a seed of doubt within me that promptly sprouted. Suddenly my body felt like something I was less in control of. And that made me very, very angry, an emotion that I promptly swallowed up.

I had very distinct dietary goals. I wanted to outlive all of these assholes and be healthy enough to dance on their graves.

I decided to talk to a nutritionist.

I was, admittedly, a bit nervous that I might start digging and discover that underneath my veneer of liking food and myself was something insidious and terrible, a nougaty center of self-loathing. I pictured some beautiful, Lycra-clad human walking through my house, throwing food into a giant plastic bag while screaming "NO!" and spraying me with a water bottle full of laxatives. What if I was opening up a Pandora's bread box here?

If I'm being honest, sometimes I look in the mirror and am overtaken by a "demand to speak to the manager because this is unacceptable" sort of energy. I didn't like that "Have you lost weight?" was by default a compliment instead of (1) none of your business and (2) a slight cause for concern because maybe I'd developed a parasite by drinking out of puddles. Also, I didn't really love my thighs? Even though they had never really wronged me in any way, I didn't understand why they weren't prettier. They could be big, but why couldn't they be *pretty*? (And, I was loath to admit it in the dark recesses of my brain, but I felt that prettiness could be imparted upon them if they were only smaller or more muscular.) Also, did anyone like their thighs? Did these people actually exist? And if they did, would they be willing to take me on as their unpaid intern?

There was another problem: I was hungry. Like, all the time. On a given day, usually somewhere between three minutes to an hour after eating, I needed to eat again. I was like a baby panda, but with less fiber in her diet.

And being hungry all the time meant that I was *hangry*

all the time. I spent my waking hours angry at everyone and thinking about pasta, which is terrifying, because I'm pretty sure that's how fascism started in Italy.

The phenomenon of hanger (a portmanteau of "hunger" and "anger") wasn't unique to me. According to Sophie Medlin, chair of the British Dietetic Association in London, a drop in blood sugar causes cortisol and adrenaline—the fight or flight hormones—to rise up. Our bodies feel as if they were under attack when we're hungry, which isn't entirely off base. (Evolutionarily speaking, it makes sense, too. A hungry person who is angry will fight for the food they need to survive.) Biochemically, Medlin says, men have more receptors for neuropeptides—the chemicals that affect the brain and can trigger hanger. So they're theoretically more susceptible to it. Yet in one survey, women—and primarily young women under the age of fifty—were much more likely to report feeling hangry than their male counterparts. Part of that may go back to how women are socialized. If we're taught from a young age that our rage is unladylike and unseemly, we'd be more acutely aware of when that feeling came up.

Even the societal messages around hanger are deeply confusing and sexist, aiming to diminish any legitimate claim women might have to feeling pissed off. Snickers came up with an entire ad campaign around the concept of it— with the tagline "You're not you when you're hungry." It started in early 2010 with a Super Bowl ad that featured Betty White playing football with a crowd of young men. She's uncharacteristically angry, until someone hands her a

Snickers bar. Upon taking a bite, she is instantly transformed back into a young man—presumably her natural form all along. Another spot followed shortly after, with Aretha Franklin on a road trip with several young men. She's complaining about the heat, and her male companions offer up a Snickers because "you're acting like a diva." Again, she's transformed into a young, pleasant man. (Liza Minnelli also makes an appearance as another young man falls prey to hunger and starts complaining.) The campaign has been so successful that Snickers has kept it going, adapting it for Gen Z. A TikTok ad in 2023 features a woman angrily texting her mom group, until someone offscreen hands her a Snickers, and she puts down her phone, happy and appeased. The lesson: Being hangry makes you whiny and demanding and is a distinctly female trait. It's as though the only time a woman *can* be angry is under the guise of hanger. Moreover, men can't feel a version of anger that doesn't involve live hand grenades without literally turning into a woman.

Locally, there was no shortage of nutritionists to choose from. Many of the ones I found were women, and according to their websites they all happened to be gorgeous, with long, shiny hair, sitting on plush chairs, wrapped in blankets, holding mugs. Dogs were often involved. None of them looked as if they'd ever been angry in their lives because it would disturb their plants' auras. Scrolling through their sites, I suddenly had an overwhelming urge to spend $8,000 at Anthropologie.

One nutritionist had a brief questionnaire on their website.

Do you struggle with keeping up motivation and
pushing past obstacles?
Are you repeatedly setting goals only to find them
unrealistic and overwhelming?
Does holding yourself accountable seem like an impossible task?

YES, OBVIOUSLY, ALL OF THESE THINGS, I AM
A WRITER. These are my main personality traits. It took
me a long while to realize that this line of questioning per-
tained to dieting and not to the fact that I have, like, seven
unfinished novels lying around my office. (If you read them,
you will laugh very hard.) (None of them are supposed to be
funny.)

Another website featured a spritely woman with a platinum pixie cut. She talked about helping people reach their
goals—from running a 10K to dropping a pant size. These
were, I should note, not my goals. She began her sessions by
having her clients record their food over several days, and I
found myself lying to her *in my imagination,* so I figured we
weren't a match.

Maybe I was going overboard with this whole project?
But also—what if I went in and found out that I actually
had a terrible relationship with food? At the age of forty-
two, I had never been on a diet and was fairly certain that
I didn't fixate about what I ate, but maybe my insistence
that I didn't fixate and my continued proclamations about
how I'd never been on a diet were a sort of fixation? Maybe
I did care? Maybe this was all a problem? It couldn't possibly be normal to want to scream at the walls at any given

hour of the day. Also, I was pretty sure I was dehydrated all the time.

I found two nutritionists whose websites felt as if they aligned with my view of food—as something that you eat several times every day, as something that needn't be tracked like a fugitive on the lam. I immediately made appointments with both of them.

My first call was with Minh-Hai Alex, a registered dietitian who grew up in the restaurant industry (her parents left Vietnam and opened a New York–style deli in Dallas). I told her a bit about my concerns. That I thought I had a pretty good relationship with food, though sometimes, due to the obligations of my work, I had to drink Flamin' Hot Cheetos–flavored soda. My biggest problem was that the food I ate during the day didn't seem to keep me full: I'd eat breakfast, and a few hours later I'd be hungry again. It was a struggle to get through to lunch, and again to dinner. By the time I finally ate, I was so ravenous I wolfed down food while getting very angry about things that I had said were totally *fine*.

I wanted tips for food that would keep me full longer and decrease my chances of being the unwitting subject of a viral video titled "Old Lady Losing It at Whole Foods."

"Why don't you have a snack?" she asked.

Honestly, imagine how bad things are that Minh-Hai was like "If you are hungry, eat," and my response was to be absolutely astonished by this radical way of thinking.

Why didn't I? Because it felt Sisyphean. I would eat my

carrot sticks and hummus, or my handful of berries and nuts (which, thanks to *Vogue,* a publication I do not even read, I had somehow concluded were the only snacks that have ever existed). And then I'd be hungry thirty seconds later because I'd consumed approximately eighty calories, which is less than what I burned getting the snack together in the first place. It never occurred to me to change these habits. I just assumed I didn't like almonds enough. Which is ridiculous, because I like almonds the maximum amount a person can like almonds, which is "barely."

If I was working on a project, I didn't want to stop to snack again and again. So I would keep going through the hunger, as if I were somehow accomplishing something. And I was! I was giving myself a headache and hating every person who ever existed, but especially my husband, because he was nearby.

Minh-Hai explained that it was pretty common for people to need to eat more than three times a day and that the breakfast-lunch-dinner model worked for very few people.

"It's hard to imagine a meal that keeps you full for six hours," she said. "Three to four hours is much more likely." She noted that it was common to eat five to six times a day (that she herself did) and that most people needed two breakfasts or two lunches.

TWO BREAKFASTS OR TWO LUNCHES. This was chaos. This was literally how hobbits ate, and yet no magazines were telling us how to get a perfect Frodo-body ready in time for summer. It made perfect sense to, like, *eat when you are hungry,* but I couldn't put my finger on why this was so incomprehensible. Until finally the words came out.

Wouldn't two lunches or two breakfasts mean that I would con-
sume too many calories?

There it was. The thing that I didn't think mattered
to me.

Minh-Hai told me that I shouldn't be concerned with
that over the course of a day. I needed to trust that I'd eat
the amount of food I needed. She advised me to think of
hunger as a spectrum—with 1 or 2 being hangry (my natural
state of being), 5 being neutral, 9 being uncomfortably full,
and 10 being a food coma. She explained that there was a
pendulum quality to hunger: If you were at a 1 or 2, you
were more likely to end up eating to the point of 9 or 10.
This was wreaking havoc on my blood sugar, causing me to
feel weak before I ate and leading me to crash after.

"But you can always trust your hunger," she said. "It's
synonymous with peeing." No one ever said that they
couldn't possibly go to the bathroom again because they'd
just gone half an hour earlier. (Though truthfully I often
had thought this. I was constantly ignoring what my body
told me it needed.)

Minh-Hai adhered to a philosophy of "body trust"—of
feeling at peace with and at home in our bodies, of tuning in
and listening to cues like hunger or exhaustion, instead of
just ignoring them. One of the examples she cited on her
website of dismissing these cues was precisely the way I had
been—by ignoring hunger because it was too early to eat or
because we'd just had lunch. The philosophy is outlined in
Hilary Kinavey and Dana Sturtevant's book *Reclaiming Body
Trust,* in which they note that most people are born with
body trust (this is why babies are so confident) and that a

thousand things can happen which may rupture that relationship as we move through our lives. Negative comments from peers and family, depictions in the media, fatphobia, sexism, racism, transphobia, homophobia, and the entire institution of junior high gym class all erode the comfort that we have in our own bodies. Sometimes we don't even realize this is happening! We just slowly start thinking that we're a less sexy version of the Skeksis from *The Dark Crystal* and this is a reasonable reflection of reality, and it's all our fault and we deserve to die alone under a pile of mismatched socks.

The stealth of this self-hate is by design. The narrative around dieting has changed drastically in the last forty years, become obfuscated, harder to even identify as that. I'd grown up seeing weight loss commercials on TV, the latest celebrity wearing fitted clothing and talking about how Weight Watchers or Jenny Craig had transformed their bodies. In the 1990s the Duchess of York, Sarah Ferguson, showed photos of herself before weight loss as she walked around a white empty space in a formfitting dress. And look, I don't recognize any monarch but the Burger King, but imagine having an *actual* royal title and simultaneously feeling as though you aren't good enough? Even Oprah— OPRAH! (whom I have met in person and it was a little bit like what I imagine it is like for devout Catholics to meet the pope?), who needs approval from no one because she is literally Oprah!—is a Weight Watchers spokesperson. There was no genre of celebrity who could escape it. While women were predominantly featured, men didn't get a free pass; even Tommy Lasorda was hawking SlimFast in 1989. The legendary Dodgers' manager talked about how after his two shakes he could eat whatever he wanted for dinner—"Even pasta!" At the tender age of nine, this commercial taught me two things:

1. Pasta—the thing my family literally ate every single day—was somehow a decadent food?

2. Tommy Lasorda, a man who surrounded himself with hairy men who were professional spitters (I didn't yet understand how baseball worked), was concerned about his body image.

In the 2010s, as body acceptance supposedly rose, a cultural shift moved us away from dieting to the world of "wellness" while still adhering to the same rules—calorie restriction and food elimination. The only difference was the goals were harder to argue against; everyone was picking up trendy eating disorders not to be skinny, or so they claimed, but to be "healthy," to improve gut flora, to boost their energy levels, even though none of that was necessarily true. Whole30—the recent wellness diet that I'd watched several of my friends submit themselves to like some weird Lenten abuse—had, according to many experts, all the medical benefits of rubbing crystals on your butt cheeks. While cutting out alcohol, lowering carbs, and reducing your sugar intake may cause you to lose weight, avoiding legumes and dairy (which the diet requires) could lead to dietary deficiencies. And the rigidity of it—the idea of being unable to engage with people in social settings that involved food, of needing to carry your own food with you, of not allowing any sort of flexibility in your diet—was counterintuitive to what a healthy relationship with food should be. And now a dangerous connection had been made: Thin was healthy, fat was not, and all of this was supposedly in our hands.

But the morality of diets was even harder to argue against now; to do so meant you were arguing against the notion of being healthy. The shifting narrative around dieting from weight loss to wellness is just another way to disguise society's total disgust with our bodies, no matter the size. We are told to embrace and love ourselves just as we are and at the same time told to change and improve ourselves through food restriction and extreme exercise. Gwyneth Paltrow built a Goop empire based on health and "clean beauty," on vitamin supplements and $1,000 "wellness table lamps" (that promise to bring the "biological benefits of natural light indoors." Basically a window). "Food is the cornerstone of health," Goop's website says, but Paltrow's most recent foray into dealing with symptoms of long COVID involved a diet that seemed like a thinly veiled eating disorder (it included beef broth for breakfast, beef broth for lunch, and then, for dinner, a sensible beef broth). And when she started working with the celebrity trainer Tracy Anderson, the discussion that emerged was how Anderson could address Paltrow's "problem areas" including her "long butt," which is *not a thing*. (Seriously, do an internet search. The only things that this phrase yields are a specific type of vacuuming apparatus and stories about Gwyneth's butt.) We are literally inventing new expressions to describe the issues we have with women's bodies. While defining the latest restrictive fad diet for someone, I realized I was also describing orthorexia nervosa—the obsessive focus on healthy eating and restrictive dietary practices that can lead to malnutrition, anxiety, social isolation, and an inability to eat in a natural, intuitive manner.

"Nobody is immune," Minh-Hai said gently, when she saw the look on my face, telegraphing the feeling that I had fundamentally failed.

She left me with one final piece of advice that I held on to like a piece of flotsam on a tempest-tossed sea. "Give yourself permission to snack," she said.

My next call was with Natalie Joffe. Natalie is a former Junior Olympic skier who, like Minh-Hai, also focused on the concept of body trust. She said that one of the problems for our culture was that we had too simplistic a view of health. It's often defined as a simple matter of weight, which correlates to your BMI (body mass index), but these measurements aren't good indicators of health. The model was well over a hundred years old, pioneered by the Belgian polymath Adolphe Quetelet. He believed that there was beauty in the statistically average form (derived from, it should be noted, a group of white northern European men), though this was a theoretical concept, found only in the ideal. All human features and all individuals deviated from this average ideal in some form or another, and so those who deviated further and further from this so-called average, those at the long tail of the bell curve, were outside the norm, and he considered them less beautiful. (Which is a bold claim from a guy whose looks can best be described as "What if Oscar the Grouch were a person?") His idea of the beauty of "normality" would be held as the standard by eugenicists (including literal Nazis) for decades to come. Despite this, BMI is still widely used in the medical community (hell, even my doctor's office noted my BMI last time I went in, and the CDC has BMI calculators on its website). It measures not how healthy someone is but solely how much they might deviate from an antiquated notion of what "average" is. The system is so broken that according to the BMI, Dwayne "the Rock" Johnson is unhealthy. DWAYNE "THE ROCK" JOHNSON, WHO LOOKS AS IF HE HAS BEEN CHISELED FROM SEXY MARBLE, IS SUPPOSEDLY UNHEALTHY.

Natalie and I talk about how "healthism" is pervasive in our society—the idea that our health is in our control. The equivalency of weight and health means that fat people are likely to be subjected to medical bias, to have their issues overlooked or dismissed by doctors, and to be blamed for any illness they experience. It's as if they could somehow heal themselves through dieting. Medical bias means that people in larger bodies have their cancer overlooked, their pains ignored, the root cause of all of their ailments attributed to their fatness. A friend of mine was recently told to lose weight while at the *optometrist*.

"Even glossy women's magazines now model skepticism toward top-down narratives about how we should look, who and when we should marry, how we should live. But the psychological parasite of the ideal woman has evolved to survive in an ecosystem that pretends to resist her," the author Jia Tolentino writes in *Trick Mirror.* "Feminism has not eradicated the tyranny of the ideal woman, but, rather, has entrenched it and made it trickier." We can't talk about food without getting pulled into the world of dieting and wellness, one that was now entwined with a particular sort of lifestyle, with a thin—pun intended—notion of feminism itself. We are no longer fighting against ideal body image, but rather against the concept of strong bodies, of healthiness, of feeling confident and powerful, of sitting on couches with long hair and cuddling dogs, drinking tea by ourselves. We are now allowed to be hungry for so many things—allowed to want more, to demand equal pay, to not want to sacrifice career for family or vice versa. But this ignores the fact that if someone asks if we are literally hungry, the only acceptable answer is no.

Natalie says it's difficult—but essential—to decouple the idea of health and weight. People can be healthy at any size, she tells me; there are a thousand other elements to an individual's health: how much sleep you get, your relationships with friends and family, your mental health, your genetics. Her philosophy is that prescribing weight loss to people in larger bodies (both she and Minh-Hai avoided words like "overweight" and "obese") is unethical.

"It would be like a doctor prescribing a patient a drug that has a 95 percent chance of not working, and a good chance that it might make things worse."

A study by the National Institutes of Health that followed *The Biggest Loser* contestants after six years found that of fourteen individuals they looked at, all but one had regained a significant amount of the weight they had lost.

There were permanent legacies of their weight loss, albeit not the ones they had intended: Their resting metabolisms were even slower now than they had been, and their hunger-controlling hormone was half of what it once was. "In short, the contestants burned fewer calories and felt less full than before they ever set foot on the ranch," *The Cut* reported in 2016.

In the U.K., a nearly decade-long study took a look at 279,000 people in larger bodies (the study uses the terms "obese" and "morbidly obese") attempting to lose weight. It found that virtually no one could. The findings were that less than 1 of every 210 men attained a "normal" weight (their words), and 1 of every 124 women did so.

And those who did, keep in mind, were now likely to feel hungrier and burn fewer calories than they did before.

Natalie explains that the practices associated with weight loss—calorie counting, exercising simply to lose weight, a hyper focus on the healthiness of food—are practices that she doesn't want to encourage in people. (The former *Biggest Loser* finalist Kai Hibbard has talked about how the show gave her an eating disorder; she was vomiting up food and her hair was falling out as she worked out up to eight hours a day. Rachel Frederickson won the fifteenth season of the show at 105 pounds, which, on her five-foot-four frame, looked skeletal. During the finale, the camera panned to the trainer Jillian Michaels, who was visibly alarmed as she mouthed "Oh my God" at Frederickson's gaunt appearance.) There was a morality tied to it—that losing weight was somehow good and gaining it was bad. Suddenly, neutral experiences—like, Natalie says, trying on a pair of pants and finding them to be too small—take on a different cadence. And because weight loss is a multibillion-dollar industry, this is something we all are convinced we can control and change.

Ostensibly, of course, all of this makes sense. But in practice, it's harder to accept. There are real implications to being fat in our society. Myriad studies have found that thinner women were actually paid more than their larger peers. For a long time, the link between poverty and being fat has always been framed as one of accessibility to certain foods. Healthier foods—fruits and vegetables and non-processed grains—generally cost more. But these findings suggested something else: that being thin has financial rewards. And there are huge societal stigmas to being in a larger body. The author and activist Lindy West has written about fatness for well over a decade. She has had to defend her own humanity for simply being larger than average.

When I bring this up to Natalie, she nods. "We live in a culture of weight bias," she says. "The system exists, and there's no denying it's real. . . . But do you want to stand for it? Or do you want to fight against it?"

It's harder to be fat in our world than it is to not be. But I was blaming the wrong thing. I was blaming the fatness, instead of a world that made it difficult.

"It's easy for you to have a healthy body image," a colleague of mine told me. "Because you aren't fat. And you fit into a lot of the categories of what we're told is beautiful."

And it's true! I make jokes about swallowing food whole

as if I were a dolphin because that's one of the things you get to do when you're "average"-sized. Except I am constantly being told I am a stupid, fat piece of garbage, too! There are, undoubtedly, layers of privilege inherent in my body. But to say that it's easier to have a healthy body image because I'm closer to Quetelet's bullshit ideal average just seems to reinforce that way of thinking—one that is so unkind to *all of us*. It's time for us to recognize that there is no us versus them, no skinny versus fat, no body type that grants you exemption from this judgment. The one thing we all have in common, the one constant feature of being a human in a body, is that someone, somewhere is going to make you feel bad about it. As Lindy West writes, "Everybody is in pain. We all suffer from this hierarchy of bodies. The people lashing out and the people pleading for help exist on the same spectrum."

Anger, when left unattended, isn't that different from hunger. It doesn't go away. It just grows, until it becomes unwieldly and you find yourself in a parking lot, watching two pigeons fight over an everything bagel and wondering if you should join in. Like hunger, anger requires you to trust yourself. To know that what you are feeling isn't crazy, or silly, or irrational. I'd suppressed my negative feelings so much they only came out when I hadn't eaten, and by then it was an uncontrollable thing, something I didn't know how to calm down except by throwing bread at it.

Angry, hungry, fat—these are things women aren't supposed to be. We need, in every single way possible, to take up as little space as we can. Violate this, and you will be made to feel as though you'll wake up and find that undefinable, nebulous thing that makes us all women has broken free from your body and is lying on the bed, like the tail of a startled lizard, still twitching, no longer a part of you.

My Batali and Bros' essays were outlets for pent-up emotions that had nowhere else to go. Putting those words out into the world was in direct defiance of what I was taught. The second I unleashed them I was told I was ugly and wrong and stupid and hateful and ugly (truly, I cannot overstate the ugliness, basically a proboscis monkey in a dress). Everyone is socialized to buy into this dynamic. Women are taught we won't be seen as lovable or feminine or that we can't have salt if we get angry. Men are taught that if they show compassion or gentleness or sensitivity, they aren't men.

In response to my posts, people I had never met told me that the food I ate was delicious and that I was wrong for disliking it, as though they were more reliable narrators than I was for my own lived experiences. That I had never experienced sexism, that there was no such *thing* as sexism, honestly what a stupid whorish thing to think in the first place. It was very tempting to backtrack, to turn tail while screaming over my shoulder, "OMG, you're right, I *am* a man-hating bitch, I'll go delete everything I've ever written, thanks!!!! P.S. I bet you *are* great in bed!"

Not because I *believed* it, but because I didn't want to be assaulted by my inbox anymore.

I briefly thought I was to blame for bringing this all upon myself. But like fatness, my anger or the way I'd expressed it wasn't the problem. The problem was how people reacted to it. Society doesn't want these things—fat people, angry women, and, God, definitely not fat, angry women—to exist in the first place. And so we blame ourselves, we suppress our anger, we don't eat, we hate what we see in the mirror.

I'm tired of feeling that way. I like who I am. I like eating. I like the creativity that emerges when I allow myself to feel my anger. It makes my writing better. This was the other component of this dynamic that no one had told us: that in being robbed of our rage, we've also been robbed of our power.

But anger, wielded properly, doesn't make a person unhinged or malicious or violent. It doesn't mean that they'll be dumping people into trash cans or slashing their chef coats with kitchen knives.

It means they cook and eat and create.

Throughout the culinary world, female chefs are expressing their feelings as they foster better culinary environments for the people they work with. Tangerine Jones, the voice behind RageBaking.com (and the Instagram account of the same name), writes that "Black folks are never allowed to admit when we're tired and why and we're certainly not afforded our legitimate and justified rage." She turned to her kitchen, a place that was sacred and meaningful to her and her community, not to lose her fury or swallow it but to channel it for good.

"I wanted to get my heart right, renew my hope and find a way forward."

She has fought hunger in her New York community, handed out treats to strangers on her commute, delivered baked goods to social justice nonprofits. She writes that she is reminded in her kitchen that "fury is fuel, sorrow can be turned into joy."

At HAGS in New York, Chef Telly Justice and her business and life partner, Camille Lindsley, aim to make their restaurant a welcoming, queer space. Both of them faced harassment and discrimination in their past roles. Lindsley, a queer female sommelier, told *Eater,* "Horrible things are said to me and to other people all the time. Sexual harassment and assault are just rampant in this industry, and racism and homophobia are rampant as well."

Justice is trans, and was told by one employer that she couldn't be out at work.

"I got very angry . . . and I never stopped being angry," she said.

How have they dealt with that anger? By opening HAGS. They've focused not just on the comfort of their guests but on the comfort of their staff as well, obliterating the stuffiness that often comes with fine dining. And obliterating the hostile environment that they dealt with. Everywhere, female chefs are challenging the long-held notion that in order to run a successful kitchen, you need to reenact key scenes from *The Shining.*

"I'm not going to get what I want by screaming. I get better food by challenging cooks in different ways," Suzanne Cupps, executive chef of Untitled at the Whitney Museum of American Art, told *Vogue.* Her background is in teaching, and she emphasizes a culture of learning in her kitchens— a radical shift from existing models where younger chefs emulate their mentors, re-creating both their dishes and their rage.

"I love to show and explore with other people rather than me getting to do all of the fun creative things and then demanding that others work the same way," she said in an interview with Battman's Chef Connection in 2018. "When you don't raise your voice too much or you don't put people down, and you have a calm demeanor, then other people follow in that way."

These feel like radical acts, but in every instance it is just women listening to their instincts. They do not ignore or swallow their feelings. They reckon with their anger, they turn it into action, they lead by example, they teach and create. In the face of so many voices telling us to do otherwise, it is a miraculous thing: to feel our feelings, to eat when we are hungry, to trust our bodies and ourselves.

17

A MOMENT IN PIE

I am standing in my kitchen, a little angry and a little tipsy. I am on step 3 of 196 of a recipe for Nesselrode pie, which you have never heard of. (No, you haven't. Stop it.) Nesselrode pie was popular for a few decades in the twentieth century, from the 1940s to the 1960s, after which it virtually disappeared, like the practice of people wearing dress hats and gloves when they went out, or day drinking at the office, or menstrual pads you had to strap onto your body like a paratrooper putting on a chute. I would argue that Nesselrode pie is the culinary equivalent of the dodo bird, except that the culinary equivalent of the dodo bird *is* the dodo bird. (Which we literally ate into extinction. Screw you, nature!) It's something supposedly delicious, now gone forever. Unless you are a ninety-five-year-old man from Brooklyn, back before it was trendy, Nesselrode pie does not exist for you.

Seymour, my grandfather-in-law, is a ninety-five-year-old

man from Brooklyn, back before it was trendy. And so, for the last twenty years, I have listened to stories of this dessert, the gastronomical equivalent of a lost love, the pie that got away. I took one look at the recipe, a culinary relic full of antiquated flavors and elaborate techniques (chestnuts, candied cherries, a custard allowed to partially set then combined with whipped egg whites), and told him I would make this freezer pie for him when the temperature in hell was suitably cold enough.

So, anyway, here I am in my kitchen, making Nesselrode pie. I am accidentally drunk. (I lied before when I said I was tipsy.) The list of people/entities with whom I have grievances is constantly being updated in my head, but is currently as follows:

- The editors of *Saveur* magazine, who keep saying things like "Stir the pot of custard constantly. Don't take your eyes off the pot. You must have your entire attention on the pot of custard or it will curdle. Don't do anything else. Maybe stop breathing for a while. While you are stirring the pot of custard, whip the egg whites into soft peaks and chop up the cherries."
- My husband, who told my grandfather-in-law that I was taking on this baking endeavor before I had completed it, thereby obligating me to finish instead of letting me abandon it and instead eat Chex Mix and play on my phone as God intended.
- My mother, who, a month earlier, made the second-worst pie I had ever eaten *in my life* in honor of my

aforementioned grandfather-in-law's birthday, thus propelling me to make this dessert as filial recompense.

- Marcel Proust, the poetic fucker.

There is a notable omission on this list; when it is your ninety-fifth birthday, you are allowed to make egregious dessert demands. You are almost a century old. When you reach triple digits, you can probably go around punching everyone in the balls and have people just be like, "Oh, aren't they an absolute *gas?*" Pretty sure AARP solidified this right.

I probably need to drink some water. I am also probably not in a condition to use my kitchen appliances. I immediately push these very reasonable thoughts out of my head. Because I have a pie to make.

Nesselrode was a nobleman, a nineteenth-century Russian diplomat who signed the Treaty of Paris after the Russians lost the Crimean War. He also liked chestnuts (which were basically the equivalent of Cadbury creme eggs in the nineteenth century). So much so that his name became synonymous with them. (I try to imagine this level of cultural culinary saturation—if people were like, "I need a Geraldine," and this was understood collectively to mean that you needed a soft pretzel the size of a Buick. It must be something close to godhood.) Apparently, he also wanted his food to get him absolutely wasted, like any good politician. And so Nesselrode puddings were all the rage in the Victorian era, and I like to think that people were absolutely getting sauced on these chunky dried fruit alcohol puddings and showing off flashes of ankle. Sometime in the 1940s, a woman named Hortense Spier (whose name we will not make fun of because *I am literally named Geraldine*) who owned a restaurant on Manhattan's Upper West Side came up with the radical idea of turning the dessert into a pie. She decided to add gelatin to the mix, because gelatin made up roughly half of the food pyramid at the time. And so she created a much lighter, airier dessert that still got you drunk. New Yorkers were delighted and showed whatever the 1940s equivalent of ankle was. (Spoiler: It was still just ankle.)

Spier started selling her confection to restaurants from her wholesale bakery. Nesselrode became a hit across the city. After Spier's death a few decades later, the bakery closed, and the pie essentially disappeared, perhaps owing to the complicated nature of the recipe and a waning enthusiasm for desserts derived from connective tissues. The author Bernard Gwertzman recounted trying to find the pie upon returning to New York from D.C. in 1987. "As far as I could determine—this was not a scientific survey, mind you—Nesselrode was apparently no more. . . . It seemed to have gone to the equivalent of food heaven."

The following year, a journalist for *The New York Times* asked local restaurant luminaries about the pie; while most were familiar with the name, they couldn't say what the dish consisted of. Today, most people I asked hadn't even heard of it.

But Seymour—Papa to his family, Si to his friends, "Old Man, I will make it look like an accident" to me—had consistently talked about it for as long as I'd known him. Online, the recipes I found were sparse and rather inconsistent. Chestnuts, once the linchpin of the dish, didn't always appear. A 1945 recipe in *The New York Times* omits them entirely, but this might have been a wartime adjustment. The dish caps off a suggested menu with asterisks placed next to rationed grocery items (breakfast is oatmeal; lunch is Welsh rarebit—four ounces of cheese accompanied by a side of pickles; dinner is baked beans with a side of spinach and coleslaw. At that point, I'm guessing that dried fruit gelatin pie would have felt like a Napoleonic level of decadence). Another recipe from 1988 involves the consumption of a lot of raw eggs, which I'm not entirely comfortable feeding to a nonagenarian, despite my earlier threats. Some recipes call for Nesselrode mix, which is no longer commercially available, but you can make a variant at home, usually consisting of some combination of dried fruits, candied citrus, almonds or pecans, coconut, and chestnuts. Some recipes call for rum. Others for brandy. My only solution is to call Seymour up and ask him what he remembers about the pie.

"I remember I ate it with a fork," he says dryly. This is not very helpful.

"That is very helpful," I say.

"You're welcome."

I ask him if there were chestnuts in the pie. He tells me he can't recall. Candied fruits or just cherries? He's not sure. I ask him again what he does remember. He vaguely describes an alcohol-infused chiffon pie with chocolate shavings on top, and some candied fruit. But then he tells me something else. Back when he lived in Brooklyn, his friends the Dilberts would bring a pie over to dinner, or he and his wife would bring one over to them. A ritualistic pastry, passed back and forth.

This was when his son, who died young, was still alive. This was before he was a widower. When his family surrounded him and his friends were close by. This is not a pie. This is a moment in time.

This is a lot of pressure to put on someone who is accidentally drunk.

The madeleine de Proust is the most famous literary device tied to a baked good, probably. Proust wrote about how the senses could bring someone back to a particular moment in time; for him, the flavors of a madeleine, an unassuming little butter sponge cake dipped in tea, were evocative of his childhood and a specific instance when his mother served him this treat. If you ever make madeleines, and I have, they are fine. A pretty dessert, but rather plain. They do not, they never can quite, have the importance they had for Proust. That's the nature of it.

Re-creating a recipe, or someone's memory of it, is a lofty endeavor. It is not simply that memories are unreliable things, malleable and transitory and a little bit squishy. But how things actually taste to us is not a constant. Our taste buds change over time; as children we are more inclined to sweetness, an evolutionary by-product linked to our survival (breast milk is, supposedly, quite sweet). As adults, this proclivity wanes. As we age, our taste buds, which once numbered close to ten thousand and regenerated every one to two weeks, have stopped rising from the ashes so readily. They decline in number, they start to shrink, our saliva begins to dry up, our sense of smell diminishes, and basically our bodies decide that we shouldn't get any pleasure from eating anymore, in order to save the tenderest bits of woolly mammoth for the younger, firmer generation who understands how to use TikTok.

Not to mention that food itself has fundamentally changed. The fruits and vegetables we find in grocery stores today are completely different varieties from the ones available decades ago. The same volatile compounds that contributed to a tomato's taste and aroma also made it more vulnerable to bruising; the produce now has a longer shelf life, but at the sacrifice of flavor. The reason artificial banana flavoring tastes so unlike grocery store bananas is that it's based on another species (we get Cavendish bananas in stores, whereas artificial banana flavoring is based on the Gros Michel variety of the fruit, which was widely available in stores until the 1950s, when it went almost extinct due to a widespread fungus). And sometimes, things just change. Most McDonald's enthusiasts will tell you about the dark day in 1992 when the chain forever altered its recipe for apple pies—opting to bake instead of deep frying them.

Layer on top of this the hazy filter of memory, and a lofty culinary endeavor becomes near impossible.

Flavor is a combination of many factors. Our tongues do not simply act alone, as anyone with a cold will readily tell you. You likely remember the diagram of the tongue, shown to you in science class sometime in the fifth grade or so, the parts of it segmented like a side of beef on a butcher's chart. The different areas denoted for salty, sweet, sour, bitter, and, unbeknownst to me when I was in school, umami (though this last flavor was discovered by Kikunae Ikeda in 1908, it would take the scientific community nearly a hundred years before they acknowledged it). The nose plays a critical role—interpreting aroma that, in conjunction with taste (and texture and temperature and spiciness), helps create flavor. It is also the sense most associated with memory. Scent is so evocative that scientists believe that kissing might have evolved from early humans sniffing one another and someone accidentally landing on someone else's mouth.

That's the problem with any madeleine de Proust; the recipe itself is merely a starting point. I could make Hortense Spier's pie exactly as she did. But that doesn't mean it would taste the same to my grandfather-in-law, a lifetime later. I settle on *Saveur*'s recipe for Nesselrode pie because it calls for ingredients that I can find online and does not require the bevy of nuts that my husband, the drama queen, is allergic to (it does contain chestnuts, but he can eat those, and I do not ask him what sort of culinary Russian roulette he played to determine all of this). I start the night before—blind baking a crust for the pie. The process necessitates lining an unbaked pastry shell with parchment and filling it with pie weights (in my case, uncooked dried beans). I'd done this once before, years earlier, but omitted the parchment, and so my home smelled vaguely of pastry and beans. I did not make this mistake twice.

The next morning, I embark on the filling. I mash

roasted chestnuts (which I have managed to find, pre-roasted and vacuum sealed, thanks to the internet) with a bit of sugar and rum. I have miscalculated the amount of liquor I need and am left with extra rum in the measuring cup. Owning to a sort of frugality I cannot explain, I elect to drink it rather than throw it out. I do not drink often and I have not eaten lunch.

So now I am drunk.

Next, I make a custard. This necessitates the separating of eggs, which is difficult if you are sober, and if you are drunk, it is basically like asking a monkey for legal advice. I manage to get three yolks and three whites in two separate bowls. The yolks begin cooking with cream and milk and sugar and gelatin, and I am diligently stirring while holding my candy thermometer in the liquid. At 180 degrees, I turn off the heat, dump in more rum and the chestnut puree, and place the entire thing in a chilled bowl to cool. The instructions say that I need to spend the next hour stirring the custard every ten minutes and return it to the fridge each time, but I don't have the time to do that, so I cool it by setting the bowl over another one filled with ice and stir until my vision goes blurry. I do not recommend this tactic. The custard is nearly fully set before I need it to be.

Saveur then instructs me to make a sugar syrup on the stove while simultaneously (HOW? I AM NOT A ROBOT. I AM NOT EVEN SOBER) whipping my egg whites into soft peaks. I then slowly beat the hot sugar syrup into the egg whites, gently cooking them, creating an Italian meringue. I do this, but I notice a distinctly fishy smell starts emanating from my eggs; apparently, this is a result of omega-3s. I begin to panic slightly. To calm myself, I eat more custard, which is extremely rummy.

I fold the egg white into the custard in a series of increasingly complex steps so the meringue doesn't deflate. I fill the pastry shell halfway, then add chopped macerated cherries (which I do not have, but maraschino is a good substitute) into the remaining filling and top the pastry shell with the rest of it. I let the pie chill for four hours.

Before serving, I top it with some artful dollops of sweetened whipped cream, more cherries, and shaved chocolate.

Given my family's predilection for setting the pastry baking bar so low as to be several feet below the Earth's crust, I tend to get a little smug when something I bake doesn't seem to be haunted by the soul of a Depression-era orphan. Many, many hours after I've started, my Nesselrode pie looks almost exactly like the picture in the magazine, I have nearly sobered up, and I am very humbly screaming "I AM A DESSERT GOD" every time Rand tries to speak to me.

Before I serve the Nesselrode pie, I sniff it, to see if the fishy scent from the eggs is still there. It is gone. There is only a whiff of vanilla and rum and something rich and creamy. I have no association with it, not yet, but it smells a little like eggnog.

I serve Seymour a slice of Nesselrode pie at dinner that night with my mother and brother-in-law, Evan, after painstakingly detailing the cooking process to him, so he knows how much to love and appreciate me.

"Does it taste right?" I ask. I know that he will tell me.

"It does," Seymour says. "The one I remember was a bit lighter. But yes. It's very similar." And he is quiet, which is out of character. He looks a little sad and a little happy, all at once.

We manage to eat half of the pie, a solid showing for five people. The flavor, for the rest of us, is something totally new. "I've never had anything like it," Rand says. It is cold and creamy, like something between a fruitcake and a custard, rummy and nutty. My associations with it now exist only there, that night, surrounded by everyone I love most. I wrap up the rest and send it home with Seymour. He hugs me tightly.

"When are you making this for me again?" he asks.

"Never," I tell him.

I am forty-two, and soon this will no longer be true. There was a time when I realistically had sixty years ahead of me, and seventy, and eighty, and a time before that when I had my entire life. An endless set of choices branching out, limitless and terrifying and exciting. Now I might have as many days left as are behind me. It's an optimistic take, to think that my time on this earth is only half through. That I will, years from now, come across the photos I took yesterday and marvel at how young I was. It's all so uncertain and there's no guarantee to any of it. As a writer, it's a maddening thing—that I have no idea how or when my story ends.

I will never be that young again. I will never be *this* young again. The constant truism of existence, of time marching forward.

I do not know what mortality looks like when you are in your mid-nineties. The idea of being without Seymour is hard to imagine. I've had him in my life longer than I haven't: twenty-two years. Some days I call him by his first name. But sometimes, I call him Papa, the way Rand does, because I realize how rare and wonderful it is to have someone in your life whom you call by a name dearer than the one they were born with.

On a phone call, Rand asks him how he is feeling, and Seymour, Papa, laughs.

"Well, you know, I'm not ninety anymore," he says.

I wonder what it is to look back at your life from his vantage point. It feels rude to ask. Instead, I simply inquire what he wants for dessert. When he tells me, I assume that this pie is just a way of reliving his own memories. I don't see his answer for what it is: a way of sharing those memories with us. That for a little while, Nesselrode pie is no longer simply a part of the past, and neither are those pastry exchanges with the Dilberts he once had. That maybe a recipe is a way of keeping the people you love alive forever.

A few days later, friends come over to dinner. I am in my kitchen, making madeleines for dessert. The homage feels a little forced, but no one seems to mind when cake is involved. As we wait for them to bake, I tell my guests the story of the pie, of how long it took.

"I'll have to make it for you sometime."

"It sounds like so much work," someone says.

"It is," I reply. But it is a small sacrifice to make, a relatively insignificant piece of time and energy in exchange for the enduring memory of a dish. The madeleines are almost done. The timer is about to go off. Tear it off the wall, hurl it to the ground, on a grand, cosmic scale, it keeps ticking. There is no stopping the clock. But sometimes we can slow it down. We can make the recipes and eat the food that reminds us of our loved ones, and it is as though they were with us. And for a fleeting moment we have all the time in the world.

ACKNOWLEDGMENTS

While I am quick to complain of too many cooks in the kitchen, the same is not true of a book—everyone who has contributed to this project has made it infinitely better, and I am grateful beyond measure for their help, their patience, their advice, and their support.

As always, I would be utterly lost without Zoe Sandler, an incredible agent, a mover of mountains, and calmer of worries. Zoe, you endure emails from me at all hours filled with existential concerns and book ideas, and always answer with patience and thoughtfulness. You are the best.

This book would not be what it is without the editorial skills of Aubrey Martinson, who saw its potential from the beginning, whose keen eye and expertise touch every single one of these pages. Thank you, Aubrey. For making me a better writer, for pushing me in all the right ways, for making this book what it is.

I owe immense gratitude to the entire team at Crown who helped make this book a reality, including Ada Yonenaka, Angela McNally, Susan Turner, Anna Kochman, Sally Franklin, Allison Fox, Gillian Blake, Emily Kimball, and Ingrid Sterner.

A huge thanks to Andy Young, for his diligent fact-checking, and for keeping me laughing.

A special thank you to Mikki Kendall for explaining to me (over Twitter!) questions I had about the *Green Book* and Black dining halls in America during the 1940s.

To Jessie Liu, I am eternally grateful for your bravery, for sharing your story, and for continuing to be a force for good in the culinary world. I can't wait to see what you do next.

To the Gretchens, thank you for believing in me (and this project) from the very beginning.

To everyone who gave me advice, who contributed their expertise, and assisted me in countless ways, and whose works are cited in this book: Thank you.

To my family: Thank you for teaching me the beauty of cooking for the people you love.

And, finally, to Rand Fishkin: Thank you for feeding me and for believing in me. You are my very favorite person.

BIBLIOGRAPHY

Amnesty International. "Crowdsourced Twitter Study Reveals Shocking Scale of Online Abuse Against Women." Press release, Dec. 18, 2018.

Basow, Susan A., and Alexandra Minieri. "'You Owe Me': Effects of Date Cost, Who Pays, Participant Gender, and Rape Myth Beliefs on Perceptions of Rape." *Journal of Interpersonal Violence* 26, no. 3 (2011): 479–97. doi:10.1177 /0886260510363421.

Cayton, Horace, and St. Clair Drake. *Black Metropolis: A Study of Negro Life in a Northern City.* Chicago: University of Chicago Press, 1993.

Cooley, Angela Jill. *To Live and Dine in Dixie: The Evolution of Urban Food Culture in the Jim Crow South.* Athens: University of Georgia Press, 2015.

"The Culinary Mystery of Nesselrode Pie." *The New York Times,* Dec. 7, 1988.

Dawn, Randee. "27 Courses, Very Little Edible: Review of Michelin-Starred Restaurant Goes Viral." *Today,* Dec. 9, 2021.

Duggan, Maeve. "Online Harassment 2017." Pew Research Center, July 11, 2017.

Eplett, Layla. "Eating Jim Crow." *Scientific American,* Mar. 29, 2016.

Frost, Natasha. "The Court Case That Killed the 'Ladies Menu.'" *Atlas Obscura,* Feb. 2, 2018.

GLSEN, CiPHR, and CCRC. *Out Online: The Experiences of Lesbian, Gay, Bisexual and Transgender Youth on the Internet.* New York: GLSEN, 2013.

Hale, Grace Elizabeth. *Making Whiteness: The Culture of Segregation in the South, 1890–1940.* New York: Pantheon, 1998.

Holt, Jane. "A Pie Named After a Russian Diplomat." *The New York Times,* Feb. 19, 1945.

Horowitz, Jason. "Of Mouth Molds and Michelin Stars: Chef Finds Fame After Epic Takedown." *The New York Times,* Dec. 23, 2021.

Iaccarino, Luca. "'Bros', il peggior ristorante stellato di sempre': Il caso e il diritto del critica." *Corriere Della Sera,* Dec. 14, 2021.

Kendall, Mikki. *Hood Feminism: Notes from the Women That a Movement Forgot.* New York: Viking, 2020.

Lew, Mike. "Beef Stroganoff Is Named for Who Exactly?" *Bon Appétit,* Jan. 16, 2014.

Martin, Ann M. *Stacey's Mistake.* The Baby-Sitters Club, #18. New York: Scholastic, 1988.

Mull, Amanda. "Americans Have Baked All the Flour Away." *The Atlantic,* May 12, 2020.

Perry, Grace. "The End of 'Ladies First' Restaurant Service." *Eater,* Aug. 16, 2018.

Petrow, Steven. *Steven Petrow's Complete Gay & Lesbian Manners: The Definitive Guide to LGBT Life.* New York: Workman, 2011.

Powell, Julie. "Being Julie, Not 'Julie.'" *The Atlantic,* Aug. 5, 2009.

——. *Cleaving: A Story of Marriage, Meat, and Obsession.* New York: Little, Brown, 2009.

——. *Julie & Julia: My Year of Cooking Dangerously.* New York: Little, Brown, 2005.

"Priceless Menu." *Time,* Aug. 18, 1980.

Pringle, Heather. "9000-Year-Old Evidence That Humans Ate Dogs." *The Washington Post,* May 16, 2011.

Pulley, Anna. "Check Please! Who Pays for a First Date in Queer Relationships?" *Chicago Tribune,* Apr. 7, 2016.

Sanders, Joshunda. "Black Women, Let Your Anger Out." *In These Times,* Mar. 26, 2019.

Schulz, Kathryn. "The Really Big One." *The New Yorker,* July 13, 2015.

Tolentino, Jia. *Trick Mirror: Reflections on Self-Delusion.* New York: Random House, 2019.

Toomre, Joyce, trans. *Classic Russian Cooking: Elena Molokhovets' A Gift to Young Housewives.* Bloomington: Indiana University Press, 1992.

Twitty, Michael W. *Koshersoul: The Faith and Food Journey of an African American Jew.* New York: Amistad, 2022.

Voss, Kimberly Wilmot. "Segregating Restaurants: How Women Got a Seat at the Table." We're History, Mar. 20, 2015. werehistory.org.

West, Lindy. *Shrill: Notes from a Loud Woman.* New York: Hachette Books, 2016.

Women's Media Center Speech Project. "Online Abuse 101." https://womensmediacenter.com/speech-project/online-abuse-101.

Wright, Daryn. "This Forgotten Cult Dessert Is Still a New York Signature." *Saveur,* Dec. 29, 2020.

ABOUT THE AUTHOR

GERALDINE DERUITER is the James Beard Award–winning blogger behind *The Everywhereist* and the author of *All Over the Place: Adventures in Travel, True Love, and Petty Theft.* Her writing has also appeared in *The Washington Post, The New Yorker*'s "Daily Shouts," *Marie Claire,* and Refinery29. She lives in Seattle with her husband, Rand. They are currently working on a cooking-themed video game (to find out more, visit SnackBarStudio.com).

ABOUT THE TEXT

This book was set in Baskerville, a typeface designed by John Baskerville (1706–75), an amateur printer and typefounder, and cut for him by John Handy in 1750. The type became popular again when the Lanston Monotype Corporation of London revived the classic roman face in 1923. The Mergenthaler Linotype Company in England and the United States cut a version of Baskerville in 1931, making it one of the most widely used typefaces today.